FROM BELONGING
TO BELIEF

CENTRAL EURASIA IN CONTEXT SERIES

Douglas Northrop, Editor

FROM BELONGING TO BELIEF

Modern Secularisms and the
Construction of Religion in Kyrgyzstan

JULIE MCBRIEN

University of Pittsburgh Press

Published by the University of Pittsburgh Press, Pittsburgh, Pa., 15260
Copyright © 2017, University of Pittsburgh Press
All rights reserved
Manufactured in the United States of America
Printed on acid-free paper
10 9 8 7 6 5 4 3 2 1

Cataloging-in-Publication data is available from the Library of Congress

ISBN 13: 978-0-8229-6508-4
ISBN 10: 0-8229-6508-9

Cover art: Photo by the Seattle Globalist
Cover design by Melissa Dias-Mandoly

For my grandmother
Ruth Justine Anderson
with love and gratitude

CONTENTS

ACKNOWLEDGMENTS

First and foremost, I want to thank the townspeople of Bazaar-Korgon for their hospitality, their friendship, and their goodwill. I owe much to their patience, to their understanding, and to their willingness to let me write about their lives and their town. In particular I would like to thank Alisher, Salima, and their children; they are longtime friends who have become family. Extra special gratitude likewise goes to my dear friend Arzikhan-eje, her children, and friends who not only assisted me with my research in every way but cared for and loved our family during my fieldwork. They made our stay, and every subsequent visit, beautiful, rich, and comfortable. Thank you for your understanding and your friendship. Thank you for making your home and your family ours. Several intelligent, hard-working young women and men assisted in various capacities with my research—thank you to Shahista, Nargeeza, Farida, Saida, Elmira, Abid, Eliza, Aisulu, and A.A. This project would have been impossible without K.D., who cared for my children with love, patience, and skill and never tired of my odd requests and expectations. You will always be close to our hearts. And to my Kyrgyz-language teachers—Dilbar-ejeke, Usubaly-agai, and Salima-ejeke—*chong rakhmat*.

Several institutions facilitated the research and writing of this book. The Max Planck Institute for Social Anthropology provided funding for research and the writing of my dissertation. The Eurasia Program of the Social Science Research Council (Title VIII), New York, funded the final year of dissertation writing. I also benefited from a one-year association with the International Institute for the Study of Islam in the Modern World, located in Leiden. In the last stages of writing the manuscript, I received support from the Amsterdam Institute for Social Science Research. Finally, my research received funding from the European Research Council under the European Union's Seventh Framework Programme (FP7/2007–2013) / ERC grant agreement 324180.

The majority of this book was first written at the Max Planck Institute for Social Anthropology in Halle, where the staff—library, IT, administrative, and research coordination—created an efficient and warm environment in which to work. The academic environment at the institute was extremely fruitful ground for thinking about religion, politics, and the postsocialist condition. Thank you to all the team members and guests who were a part of the project on Religion and Civil Society at the MPI. A special thank you, of course, goes to Juraj Buzalka, László Fosztó, Monica Heintz, Krisztina Kehl-Bodrogi, Vlad Naumescu, Mathijs Pelkmans, Johan Rasanayagam, Manja Stephan, and the late Irene Hilgers for their camaraderie, intellectual engagement, and well-timed insights. Thank you to the many friends and colleagues at the MPI over the years for the thoughtful conversation and input, especially Judith Beyer, Olaf Zenker, and Jutta Turner for the cartography. I am grateful to my "unofficial" supervisor, Lale Yalçin-Heckmann, for her warmth, her guidance, and all of her comments and to a seminar at the Martin Luther University organized by Richard Rottenburg. Finally, I would like to thank Chris Hann, my supervisor, who nurtured a rich academic environment and provided a rigorous program that challenged me at every turn. This book has benefited greatly from his insight and guidance from beginning to end.

The intellectual journey that helped shape this book neither started nor ended in Halle but continued through dialogue with scholars at various conferences, summer schools, and institutes over the years. I would like to thank Alex Strating of the University of Amsterdam (UvA), my first guide in the world of anthropology. For thinking about Islam and the idea of modernity, I benefited greatly from conversations with scholars at the International Summer Academy's "Islam and the Repositioning of Religion," convened by Armando Salvatore and Georg Strauth, and the International Institute for the Study of Islam in the Modern World (ISIM), some of whose associates also commented on portions of this book. Three chapters of this book were previously published and therefore benefited from the skilled attention of the editors of those volumes. Thank you to

Deniz Kandiyoti, Filippo Osella, and Benjamin Soares. This book also benefited greatly from everyone at the University of Pittsburgh Press, including the comments of the peer reviewers, the assistance of editors Peter Kracht and Douglas Northrop, and the copyediting and production team.

There are many to thank at the University of Amsterdam—colleagues and dear friends who either read portions of the manuscript, talked with me endlessly about it, or supported me in the very emotional journey of writing. Thank you to Anneke Beerkens, Marten Boekelo, Peter Geschiere, Erella Grassiani, Tina Harris, Olga Sezneva, Rachel Spronk, Yannis Tzaninis, Oskar Verkaaik, and especially Artemy Kalinovsky. I also want to particularly thank Annelies Moors, who has supported me in the writing of this book for many years. I have greatly benefited from her comments on the manuscript specifically, but more generally from ongoing intellectual conversation and friendship.

Thank you to Mathijs Pelkmans, who gave so much during a long, crucial period of this project and who was above all a critical intellectual sparring partner and companion. This work bears the imprint of our decade-long conversation. Thank you to friends and family whose interest, good humor, and practical support at various points over the years enabled me to keep going—Mark Genszler, Issa Niemeijer-Brown, the Pelkmans and Dijkman families, Erin Stowell, Lois Thorpe, Tom Vandenberghe, Debbie Charles, Jessica Jordan, Christina Chandler, and Katherine Jordan. To Alex Niemeijer-Brown, for our conversations about this book, for our trips around Dam Square, and for much, much more, thank you, dear. You more than anyone helped me find the strength, endurance, and insight needed to complete this project.

My parents, Ben and Marianne McBrien, have always supported my interests and desires, assisted me through trying circumstances, and cautioned me to keep perspective and balance in life. My completion of this book is as much a result of their lifelong parenting work as it is of my own academic efforts. To my daughters Sophie and Emma, who have grown up with this project, you have been sources of levity, purpose, and, above all, love. And finally, to my dear grandmother, Ruth Justine Anderson, to whom this book is dedicated—no one has taught or inspired me more. Onward!

NOTE ON
TRANSLITERATION
AND TRANSLATION

All translations from Kyrgyz and Uzbek are my own. I have used the American Library Association–Library of Congress (ALA-LC) System for the transliteration of Russian words and the 1979 romanization system developed by the US Board on Geographic Names and the Permanent Committee on Geographical Names for British Official Use (BGN/PCGN) for the transliteration of Kyrgyz words. I have made exceptions for proper nouns with widely accepted English spellings, as well as certain Arabic-derived words used in Kyrgyz and Uzbek with commonly accepted English spellings (e.g., Moscow, Akaev, Shari'a, Quran). This is true also for the word *bazaar*, which derives from Persian and is found in the town name Bazaar-Korgon. Certain terms—such as *namaz* or Noruz—are cognates in Kyrgyz and Uzbek, usually with slight differences in vowel pronunciation (e.g., *namaz* versus *namoz*, Noruz versus Navruz, *atincha* versus *otincha*). Since to switch from one language to the other throughout the text would create more confusion than clarity and since my literacy in Kyrgyz is higher, I have chosen to use the Kyrgyz words throughout for simplicity.

cartography: Jutta Turner   base map: http://www.lib.utexas.edu/maps/commonwealth/kazakhstan_physio-2001.jpg

Map of Central Asia with fieldwork site, Bazaar-Korgon, indicated.

FROM BELONGING
TO BELIEF

FIGURE I.1. Lenin statue, Bazaar-Korgon main square. Photograph by the author, 2004.

FIGURE I.2. Bazaar-Korgon *rayon* government offices. Photograph by the author, 2009.

INTRODUCTION

The main roadway leading to Bazaar-Korgon, Kyrgyzstan, follows a most un-flattering route. Capitalism's failures flash by the window first—a defunct joint venture cotton-processing plant to the right, to the left a row of houses, their crumbling accouterments exposing shoddy quality. Next, the decay of Soviet progress unrolls before the eye—dilapidated government buildings, rundown apartment blocks in desertlike surroundings, a public park yellow with brittle vegetation, and empty concrete casks that were once a fountain. The road widens as it enters the town square and nears the main market and bus station. Flanking the square, two objects come into view: a statue of Lenin and a mosque.

Lenin stands to the right against a backdrop of mountains. His outstretched arm strongly calls the viewer's attention upward and forward. In the 1980s, it literally guided the viewer's eye across the square to the newly built district government offices, indicating the fruition of local development projects and the seat of local power. It likewise called the viewer's mind to thoughts of a larger collective and its communal fantasy. The figure of Lenin was intended to inspire visions of an imminent future of unparalleled modernization—an imagined communist utopia. This future included universal atheism, the ultimate goal in this particularly virulent project of Soviet secularism. More complicated than that, the

3

FIGURE I.3. Bazaar-Korgon rayon Friday mosque. Photograph by the author, 2009.

FIGURE I.4. Taxi drivers waiting for work. Photograph by the author, 2004.

statue simultaneously called to mind much larger, more tangled webs of hopes and failures, power and control.

Although the Red Banner of the Soviet Union is gone, the government offices remain, now marked by the emblem of the independent Kyrgyz republic—a white hawk on a backdrop of blue. But the building shares its favored position with a teahouse and a mosque; the viewer's eye no longer effortlessly toggles between the symbols of socialist hopes and the enactment of socialist power. The view is now interrupted by what forms the focal point of the skyline—the mosque. Remarkable in size and position, if not in beauty, the mosque juts from the last bit of hill before the square narrows into the dead end that marks the eastern edge of the town's bazaar. The mosque, built in the 1990s, directs the viewer's attention to nothing but itself. Its impression lies only in its size and its mass, which some have likened to a fortress. The mosque started as a community initiative in a new political environment, one that created and signaled the townsfolk's self-understanding as Muslims. Freedom of conscience, newly privatized land, and private donors made building the mosque possible and through its construction a sense of development and progress—the promise of capitalism—emerged. The project marked Bazaar-Korgonians' first move in a new institutional arrangement and indicated the town's growing fluency in new arenas, providing hope for what they imagined would be a successful "transition" to capitalist democracy.

Just beyond the town square, girls sell bubble gum at makeshift roadside stalls, dozens of out-of-work men peddle their driving skills for next to nothing, old men rest next to donkey carts and chat with one another. A close look reveals outhouses in the lots next to the government building, chips of marble from Lenin's platform, and trash blowing around the park. The fountain's water stopped flowing long ago. Townsfolk queue outside government offices, waiting for the chance to genuflect for the paltry funds and the little influence the district leaders can still arrange. These, too, are symbols of projects imprinted on Bazaar-Korgon, projects gone awry amid false intentions, hidden power, poor planning, misconceptions, and just dumb stupid luck.

Despite their presence, neither the people nor the peripheral decay draws the eye. Lenin and the mosque retain that role, but they suggest a startling fact: the mosque construction did not seem to necessitate the removal of Lenin's image.[1] The two stand together well into the twenty-first century. They neither precede nor follow one another in the way teleological narratives sketched their ideological and material regimes—atheism and Islam, socialism and capitalist democracy. The synchronic presence of Lenin and the mosque creates a difficult terrain to interpret. Residents' reflections on the scene and the political and economic environments it represents reveal a complex, contradictory evaluation in which there is no clear winner. This book is concerned precisely with how this complex, sometimes contradictory landscape of religion and politics came to be, why it was so variously interpreted by Bazaar-Korgonians, and what together this says about secularism.

Based on fourteen months of fieldwork conducted in 2003 and 2004, this book examines the way in which Bazaar-Korgonians constructed a post-Soviet religious landscape as they moved from socialism, with its state-enforced atheism, centrally planned economy, and limited access to ideas, goods, and people beyond socialist borders, to its current state of capitalist democracy, liberal secularism, and globalization. It looks at the clothes Bazaar-Korgonians wore, the buildings they constructed, the way they married, and what they watched on TV in order to find out how they were constructing themselves as Muslims and—through their diverse opinions and in conversations with one another— what they (variously) made and understood Islam to be. It charts how Bazaar-Korgonians began labeling those who were "interested in Islam" or those who might be "terrorists" or "Wahhabis" and how these labels and notions related to regional, state, and global discourses on religion and extremism, past and present. In short, it looks at how all Bazaar-Korgonians—regardless of whether or not they veiled, prayed, abstained from alcohol, or visited a shrine—created, lived, and evaluated religion and debated what it meant to be a Muslim in a post-Soviet, Muslim context.

Religious life in Bazaar-Korgon in the early 2000s was public in a way that was impossible in the late Soviet period. The flourishing of religion was consistent with many of the piety movements being described at that moment by anthropologists around the world, though with notable differences, as this book details.[2] Regardless of whether and how the townspeople imaged and followed Islam, religion, as well as the freedom to practice it, was nearly universally lauded among my interlocutors in Bazaar-Korgon. In fact, freedom of religion remained one of the most popular aspects of the post-Soviet period in Kyrgyzstan, even while disappointment with democratization and the transition to capitalism had already become a normal part of everyday life.[3]

By the 2000s, Bazaar-Korgon had become known throughout Kyrgyzstan as a place where something was happening with Islam. The public space of the new political order had created room for Bazaar-Korgonians to live Islam in locally novel ways. Those "interested in Islam" (*dinge kyzyktuu bölüp kaluu*) or those who had "turned and gone to Islam" (*dinge burulup getkin*) sought out local religious teachers to instruct them in Quranic recitation and proper ritual performance or began to "call others to Islam." Women, but also some men, changed their mode of dress to fit what they perceived to be proper and modest for Muslims. Some began eschewing certain rituals and modifying others to make them more pure

FIGURE I.5. Bazaar-Korgon. Photograph by the author, 2004.

and Islamic. Debate ensued about what proper Muslimness (*muslumanchylyk*) should be.

At the same time, however, many, if not most, residents also expressed a sense of discomfort with particular interpretations of Islam being publicly articulated in town. These formulations emphasized a notion of Muslimness that differed from the widespread and dominant one of the late Soviet period. The public Islam gaining ground in the 2000s challenged established notions that Muslimness was a matter of collective, ethno-religious belonging. Locally new discourses insisted rather that "Muslim" was primarily, if not exclusively, a category of belief. The notions and practices that most residents asserted to be an inherent part of Muslimness were not accepted as religion in these formulations. This challenge forced many Muslims in Bazaar-Korgon to rethink their Muslimness. This was often troubling.

The central argument of this book is that the unease felt by the majority of townsfolk was not only about specific ideas of Muslimness. It was equally about the broader, underlying notion of religion implicated in the new interpretations of Islam in town. The conception of religion held by the majority of Bazaar-Korgonians differed significantly from the locally new variants circulating in the region—ideas that premised the notion of belief and conviction.[4] Their ideas about religion had more to do with collective belonging, and they had been cast by the modernizing campaigns of the Soviet Union and its political project of secularism.

The power and authority of a modern, secular state, Talal Asad (2003) argues, emerge in part from the state's control over the definition and place of religion; it therefore perpetually monitors and regulates these qualities, limiting the concept of religion to that of internal belief. While Asad and those building on his work are often careful to indicate that this is a notion of a liberal, secular state, the analyses rarely address the liberal/nonliberal distinction and its implications. The first wave of literature on secularism was, for example, far more concerned with discussions of religion and the secular in light of one another. As a result, a certain fluency and care in interrogations of these concepts vis-à-vis each other developed, but, as Charles Hirschkind (2011) has pointed out, there is considerably less precision in the use of the term "secular" as it relates to the notions "modern" and "liberal." Hirschkind is concerned with ferreting out the differences between what is secular and what is modern in his investigation of the secular body. In contrast, I examine a secular definition of religion to explain the secular as a concept distinct from the liberal.

I suggest that what we have taken to be the modern secular definition of religion is merely its liberal secular variant, produced by states dominantly operating in this register. The Soviet Union, whose political economy was distinct from, though certainly bound up with, liberal traditions, had logics that produced and were predicated on alternative ideas and practices of society, polity, economy, subjects, the secular, and—not surprisingly—religion. These logics had much less to do with "internal belief," individualism, markets, and subjects supposedly free from intervention and much more with interpersonal affiliations, organized collective action, and the alteration of structure and generative action to transform the subject or society.

My assertion is that religion as internal belief is a particular form of religion suited to a secular, liberal logic. But the shape of religion would necessarily differ in a modern state constructed through congruent but alternative scripts. Religion in the Soviet Union is one such case. The Soviet atheism campaigns—a particularly virulent version of secularism—have largely been viewed only as an attempt to eradicate religion, rather than examined for what they, however inadvertently, sustained, altered, and created.[5] Yet, the attack itself was the work of definition. It presupposed an idea of religion—the thing that would be attacked—or at least the idea of an unacceptable, backward, threatening religion. These attacks delineated certain elements often bound up with Islam and Muslims and therefore, presumably, with religion by condemning and outlawing them. They were vilified and delegitimized—labeled as antiquated, violent, or false.

At the same time, other state policies and practices inadvertently nurtured another notion and practice of religion. Religion in this way was allowed, ignored, or promoted. In Central Asia, both a space for and an idea of religion emerged, for example, as part of an inchoate national identity. Acceptable religion became increasingly tied to home-based practices and life-cycle events where it was consciously ignored, unwittingly missed, or tacitly tolerated by local and distant state authorities (e.g., Abashin 2014; Rasanayagam 2011; Hilgers 2009; Kehl-Bodrogi 2006). Religion thusly defined and practiced was cultivated and validated by the state in part through efforts like the nationalities policies (korenizatsiya). Religion became wrapped up with national forms of belonging, and the performance of this ethno-religious national identity became necessary to gain access to power, resources, and advantages. Religion in this way—religion as belonging—was a functioning public category; in this manner and in these spaces it did not threaten the state's authority or the rationale of its existence. Rather, religion thusly understood and enacted emerged in tandem with Soviet secularism as an intertwining of several policies, measures, and visions; this notion of religion was necessary for the power and being of the Soviet secular state.

The Soviet Union was an instance of nonliberal secularism; understanding and comparing it to Western variants helps illuminate that which is secular (and/ or modern) as opposed to that which is liberal. My argument is that the notion of interiorized belief of the individual as the inherent characteristic of modern secularized religion is merely its liberal, Western variant. It is a conceptualization and enactment that fits liberal logics and the exercise of Western power as it unfolded historically. Soviet modernization followed another course, one that from the outset was more oriented to interpersonal affiliation and organization.[6] Its vision of the secular and the notion of religion it created necessarily fit these contours; they were co-constituted in the same historically evolving conversation. But they also played on preexisting ideas of religion—as they existed in the Russian Empire and its encounter in its borderlands, including Muslims in Central Asia—thus picking up another side of religion disregarded or ignored in liberal modern projects: religion as a mode of belonging.

When, in the post-Soviet period, other notions of religion were given more space to circulate and flourish in the region, they challenged this widespread, Soviet-era notion of religion. In Bazaar-Korgon this meant that many townsfolk were being challenged not only about specific ideas or practices of Islam but also about the nature of Muslimness and therefore implicitly, the nature of religion. In this way I chart my interlocutors' struggle as one in which they were being challenged to move from a Soviet-era definition of religion (which was essentially about belonging) to a liberal one (in which belief was the necessary condition), hence a shift from belonging to belief.

Belonging, Belief, and Secularism

To use the words *belonging* and *belief* in the title of a book on religion and secularism is to immediately call to mind the influential work of the sociologist Grace Davie on religion in Britain and the two pieces whose titles contained the phrase "believing without belonging" (Davie 1990, 1994). The question around which Davie (1994, 2) framed her work was why "the majority of British people—in common with many other Europeans—persist in believing (if only in an ordinary God), but see no need to participate with an even minimal regularity in their religious institutions." Davie was essentially wrestling with the question of religion's presence in the modern world, a fact that presented a problem for many sociologists because the secularization thesis had predicted religion's demise. The "believing but not belonging" British, and the particularities of their persistent faith, were only one element of the conundrum. The public return of religion in the 1980s—in the American Moral Majority, the Iranian Revolution, Indian nationalism, the Polish Solidarity movement—troubled the secularization thesis, as well as its proponents, more profoundly. Peter Berger (1999, 2) assessed this situation and declared that "the assumption that we live in a secularized world is wrong" and that the body of work "loosely labeled 'secularization theory' is essentially mistaken." Other sociologists, notably José Casanova (1994), wondered if instead the secularization thesis should be revisited and re-evaluated, rather than dismissed. Instead of a unitary notion, he argued, the thesis had three core ideas. The presence of public religion troubled only the predicted decline and privatization of religion. The thesis of differentiation—the idea that religion, politics, economics, society, and so forth, became disentangled, differentiated, and increasingly autonomous spheres in the modern era—could still be upheld, he argued.

Danièle Hervieu-Léger (1990) too called for rethinking secularization and began framing her work not around secularism per se but about how "religion organizes itself" in the condition of modernity, and she did so by decoupling secularization and modernity. Religion was a "chain of memory," and many modern Europeans were to be understood as amnesiacs (2000). By 2006, she was examining "high modernity" in Europe and arguing that in "religious modernity" in Europe there was a "dual tendency" toward "the individualization and subjectivization of beliefs on one hand, and deregulation of the organized systems of religious belief, on the other" (2006, 60). In contrast to Hervieu-Léger, Casanova (1994) argued for the very public role of religion, moving away from the individualization and, somehow by implication, the private religion at the center of Hervieu-Léger's 2006 argument. This is perhaps because Casanova's focus was wider, examining the United States, Poland, and Spain, for example—countries that in one typology or another had long been seen as exceptions or variations on the (northern or western) European rule.

What was perhaps common to all their work, including that of Davie and the influential David Martin, was a re-evaluating of the role of Europe as a model of and for secularization in modern societies; it became instead merely a historical option. Modernity, for these sociologists, could lead to secularization, as in Europe, but it might also include religion that would be molded and shaped to its particular form. Berger (2006, 153), for example, argued that secularization was not a necessary corollary of modernity, but that pluralism "of worldviews, values, etc., including religion, very likely was."

Casanova's work played an early and influential role in my own thinking about secularization and religion. Despite my forays into the literature, however, it never formed a central part of my approach. His influential book specifically, and the sociologists' vast work on religion and secularization more generally, never proved as fruitful as I had hoped for interpreting the (post) Soviet religious landscape of Kyrgyzstan. Davie's impressive corpus was no different. Thus, despite the similarity in title, my book is not meant to reflect Davie's work nor does it draw on her central argument to make its own. This is in part because underlying Davie's analysis, and much of the sociological literature, is a bias that limits its use in analyzing religion and secularism outside of Europe, a critique lobbed as early as 1965 by David Martin, the eminent sociologist of secularization. He argued that secularization as a concept was faulty, because, among other issues, it had "roots in rationalist and historicist ideology" (Martin 2005, chap. 10).

Martin's critique and injunctions are extremely insightful, and an approach similar to his shapes this book, though I came to it by way of the anthropologist Talal Asad. Asad's influential work on the secular was predated and undergirded by his genealogy of religion, including his evaluation (Asad 1993, 27–54) of fellow anthropologist Clifford Geertz's (1973) universal definition of religion. It is there that his argument converges with Martin and his criticisms of theories of secularization. Asad argued that instead of the catholic description Geertz intended, the famed scholar had produced a parochial one. Geertz's definition, Asad (1993, 43) asserted, was a historically specific description crafted from within a Western "modern landscape of power and knowledge." It was situated in a contemporary notion of the secular that emerged from a postreformist, Protestant tradition of Christianity as it had developed in tandem with modern forms of the state, knowledge, the market, and the subject. Geertz's definition was, Asad (1993, 47) contended, one rooted in an idea of religion as individual, internalized belief in which belief was a "state of mind" rather than, for example, a "constituting activity in the world." It was, in short, not universal; it was a modern, secular definition par excellence.

In deconstructing Geertz's definition, Asad illustrated the located nature of social science understandings of religion.[7] The definition of religion we are most given to work with is not universal but rather that postreformist, secular conception that Asad identified in Geertz's work, one also seen throughout the sociological literature, as argued by David Martin (2007), and the anthropological literature, as indicated by Chris Hann (2012). Martin (2007, 144) argued, for example, that "the master-narrative favored by sociology has privileged the individualizing potential and inner-worldly asceticism of Protestantism," a view that needs to be reformulated, he argued, by paying attention to critiques coming from Catholicism, Anglo-Catholicism, Orthodoxy, and Evangelical Protestantism. Hann (2012) and Hann and Hermann Goltz (2010) argue similarly; their alternative analysis is informed by studies of the Orthodox Church and, importantly, of religion in former socialist states. The bias identified by Asad, Martin, Hann, and Goltz is precisely one of the reasons that observations and analyses made by the sociologists of religion discussed above lack analytical purchase in postsocialist regions where Islam and Orthodoxy (not to mention others) were the religions that shaped the secular and projects of secularism. But this is only the start, for not only are there different religious traditions in these regions, but these regions have also have strikingly different (histories of) political economy than western Europe. Thus, the sociological notions neither mesh with the specific conceptions, practices, and institutions of the religions in question nor do they fit the political and economic histories of the region, including their particular projects of secularism and notions of the secular with which they are bound up.

Much of the recent work on contemporary secularisms, largely though not exclusively in anthropology, in contrast has shown the ways each specific project of secularism is bound up with particular religions, histories, and political economies; what kind of subjectivities and sensorial experiences each secularism produces; how secularism is created, negotiated, and contested; how it functions as a mode of power, problem space, or political medium; and, importantly, how religion and the secular are tangled and interwoven.[8] This subfield has flourished and produced rich empirical and theoretical insights. As James Bielo (2015, 119) has argued in a review article of influential interdisciplinary publications, "secular studies has come of age."[9] Yet there is, he asserts, nonetheless a noticeable bias in the corpus to date—namely, the consideration of a narrow range of state secularisms, with the former socialist world being a notable exception.

It is only relatively recently that researchers have begun to delve into the specificities of Soviet secularism (e.g., Luehrmann 2011; Smolkin-Rothrock 2010; Wanner 2012). Here a significantly different political, economic, philosophical, and religious history shaped a particular political project of secularism and all the ideas, practices, objects, and institutions bound up with it. Victoria Smolkin-Rothrock (2010, 1) seems to question the secularity of the Soviet Union, arguing that in the postwar period those involved in Soviet atheism campaigns began to cultivate a "Soviet spirituality" they thought was needed to "fill the 'sacred space' made empty by the regime's war against religion." Catherine Wanner and Sonja Luehrmann both implicitly contest Smolkin-Rothrock's approach. Wanner (2012), for example, eschews dialectics of enchantment as a means of studying religion and secularism in the Soviet Union. Taking an Asad-inspired approach, she argues that secularism is, in essence, about the control of religion rather than its negation. She therefore argues for understanding the ways in which Soviet secularism affected and altered religion, claiming that "historically shifting needs of governance" were the generators of ideas about and practices of religion in the Soviet Union (2012, 9). Sonja Luehrmann (2011) argues that there was something more in Soviet secularism than just the replacement of religion with the secular—a cinema for a church, for example. Rather, theorists of and materials about Soviet atheism saw "the need for atheism to be substantially different from the religious sensibilities it sought to replace" (2011, 7). At the heart of this was the notion of exclusive humanism. Luehrmann asserts that Soviet secularism diverges from Western variants regarding ideas about "privatized religion" or "individualism" but converges on the idea of "exclusive humanism" (2011, 8) as the aim of its project.

Like Wanner, I take an Asadian approach in my study, and like Luehrmann, I am interested in similarities and differences between Western variants of secularism and Soviet ones. My particular interest lies in the concept of religion that Soviet secularism formed, a terrain largely unproblematized in both (post) Soviet studies of secularism as well as the broader literature on the topic. The liberal, secular definition is usually assumed by default. A notable exception is Kristen Ghodsee (2009), who likewise problematizes the concept of religion in her exploration of secularism in postsocialist Bulgaria and similarly finds an idea of religion that foregrounds ethnonational belonging rather than internal belief.

I understand the categories of "religion" and "the secular" to be parts of larger logics that are, importantly, co-constituted in given political and economic environments, in dialogue with particular religions over time. Because of the very specific struggle of my interlocutors, the aspect of secularism in which I became interested was its definition of religion. What I saw in post-Soviet Bazaar-Korgon was a debate over the nature of religion. What was being contested, I concluded, were two different ideas about this, each produced by a different project of secularism. I therefore began to interrogate what religion, as a concept, must have looked like during the Soviet era. This in turn led me to examine how this idea of religion emerged from a context shaped by, among other things, practices and ideas about religion in the Orthodox Church, a Russian imperial encounter with Islam in Central Asia, and the very specific nature of the Soviet state and economy. My interests thus diverged from the sociology of religion/secularism, in which religion often appeared, by default, as individual, internal belief and in which such ideas were premised on the structure and functioning of the Catholic Church and the Protestant denominations, as well as their doctrines, habits, conceptions of time or the soul, and truth, for example, as well as on the particularities of western European states and their histories. The "believing without belonging" referenced in the titles of Davie's article and book is just such a case.

In a revised edition of her book on religion in Britain, Davie (2015) looks back at the popularity of the phrase "believing without belonging." She is careful to reiterate that the terms she employed should "not be considered too rigidly" (2015, 79). With this injunction in mind, it is nonetheless important to sketch out that, generally, for Davie, belonging seems to be connected to practice in and attendance at the church as institution. Already at this point, Davie's ideas prove insufficient for my study of Islam in Kyrgyzstan. Using only a very general concept of Islam that elides all variation in interpretation and practice among Muslims in space and time, we see that in Islam "belonging" does not mean to link one with an institution; it has more to do with community and relationship to people and God—the *umma*. Davie also mentions practice. Here too her conception proves to be too firmly rooted in a particular religious tradition to make it useful for my analysis. Practice, in a Protestant tradition, diverges from that rooted in Catholicism or Orthodoxy, for example, as it does from the various interpretations of Islam and other religions of the former socialist world. Therefore, when I invoke the words *belonging* and *belief*, I have different notions and a different process in mind than Davie. Belonging and believing mean different things in Soviet and post-Soviet Central Asia than they do in western Europe.

But this is not the only difference in my analysis, for in using these words I am not attempting to describe the habits or ideas of particular religious practitioners, as Davie was. I use these words—*belonging* and *belief*—as heuristic devices, not to indicate what people are or are not doing but to point to what I believe are two different notions of religion formed by two particular projects of secularism.

What was Soviet secularism? On what notion of the secular was it premised? These are questions I cannot definitively answer in this introduction. A partial answer may be found in a genealogical investigation of religion and the secular as they emerged from Russian Orthodoxy, which would be a study similar to Asad's on European Christianity. The burgeoning work on Eastern Christianities is already revealing fascinating insights in this vein, a few of which are relevant for my discussion here.[10] This literature shows, for example, a specific conception of "the person" in Orthodoxy, one that differs from liberal notions of the individual (Hann and Goltz 2010; Hirschon 2010; Agadjanian and Rousselet 2010). Personhood, in some instances, is understood as bestowed by God and can be realized only in Holy Communion, which carries a social sense of being part of a larger collectivity (Agadjanian and Rousselet 2010); it is the idea of a socially embedded person (Hirschon 2010). Working from these concepts—instead of ideas about individuals, for example—necessarily leads to alternative conceptions of religion and the secular. Similarly, ideas about the relationship of the material/immaterial (e.g., Hanganu 2010; Luehrmann 2010; Rogers 2010), conceptions of the church and the idea of the community of believers (Hann and Goltz 2010), or ideas about mediation, practice, or interiority and exteriority all lead to an idea of religion that diverges from liberal ones. And because these notions of religion arose not only in Russia but throughout the vast territory of the Russian Empire and the Soviet Union, among a variety of people and their religions, in a multiplicity of political expansions, encounters, and appropriations, the same kind of analysis is necessary for these various contexts if a fuller, more complex idea of religion and the secular in Soviet secularism is to emerge.

Such an analysis is too vast a project for this book. My argument is but one contribution to this effort. In the remainder of this introduction I look at policies, programs, and approaches of the Russian Empire and Soviet Union in order to get at some of the general, underlying logics, including the notion of religion, at work. Based on the secondary historical literature, I give a sense of the category of religion I think the Soviet state casted and authorized in Central Asia, how it related to preceding Russian imperial notions of religion and Central Asian ideas and practices of Islam, and the way this concept of religion looked and worked by the end of the Soviet period. This category of religion was at play when alternative, primarily liberal notions of religion confronted many of my interlocutors in the early post-Soviet period.

Notions of Religion in the Russian Empire

The concept(s) of religion that were at work in Soviet secularism and that emerged from it came from prevailing conceptualizations in the Russian imperial period. My aim in this section is not to provide a systematic account of Russian imperial attitudes, policies, and institutions regarding religion generally or Islam specifically over the empire's very long history and in its encounter with many different groups of people. Rather, I simply attempt to sketch some of the general qualities of religion as it emerged. The notion of religion as a defining, essential characteristic of a people was prominent in Russia before the imperial expansion. Michael Khodarkovsky (1997, 17) argues, for example, that "religion defined the aggregate identity of Russians in premodern Russia." Religion was also a means for classifying non-Russians within Russia's borders. Andreas Kappeler ([2001] 2014) argues that religion in premodern Russia was the primary means for classifying its population, for while individuals could, and often did, speak multiple languages, especially among the middle and upper classes, a person could have only one religion. As the empire expanded, this understanding of religion as an essential element of collectivity carried on in the Russian imperial encounter with the "others" that occupied the lands to the south and the east. Language was one of the primary markers of difference used in the earliest years of Russian expansion (Kappeler [2001] 2013, 14), but territory, kinship, and religion were likewise employed in the project of classification and difference making.

As the empire expanded into non-Christian lands, religion as a differentiating factor became more prominent (Kappeler [2001] 2013, 15; İğmen 2012, 11). Russian imperial actors, researchers, and intellectuals began the process of identifying and classifying the "other" in their expanding empire. Curiosity about the nature of the other, which extended to delineating who they were and sketching a normative evaluation of them, began, as Yuri Slezkine (1997, 30) argues, under Peter the Great and his "mentors"—Germans interested in travel, study, and classification. Among scholars and other elites, religion was initially understood as the essential and most basic defining element of a people, a category that subsumed all other markers, including dietary habits, sexual and kinship practices, and relationship to land (32). However, the place and understanding of religion began to shift in and through these investigations; religion became one element among the others and it increasingly became seen as the spirit or culture of the people (33). The various peoples of the empire were classified as distinct from each other, often in an evolutionary scale, and from Russians, who were therefore co-constituted in this dialogue; the consolidation of Russians as, among other things, essentially Christian, became more pronounced. It seems that religion at this moment was often spoken about not in terms of belief but, according to Slezkine, with reference to "ethical and liturgical precepts collectively known as 'law'" (33). Material culture, dress, and bodily fashioning were likewise tied up with this notion of religion (Frank 2012, 64–75).

This concept of religion as concerning the spirit of a people and the regulation of their community took hold and became widespread in various strata of the population throughout the empire at least partly because it was one of the classificatory elements used when delineating, understanding, and, importantly, ruling the various peoples. As Robert Crews (2006, 8) argues, while "modern scholars tend to conceptualize this diversity [of the Russian imperial population] in terms of ethnic or national categories . . . tsarist elites consistently viewed the heterogeneous peoples of the empire through the lens of religious affiliation." It was the means through which the ruled were made legible and governable. Religious leaders, for example, were used as a strategic means of exercising authority. Religious affiliation also played a role in the determination of tax regimes or army service. As late at the early nineteenth century, religion was still the primary criterion for legal identification, even above language (Kappeler [2001] 2014). The "nomadic people" of the Russian Empire were at that time, for example, prominently referred to in legal documents by the term *inovertsy* (of a different faith) ([2001] 2014). The term *inorodtsy* (foreign-born) appears for the first time in a proposed statute in 1798 ([2001] 2014), though Paul Georg Geiss (2003, 154–55) notes that in administrative contexts in the early nineteenth century, the criteria for use of the term still had more to do with religious affiliation than other indicators.

In being ruled this way, imperial subjects were drawn into a logic in which religion was, in part, a means of presenting, maneuvering, contesting, and understanding oneself in reference to a collective body and the state that granted rights, privileges, and resources in these terms (Geiss 2003, 2, 10). Over the long history of Russian imperial rule, difference and collective rights were the basis of governance and the means by which subjects connected to the polity (Burbank 2006). Even in the mid-nineteenth century, when there were liberal calls for reform of this policy in the direction of universal rights, "officials defaulted in practice to the habit of manipulable, unequal rights" of "natural" collectives (Burbank 2006, 400). This conception of rights and rule persisted to the beginning of the twentieth century and, Burbank argues, continued to inform ideas into the Soviet period.

Religion became a primary mode for Russian rulers to understand and control their populations for at least one other important reason. Religion was understood as an effective way to govern—in terms of the classification of the populations and in the utilization of laws and leaders—because it was seen as a "comprehensive system for discipline" that would ensure "personal salvation" as well as the "general good" contributing to public order, morality, and ethics (Crews 2006, 42). Policies regarding non-Orthodox religious groups, however, changed over time. Under Peter the Great there was a time of forced conversion to Orthodoxy simultaneous with certain moves toward religious freedom (Kappeler [2001] 2013), though Geiss (2003, 154) classifies the tsar's general approach as anti-Islamic. Catherine the Great initiated a more flexible and pragmatic stance toward religion (Kappeler [2001] 2013), and under her there was an "Islamic-Tatar" renaissance (Geiss 2003, 154). Catherine II is often understood to have evaluated Islam as favorable or more evolved vis-à-vis other religions in the empire.

Religion was understood not only as elemental to a people's collective belonging and a means for exercising power over them but also as intrinsic to their character and their collective morality. While there had long been an ambiguous relationship between the Russians and the nomads and Muslims of Asia, Kappeler ([2001] 2013) argues, the normative evaluation of the differences took a negative turn toward the late seventeenth and early eighteenth century, when a marked sense of superiority developed and religion became the prominent cleavage between the two. Under Catherine the Great, this situation worked itself out in terms of "civilizing missions" (Kappeler [2001] 2014). Russian orientalism in Turkestan, for example, objectified and essentialized all that was "other" among its Muslim populations as being located in Islam. "'Fanaticism' came to be the defining characteristic of Central Asia," Adeeb Khalid (1998, 51) has argued, and this, he asserts, was "seen to reside in Islam." The understood antidote was civilization, modernization, and enlightenment. What is important for this discussion is not the normative evaluation—flattering, praiseworthy, derogatory, or demonizing—of a religion but the work that the category of religion was doing: it was summing up a people and their qualities.

Religion as a category emerged as an idea of people together—both their spirit or essential defining traits and the way they regulated their communal life. This movement was concomitant with changes in conceptualizations about collective belonging itself. There were contradictory, sometimes ambiguous normative evaluations of religion, but the contours of religion as a category of belonging were more cohesive and clear.[11] Religion in imperial Russia was about collective belonging, collective ethics, and a communal ethos. It was understood as an important element of control in a state with a diverse population; it was an essential element of identity for those populations and the means by which they could be recognized.

It would be a mistake to see these ideas about and modes of ruling through religion as disconnected from ideas and practices prominent in Europe or other regions of the world likewise undergoing changes in notions and practices of religion and collective belonging. Certainly liberal notions of religion, which premised "belief" as central to religion, were to be found in the Russian Empire.[12] But the relationship was complex, and intertwined were dialogues with two broad strands of European thought—liberalism and romanticism—the latter more akin to the ideas of "belonging" I have sketched here.[13] Despite this, the idea of religion as belonging held prominence. Moreover, more widespread and institutionally practiced sets of ideas, predicated on interpersonal, collective notions, were also prominent in the region, effecting and shaping not only an emergent sense of religion but also notions and practices as diverse as citizenship, economic relations, the self, or political authority, for example. This is important as the idea of religion in Soviet Central Asia developed in tandem with that of the modern nation.

Religion and Belonging in Soviet Central Asia

An understanding of religion as collective belonging and the regulation thereof were prominent in Central Asia at the end of the Russian imperial period. It was continuously evolving and being constituted in conversation with altering and emerging forms of collective identity. A prominent one at the moment was the modern idea of nation. The two ideas continued to intermingle and co-constitute one another during the onset of the Bolshevik Revolution and eventually the start of the antireligious attacks in Central Asia. The interwoven nature of these notions is apparent whether we look, broadly speaking, at ideas in Orthodox Christianity, at concepts prominent among elites and distant state authorities involved in the modernizing campaigns as the Soviet Union began to take shape, or at those ideas more locally connected to Central Asia and to Islam as it existed in the region. The notions held by these various actors were not identical by any means, but the overlap provided, in part, the vocabulary through which they conversed and mutually constituted one another. From this history, ideas and practices of religion and nation developed simultaneously in Central Asia. It is to a discussion of this development that I now turn.

Modes of collective belonging in Central Asia prior to the consolidation of power by the Russian Empire in the mid- to late nineteenth century were tied to social and economic status, guilds, language, lineage and other kinship groups, settled and nomadic patterns of residence, and Islam (Khalid 1998; Geiss 2003; Edgar 2004, 18; Finke 2014). These modes were overlapping, competing, and deeply intertwined. By the late nineteenth century modern ideas and projects of the nation had begun to develop and circulate in Central Asia, and, as in Russia, they were multiple, divergent, and sometimes conflicting. In Central Asia some of the earliest deployments of the idea of the nation for modern political projects came from, among others, the Jadids, who themselves were in conversation with their European Russian counterparts as well as with modernist movements in the Ottoman Empire and throughout the Muslim world (Khalid 1998).

Russian officials were already commissioning and utilizing ethnographic data to classify and govern imperial subjects. Bolsheviks continued this following the revolution and in the early 1920s, even as their notions of the relationship of Central Asian nations to the Russian nation in a now socialist union differed significantly (Khalid 2006). Ideally, in communist ideology the nation would be bypassed. In order to arrive at this end-point evolutionary state, however, many of those shaping the earliest Soviet policies and projects were convinced that the various peoples of the Soviet Union had to pass through the proper stages of development, moving through full nationhood, before they could achieve a postnational state.

An early step in this process was an ethnographic effort to identify, delineate, and classify the various peoples of the Soviet Union. Tsarist-era romantic ideas of the nation informed decisions about what kind of "material" should be utilized to classify the nations. Francine Hirsch (2005, 164) points to "local cultures, religions, kinship structures, *byt* (Russian: everyday life), physical type, and languages" as the primary elements being considered. The material needed for the national repertoire of traditions of each ethnonational group—national dishes, language, clothing, instruments, and heroes—was largely gathered by Soviet ethnographers. However, the cultural forms were not invented ex nihilo; they were largely based on existing material.[14] But this material was then systematized, standardized, displayed, and taught to the "titular groups" involved, as well as to other nationalities. The actions, policies, and unintended consequences of these efforts by Soviet authorities, in dialogue and power plays with local national elites, created national boundaries, facilitated the formation of ethnonational consciousness, and encouraged the gathering of "cultural stuff" that was associated with each nationality (Grant 1995; Slezkine 2000; T. Martin 2001; Hirsch 2005; Pelkmans 2006). The need to mobilize national identity in order to access power, resources, and social rewards within the command economy of the Soviet Union made the adaptation of these identities essential for survival and advancement (Kandiyoti 1996; Hirsch 2005).

Religion was an essential element in the classification of the various peoples, as well as in the emerging nationalities and nations identities (Hirsch 2005, 101–227). Similarly, things like byt, which included ways of dressing, eating, and cooking, as well as household-related rituals or life-cycle events, were likewise elements drawn upon in the conceptualizing and constructing of nations (Northrop 2004, 51; Kamp 2006). These things were, for most Central Asians, likewise tied up with being Muslim. Thus religion—being Muslim—was being intimately intertwined with the emerging sense of the Kyrgyz or Uzbek nation, for example. This process was fraught with power plays and competing narratives and riddled with contradictions. And, just as these elements were being gathered up and prioritized as essential components of the emergent nations, other programs and policies of the Soviet state were labeling them as traditional at best and as backward, ignorant, or threatening at worst. These elements were being cultivated so that they could be surpassed. This is one of the essential contradictions of a modernizing regime: the modern can only exist in reference to tradition; tradition must be created for the modern to come into existence, and yet the modern is always anticipating and aiming toward tradition's demise.

Soviet Secular Production of Muslimness

Soviet atheist campaigns occurred concurrent with the creation of nations, and a similar counterintuitive and somewhat contradictory effect resulted from them. As Soviet officials, antireligious activists, and local and national elites who supported these efforts attempted to eradicate religion, they were in fact involved in defining what religion was. These definitions were then further shaped by those who opposed the antireligious efforts and by those who were forcibly drawn into the rather virulent material conversation. In this process, a particular category of religion was produced.

The antireligious campaigns of the early Soviet period were among the most militant, violent, and thorough of the twentieth century. They were in fact an attempt at atheism. The state endeavored not only to regulate religion—by creating a space free of it—it tried to eliminate it, in at least three particular moments over the seventy years of Soviet history. The antireligious campaigns of the early 1920s included propaganda drives aimed at teaching Central Asians that religion was false and science had triumphed over it (Keller 2001a, 2001b), as well as anticlerical measures that targeted traditionalist clergy and initially supported reformers (Keller 2001b, 69–140), such as the Jadids in Central Asia (Khalid 1998). Those involved in the campaigns took the Orthodox Church as a model of how religious life was structured and on that basis targeted what were interpreted to be Islam's primary institutions and leadership (Keller 1992), though Muslim activists argued against the efficacy of this approach (Keller 2001a).

These early years of the Soviet Union modernization and antireligious campaigns were rather unsuccessful. Leaders of these movements therefore changed tactics multiple times and tried various means to discredit Islam throughout Central Asia. In the Fergana Valley, they ultimately squared their attack on byt—notions of everyday life—as embodied by women and the home (Northrop 2004). They aimed their efforts at veiled women, arguing that their imprisonment in the *paranji* represented the evils of fanatical Islam.[15] Unveiling women was seen as tantamount to their liberation. The campaign was simultaneously part of attacks on religion and a push to speed up the cultural modernization of the region.

Early effects of the *hujum* (attack or assault), which began in 1927, varied.[16] While some embraced the movement, others rejected it. Discussing the campaigns in Uzbekistan, Marianne Kamp (2006, 134) notes that "unveiling had supporters and opponents from every social class and group within Uzbek society. There were women who unveiled in opposition to their families, and women who remained veiled in opposition to their families." As with the establishment of nations, this process too was riddled with conflicts and power struggles. The very same elements that had been used to classify and codify peoples and create nations—manner of dress or religion—were being targeted, for example, as repressive, patriarchal, or backward (see Edgar 2004, 13–14). Those opposed to the hujum read it simultaneously as the continued encroachment of Soviet power into community structures and local power, an attack on Islam, and a threat to the Uzbek nation (Kamp 2006, 186–87; Northrop 2004, 185–87). The Soviet state had begun to extend its reach into people's lives (Kamp 2006). The veil became, for a time, a centralized and valorized element of the emergent Uzbek identity as it was attacked by those involved in the atheist campaigns.[17]

While these early attacks on Islam were ineffective, long-term efforts succeeded in nearly eliminating central Muslim institutions and practices, including institutions of religious learning, religious authority, and collective worship. *Waqf* property was confiscated. Religious leaders were killed or deported. Religious education and chains of knowledge were interrupted. A change of alphabet was forced—from Arabic to Latin and finally to Cyrillic—at least partly to prohibit access to philosophical, legal, and literary texts used by religious specialists of the region (Shahrani 1995, 278). Although some of these texts survived until the post-Soviet period and, at least in Bazaar-Korgon, were cherished as links with the past and held up as evidence of a chain of religiosity and scholarly learning, the material in them was largely inaccessible to those who secretly owned them. Fasting at Ramadan and collective prayer were prohibited. Veils were forcibly removed. While the process was uneven, the power and reach of the state were both extensive and brutal. Through these campaigns then, not only were institutions, knowledge, practices, and sometimes people eliminated but particular elements of Muslim life were evaluated and continuously classified by state actors as improper, fraudulent, threatening, or outdated religion; religion became something that needed to be continually regulated and/or eliminated by the state.

Concomitant with struggles against religion were the promotion of Soviet ideals and modernization projects. While women were unveiling and being unveiled, they were also being offered new possibilities for work, recreation, and home life. Notions of gender equality were promoted and discursively tied to the Soviet modernization projects. While it has been argued that the dream of creating a "Homo sovieticus" was never achieved, the Soviet period did transform, and had lasting effects on, the inhabitants of the union.[18] During the Soviet period, primary reference points for identification shifted from regional, tribal, and occupational groups to an ethno-religious nation. Mass education became universal, as did an appeal to texts and the interpretation of them as sources of legitimacy and knowledge. Rational, scientific investigation was touted as a means of personal and societal advancement, and certain technological accomplishments—both small ones at the local level, such as electricity, plumbing, and the telephone, as well as prestige projects, including steel plants and a space program—helped shore up faith in these ideals. The command economy and collective agriculture transformed not only means of production and modes of consumption but also ways of acquiring and exercising status, influence, and goods (Humphrey 2002).[19] Moreover, as argued above, access to goods, resources, favor, power, and social life was conditional upon proper performance in this ideological environment, helping to ensure its continuation. Important within this was one's belonging to a particular ethno-religious nation.

Amid the attack on religion on the one hand and the promotion of scientific atheism, progress, and modern life on the other, there were Muslim practices, spaces, and ideas that escaped the antireligious campaigns. These notions and practices, equally bound up with the concept of Muslimness, persisted, though of course not unchanged (Shahrani 1984). Many of these things, such as the marking of life-cycle events and rituals related to the home, were connected to the domestic sphere and the concept of "everyday life" (byt) that had been valorized as a key component of national culture (Hirsch 2005; Northrop 2004). They also included things like mode of dress, language, or food. These were at times lauded—as when national traditions were displayed at school festivals—and at other times simply left alone or unrecognized—as when food was cooked in oil on Thursdays for the sake of the ancestors. Likewise, rituals surrounding death persisted, shrines were visited, and appeals to saints made. These practices continued for a variety of reasons. As Bruce Grant's (2011) interlocutors in the Caucasus indicate, they continued perhaps even because authorities feared the power of a saint or because of the complicated negotiating of powers between local authorities and practitioners of religion, who were sometimes one and the same (Abashin 2014; Grant 2011).

The antireligious campaigns were most virulent during Stalinism. Attitudes toward and policies and plans regarding religion eased in the immediate postwar period, and we can speak of a regulation of religion across the entire Soviet Union during this time (1943–47). The easing of antireligious pressure brought about an increase in religious practice, which worried officials and led to a much firmer approach from 1947 to 1954, though without the violent repression of the 1920s and 1930s (Ro'i 2000, 10). Another period of permissiveness prevailed from 1955 to 1958, followed by yet a third wave of heavy repression under Khrushchev from 1958 to 1964 (Ro'i 2000, 10; Tasar 2010, 4). From the mid-1960s onward the approach was generally one of toleration, though it was a negative tolerance in which religion was discouraged and treated as a necessary evil and efforts were still made to "educate" the population about their false beliefs.

During the early and mid-Soviet period many elements seen as inherently part of being a Muslim were not included in the attacks on religion and were inadvertently tied into a sense of national identity. However, those leading the renewed attacks on religion in the postwar period became alert to the way these forms and practices of religion were interwoven with national identity. Attempts to eradicate these practices followed, along with, in some cases, efforts to separate what was "religion" and what was "culture," and then promoting the latter in an effort to eliminate the former (e.g., Ro'i 2000, 698–99). It was largely impossible to make this distinction, however. One reason is that what was considered non-religious in Moscow could easily be construed as essentially Muslim in Central Asia or adopted as such in power struggles between local and distant elites (698–99). Another reason is that religion and culture had become even more interwoven for Muslims of the region, as well as for many other religious groups across the union (682–700). In her research on religion in the Volga region, Luehrmann (2012, 288, 295) points to two important reasons the effort to separate religion from culture failed, namely, the inability of policy makers and planners in Moscow who crafted the broad framework of antireligious campaigns to adequately conceive of both the meanings and functions of religion in local life, as well as their contradictory stances and inability to come to terms with "the difficult nexus between religion and communal identities."

Thus, despite reinvigorated attempts to eradicate religion as manifested in domestic spaces and life-cycle events, Muslim practice and an idea of Muslimness as tied to national identity continued. Examining the postwar era, Eren Tasar (2010, 61) indicates that Muslim practice was possible at times and in certain spaces because there was an overlap in the moral vocabularies of different traditions: "Central Asian (community, family, dedication to one's region or locality, respect for elders), Islamic (sacrifice, charity, erudition, devotion to one's homeland), and Soviet (sacrifice, love for the homeland, labor)." This palimpsest of values made some practices resonant and become positively readable in different, overlapping registers. Johan Rasanayagam (2011), examining the late Soviet period, argues that the coexistence of Muslim practice and selfhood within a Soviet secular state was made possible through the kind of deterritorialized milieus Alexi Yurchak (2006) has described. In these spaces of sociality, which were opened up by state discourse and action, members could, among other things, act and create themselves as Muslims in ways that were not necessarily inimical to or in support of the state (Rasanayagam 2011, 77). Or, as Rasanayagam (2014) would later argue, Muslimness flourished because the notion of a national culture was located between the politicized categories of backward, premodern tradition and fully enlightened Soviet culture. It was a form that could supposedly be "filled" with socialist content (see Pelkmans 2005, 2007). However, because it was the space allowed for life-cycle rituals linked to a sense of being Muslims, for most Central Asians it was likewise the space left for constructing oneself as a part of a moral community (Rasanayagam 2014, 11, 14).

It was not only that Muslim practice remained that is important for this argument. The practices that remained, the ideas that persisted, the objects and the spaces that continued were altered to address the new political, social, and economic environment. Muslimness ultimately became inseparable from an emerging national identity; it was an element that was at once tolerated, ignored, or unseen by the state but sometimes found acceptable, mobilized, acknowledged, or even celebrated. The nationalizing policies of the union, as they emerged over the century, continued to stimulate the development of an institutionalized, folklorized sense of nationality that included Muslimness.[20] An international political union that wanted to go beyond nationalism and a rational scientific state that wanted to eradicate religion had unintentionally created nations and a sense of ethnonational identity that was inextricably bound up with religious belonging.

The emerging category of religion therefore began to take shape through at least two means: the attacks on it in the atheist campaigns and the consolidation of it as a part of national belonging. In the former (the process of eradication), we see the state drawing a boundary, finding, identifying, monitoring, and eliminating or destroying those elements of religious life found to be inadmissible—the ones that would threaten its ontology. But perhaps most important for this discussion is the latter process. At the same moment that the secular state mapped out what "religion" was not allowed, being Muslim as an element of national culture (not as personal religious affiliation or faith) became an acceptable referent for public identification and at times necessary for successful participation in a multinational/religious political union.

The nationalities policies of the Soviet Union, which made these identities critical for advancement and for the acquisition of resources (Kandiyoti 1996) and which built what Terry Dean Martin (2001) has called an affirmative action empire, entailed a constant awareness of one's own specific ethnonational/religious identity and its difference from the other nationalities of the union. In essence then, there was a persistent discussion, a perpetual renegotiation and deployment of an idea of religion as well as a specific concept of Muslimness that was tied to a collective, now national, identity. Importantly, the performance of this identity counted, not only because of the moral registers it hit, the sense of belonging and meaning it gave, or the space it made for creating oneself in reference to Islamic tradition. The performance of this identity was essential for the creation of oneself in public secular life, the acquisition of land and other resources, the ability to apply for academic positions, and a whole host of other practical elements of daily life necessary for survival and well-being.

Central Asians were not isolated, interacting only with one another. Muslimness was understood as part of being Uzbek or Kyrgyz; it was also understood that all nations within the Soviet Union had a religious component to their national identity. Nations were, in part, defined by their religion, as they were by their dress, their language, the dishes they prepared, and the way they married, for example. The construction of national cultures and belonging was always a contrastive one; Muslimness was juxtaposed to, for example, the Christianity of the Ukrainians or Russians (or compared to the Muslimness of the Kazakhs, Tatars, or Azerbaijanis), a trait already present in the early imperial period. Displayed in museums, shown on posters, discussed in textbooks, promoted in affirmative action policies, and celebrated in festivals, the nations were created in contrast to one another and along an axis of set components. And these were not distant others; Slavic populations settled in Central Asian regions. Central Asians traveled and studied throughout the union. All nationalities fought together in war. National culture, which included religion, was created, celebrated, discussed, and displayed (Hirsch 2005).

Returning to my interlocutors, one of the primary challenges they felt in the post-Soviet period, when alternative interpretations of Islam appeared in the region, was to their understanding of themselves as Muslims, which they defined primarily based on birth into the community, adherence to rituals and norms often related to the home and life-cycle events, the wearing of certain kinds of clothing, the cooking of certain kinds of meals, and belief in God. In short, there was an understanding of a community of belonging that was simultaneously religious and ethnonational.

Nonliberal Logics and Secular Religion

The secular state delineates religion's space and its definition. It does so in conversation with religious actors who live, act, and create from within the ideational-material logics of the system; it is the environment within which they form themselves, their communities, their ideas, their material objects, their systems of knowledge, their particular positions of power, their critique and efforts at change, and their religion, all in a manner that can be heard and carried out in these logics. My assertion is that in the Soviet Union—for various material and ideational reasons—the idea of community, and of practice, became highlighted and centralized in the category of religion, much as internalized belief did in liberal variants of religion. Both were formed through a political project of secularism, but with alternative notions of the modern and the secular. Using this articulation of religion was necessary for material survival and flourishing with the Soviet Union, as discussed above, because of the way access, rights, and resources were granted. It likewise made sense to Muslims because an idea of religion that centralized belonging and praxis fit with ideas and practices of Islam in the region at that time.

Religion developed through and as an understanding of collective belonging as employed, for example, in the administration of distant territories and in historical-evolutionary ideas of human society and its development. At work in this construction of religion—however intended, implicit, or inadvertent—was the logic of Soviet modernity and one of its key ideas, the interpersonal. The Soviet state's vision, organization, and attempts to transform society prioritized and presupposed the interpersonal—the notion that society should be transformed through and on the basis of collective action. Ideas of citizenship more rooted in joint responsibility, for example, or economics premised on redistribution articulated these logics.[21] So did ideas about communal effort being the mode of societal transformation, with the object of change being the collective itself.[22] They were conceptions that resonated with and developed in part from ideas within Islam and Orthodoxy as understood and practiced at the time. These logics developed into particular conceptions of nations and citizens and informed the way individuals understood their participation in, resistance to, ambivalence about, or survival in the socialist political economy. The development of a concept of religion—both material and ideational—was tied to and co-constitutive of this set of ideas and material practices.

I understand the logics of a state, as well as its particular modes of power, to be rooted in and bound up with the mode of production, and following Hann (2012) and Asad (1993, 2003) I want to understand the way these modes directly and indirectly affected religion, including its categorical definition and its space. Religion as collective belonging fit within socialism's broader logics and modes of power and was consistent with the particularities of the Soviet modernizing regime. But this state and its practices and ideas were not liberal. Internal faith and privatized religion fit the liberal logic of the autonomous individual—a logic that gives inspiration and drives things like the American Dream while simultaneously serving as the basis of power that keeps individuals captive to the state and the market, leaving them precarious, fluctuating, and atomized without recourse to social support. It fits with ideas of ethics and conscience as a personal matter (Asad 2003, 247), with ideas about technologies of power producing subjects that police themselves (247). It was another logic that gave the idea of religion as collective belonging its context—a logic that inspired the dream of socialist citizens collectively working for the common good, that saw the transformation of society and its material structures as necessary for moral regulation, and that simultaneously enabled and consolidated power in the hands of the party-state, which could, in the interest of the collective and on the authority of determining that good, dominate the state's subjects and their will. This logic worked through and on the basis of collectives, co-creating and objectifying them, in some cases where they did not exist, so that later they could be surpassed and in the meantime could be used to create and police socialism.

In liberal secularism, acceptable religion could be the faith of an individual believer in a space (the private) that was removed from politics. The Soviet state's reach into the home and the politicization of private life left little space for this conceptualization or practice of religion to be legitimate (Luehrmann 2011, 9). Liberal variants of religion meshed with overarching liberal economic and political practices and ideas—that of the individual, of the self-made "man," of a social transformation brought about by individual change, of social needs met by nonstate actors. Models and practices of state, economy, and politics in the Soviet Union were different, necessitating a different idea and enactment of secularism and ultimately of religion. Bolshevik and later Soviet models of societal change, for example, began with the proper construction of social and economic institutions, or aesthetic and cultural practices, which would then result in the alteration of individuals. Rather than truth springing from within the individual and leading to the transformation of society, structural change brought about by collective effort would generate individual transformation (see Wanner 2007, 33).

Luehrmann's (2011) work on secularism in Russia's Volga region is particularly informative here. Luehrmann analyzes the techniques of activists involved in the antireligious efforts of the late Soviet period. She describes how underlying notions of the collective alteration of society worked out in practice, showing the shape and nature of the Soviet publics that enacted them in the late Soviet era. Luehrmann's understanding of Soviet secularity is located in what she calls, building on Charles Taylor's work, its "exclusive humanism"—the idea that social relations do not include nonhuman agents and that society must be shaped and constructed with "human contemporaries [as] the only possible partners in action" (2011, 7–8). For Luehrmann, secularism in the Soviet Union was not premised on a notion of individualism or privatized religion. Instead it was constructed through a didactic public in which "the primary object of intervention was often society as a whole, rather than individual selves" (10). Here, there was a notion of the "'malleable self' open to the influence of outside forces" in which "efforts to become a new person were inseparably tied to learning how to change others" (10). Rasanayagam's (2014) work on Islam in Uzbekistan points to a very similar conception and practice. He argues that the Soviet project in Central Asia should be seen as a civilizing mission that sought to move people beyond premodern traditions to a place of high culture, of civilization, and this was to be done through the transformation of the human subject: "the New Soviet Person was to enter society as part of a collective, achieving his or her human potential in the pursuit of collective, rather than individual, goals . . . worked out through the capillaries of society, in the workplace, in leisure activities and living space, and through practices of peer and self-criticism" (2014, 6–7).

Luehrmann's and Rasanayagam's ideas are useful here because they reveal both the underlying logics of Soviet power broadly and the particular way societal alteration was understood, both of which are inextricably tied in with the construction of religion. First, their work demonstrates that in theory there was no space free from the reach of the state, and thus the "private" was a space into which the state could legitimately intrude. This does not mean that the state always did intrude in practice, but it points to a different conception of what private and public were, what spaces were legitimate sites of political action, and what the nature, form, and aim of this action were. Second, there was a set of notions about transformation occurring through generative collective action, whether this was done in reference to the state, through party programs, via prestige projects such as steel plants and dams (Kotkin 1995; Kalinovsky forthcoming), or in local forms of sociability and conviviality, and also whether this was done in support of or in contrast to state-led activities or ideas or—as Yurchak (2006, 9) has pointed out—"in ways that did not fit either/or dichotomies."

As a secularizing regime, the Soviet state was constantly identifying and locating religion, drawing boundaries, and defining, in discourse and practices, the difference between acceptable, tolerable religion and threatening, improper religion. The latter category was perhaps the most easily identifiable—those things targeted in the antireligion campaigns—religious texts, knowledge and practice of certain rituals, certain forms of dress, authorities and teachers, and so on. The former category, in a society that sought the total eradication of religion, was inimical. In practice, however, much was tolerated and inadvertently cultivated "in the meantime." Religion, as allowed (explicitly and tacitly) by the state, signaled less the internal belief of an atomized individual—safe in private space from influencing politics—and more an ascriptive attribute of national belonging.

In saying that religion as a part of Soviet secularism was primarily about belonging, I am not arguing that "belief" was eliminated. I am not arguing that Kyrgyz or Uzbek Muslims did not believe while identifying as Muslims or participating in rituals, or that they necessarily did. I am not asserting that belief and truth claims were unknown to them. In making this argument, I am not asserting anything about how they understood the concept of "belief" itself nor about the experiences they had when engaging in ritual, for example. That is not the point. The point is on which grounds religion could legitimately be discussed, appealed to, or understood in reference to, or as allowed by, the secular state, and in what ways religion fit the modern logics in which it was located and generated. What I am pointing to are the ways that the category of religion was co-constituted in dialogue with and tacitly, inadvertently, explicitly, or otherwise allowed by the state. In which space and form did the state allow for religion to be articulated? When was "Muslim" an acceptable referent for public identification? Religion could be invoked, but only as it announced national belonging.

The contrast with liberal variants of secularism, in which religion as belonging is excluded and invalidated by state actors and legal systems, becomes clear in examples found in Asad's (2003, 139–40) and Saba Mahmood's (2009, 79–83) work.[23] In both cases, we see a legal environment that invalidates a definition of religion premised on belonging in favor of one founded on belief. Actors can maneuver in these realms and on the basis of these laws only if they abide by and articulate themselves in reference to these definitions. In the case of Soviet Central Asia, collective belonging, on the other hand, was the only basis upon which religion could be positively, publicly defined or appealed to (even if the space for it was highly curtailed and limited when compared to religion in European or American contexts). Doing so with reference to faith or belief would have been impossible.

I do not want to overemphasize the distinction between liberal and non-liberal. They are both forms of modern power, carrying broad similarities, and certainly in the Soviet Central Asian case the idea of individual belief was not absent, nor has the notion of communal belonging disappeared from ideas about religion in Western contexts.[24] In fact, both individual and communal categories of religion are to be found in both liberal and nonliberal settings (Lehmann 2013); both are modern conceptions that were crafted while notions of the secular, as well as secularizing regimes, were emerging. They are treated and evaluated differently, however. Certain elements are highlighted and become more essential to conceptualizations in the Soviet case than in the others, and these are directly linked to the secular state that legitimizes religion and whose exercise of power and its creation of subjects follows this same logic, a logic tied in with its material regime.

The question remains: without a focus on the individual, on internal belief, on religion defined as a set of internal truth claims, was the notion of religion in the Soviet Union a *modern* notion of religion? It was articulated by self-proclaimed so-called moderns and in a manner in which those deploying the idea did so from the stance that religion was something that had been or needed to be disentangled from politics, economics, or science, a Latourian articulation of the modern (Latour 1993). It was developed within the broader logics and endeavors of a state that had secularism and modernity as its self-proclaimed political project, an Asadian view of modernity as a historical epoch (Adad 2003, 14). It was connected to and premised on "a particular form of power and knowledge" that worked itself not only into the construction of an abstracted, universalized concept of religion but into new kinds of states, science, and subjects (Asad 1993, 43) and ways of organizing production.

Another way of putting it is that a modern state is, among other things, predicated on a particular mode of power. This power is legitimated, in part, through a supposed separation from religion and the right to delineate the proper boundaries, scope, and power of religion. In short, a secular state of self-proclaimed moderns can do nothing other than produce a modern form of religion; that is its ontological necessity, though of course the production and maintenance of such a notion takes time and proceeds unevenly. But here the secular takes on its particular Soviet form through its unique historical development in a Russian conceptualization of the secular that arose in part through its encounter in Central Asia.

Returning to the discussion of a secular, liberal notion of religion, there is the simultaneous, often contradictory program of liberal democracies that tolerate religion, and make space for its existence, but whose own power is invested in controlling, limiting, and enervating religion and whose modernizing narrative constantly waits for its demise. Religion's space then is left to the private belief of the individual—its primary defined trait—and the community of the faithful as they live and practice together—secondarily understood and defined by prior ascension to faith. This faith must be tolerated and respected or at least treated equally by the state in accord with the appeal to human rights. This ideally individualized religion is part and parcel of a larger frame of material and ideological practices and notions in a capitalist democracy in which the flexible, autonomous, individualized, rights-claiming self is fashioned in a neoliberal environment.

In the Soviet Union, there was another set of (contradictory) logics at work. There was a drive to actively eliminate religion simultaneous with the cultivation of collective belonging in a multinational environment that utilized religion as an indicator of the nation's character.[25] This occurred in a context in which rights, access to resources, and modes of development were connected to collectivities. Religion never needed to be fully disentangled conceptually from culture. Nations, their characteristics, and the people who belonged to them were understood as a necessary element in the social evolution that would lead ultimately to communism. They likewise became central as means of control and modes of organized change. Socialism and ultimately the communist ideal did not depend on removing religion from national culture. It was celebrated in the historical-evolutionary moment of socialism that would be superseded completely as nations melted away and communism was reached. These national cultures would someday be replaced by a nation-free, religion-free, atheist-communist utopia. Religion would disappear when the material and ideological transformation of society was achieved, when the need for religion was no longer present because of collective structural alteration, because of the elimination of capitalist enslavement and premodern socioeconomic structures, and when enlightenment appeared as a result of public education. In the meantime, however, the group-oriented, collective identity of the nation, the religious-cultural community, fit within the material-ideological logics of the Soviet system.

Returning to the definition of religion among moderns, my proposition is that religion in a secular state does not always have to be individualizing and it does not always have to be premised on internal discourse above practice—this is its liberal variant. It's quite a self-evident claim on the one hand, as that is one of the essential definitions of liberalism. The Soviet variant turned out to be one in which collective belonging—benign and promoted in folklorized scripted forms, unrecognized in its tie to domestic spaces, targeted but not eliminated, or allowed by low-level leaders because of its importance to life-cycle events— came to be the quality that defined religion. The specific historical conception of religion in a nonliberal, secular environment was about belonging, not belief. Confronting the liberal idea of religion and the secular was the essential struggle and discomfort many of my interlocutors faced when the Soviet Union collapsed, when new ideas about religion, Islam, and being Muslim entered the region, and when the entire political economy was transformed.

CHAPTER 1

ON BEING MUSLIM IN BAZAAR-KORGON

The townscape of Bazaar-Korgon is low and sprawling. Walking, it takes at least an hour and a half to traverse the town. In most quarters earthen walls line dusty streets, creating a landscape that, to the unfamiliar eye, becomes a maze of identical roads. The glare of a midday summer sun blinds those who dare venture out in the heat that tops 40 degrees Celsius. At the right time of day, however, nearly all the year through (winters being mild out of doors in the sun but bone-chilling in an unheated room) the streets are alive with activity. Women and girls gather at public water sources, socializing while they wait to fill their buckets. Groups of young men and boys stand or crouch on corners and other points along the roadside, not waiting for anything in particular, just talking and passing time. Few residents own cars, so most walk, stopping along their way to greet friends, neighbors, relatives, or acquaintances; the demands of this kind of everyday sociability make an already long walk even longer.

Five wide, paved streets cut through Bazaar-Korgon. On one of these lies the current town square, where one of the town's two Lenin statues stands. On the southwest edge of the square, on the hill overlooking the bazaar is the district Friday mosque. Close inspection reveals that the wider mosque complex is incom-

FIGURE I.I. Bazaar-Korgon. Photograph by the author, 2003.

plete; one sees the foundation for a minaret never built, the makeshift facilities for ritual ablutions, the groundskeeper's flimsy hut, two of its walls consisting merely of a sheet.

The construction of the central mosque, begun in 1993 and completed in 1999, was nearly universally supported by townsfolk. Perhaps this unanimity was because during the 1990s, when all else was falling apart in town, it was the one concrete sign that postsocialist dreams might be realized. This particular project was important because its realization, involving foreign donors, symbolized successful participation in new political and economic arenas. It was also an expression of newly gained religious freedom and the ability to assert oneself as Muslim in public. The mosque was "the transition" to capitalism and democracy happening; through it, residents imagined that the dream of transition might still be fulfilled, despite the massive economic downturn of the early post-Soviet years. Its construction even moved forward through the mid- to late 1990s, when Kyrgyzstan's economic decline reached its nadir.

Just to the northwest of the mosque is the bazaar. It too was emblematic of the transition.[1] In the Soviet period there had been some light industry in town and a series of other state-run enterprises, but most residents had been engaged in agriculture. The town had basically been two large state farms. The

FIGURE 1.2. Foundation for a minaret never completed. Photograph by the author, 2004.

closure of the factories, the cessation of collective farming, and the distribution of agricultural land among residents in the early 1990s left large portions of the population unemployed. With no other jobs in sight, countless townsfolk and residents from villages in the region tried their luck in the new marketplace—as petty merchants in the bazaar. Sadly, most were not able to reach the state of

FIGURE 1.3. Particleboard and sheet-covered hut for groundskeeper of the rayon Friday mosque. Photograph by the author, 2004.

affluence they equated with democracy and capitalism. In fact, most remained impoverished.

If the bazaar failed to fulfill the economic promises of capitalist dreams, it faired better in providing for the realization of other liberal promises—freedom of conscience, press, and assembly. The bazaar had become a place to produce, sell, and consume ideas in the form of books, pamphlets, audiocassettes, and CDs. It was also a major node of social interaction and a location where those wanting to get a message across could advertise. And while these advertisements generally concerned new products or the announcement of events, the public space of the market had also served as a venue for conveying Islamic messages.

There is a story that sometime in the year 2000 men stood in front of the bazaar and called listeners to come "close to Islam" (*dinge jakyn*). None of my acquaintances could say who the men were, but gossip was that they were "Wahhabis" or members of Hizb ut-Tahrir.[2] The veracity of this evaluation is suspect, but what is interesting is the impression this event made on residents; the story was retold to me many times as evidence of what was happening in Bazaar-Korgon. Other indicators of change offered to me were the new ways women were wearing headscarves and the increasing number of women doing so. Residents also pointed to the rising number of men, especially young boys, attending mosques, and they mentioned the home-based Islamic study groups that had proliferated in town. Unlike the construction of the central mosque, however, these displays of Islamic behavior were not as positively evaluated.

Residents of the community read these signs as indicators that the actors adhered to interpretations of Islam and held conceptions of Muslimness (*musluman-chylyk*) at variance with the public norms of the late Soviet and early post-Soviet era. This challenge stirred debate in the community, especially among those who did not refer to themselves as "close to Islam" but who considered themselves Muslim nonetheless. What did it mean to be a Muslim in Bazaar-Korgon at the turn of the millennium? This book is premised on the idea that the answer to this question was up for debate; the hyperinterrogation of this notion—the fearful attitude displayed by some and the playful shaping of it by others—was in fact the most salient aspect of religious life and of discussions about religion in the community.[3] The space for this debate is what made religious life in turn-of-the-millennium Kyrgyzstan so unique, compared to, for example, neighboring Uzbekistan (Rasanayagam 2006c) or the situation in the Soviet period. This book is about these discussions.

However, this assertion does not mean that religious life per se was what was most pressing in the lives of Bazaar-Korgonians at the turn of millennium. For most residents, dealing with the economic and social dislocations of the postsocialist period was the most urgent issue. Kyrgyzstan's economic decline reached its nadir in 1998. By 2003, when the research for this project started, residents were still climbing out of that spiral and were just barely beginning to meet their daily needs (see Reeves 2012, 108–9). Yet the ability to feel "normal" and the ability to return to some sort of familiarity or regularity (see Zigon 2009) in the everyday workings of the new political, economic, and social situation were still far off. Joma Nazpary (2002, 1–19) has discussed this period in Kazakhstan in terms of "chaos," while Caroline Humphrey (2002, xvii) has employed the term "radical uncertainty" for the Russian situation. In 2003 and 2004, residents of Bazaar-Korgon were living in this chaotic, uncertain time and looking back to the Soviet period was a ubiquitous activity. It was a consciously "post" environment.[4] It was no different for those who were actively engaged in learning about or being close to Islam. The insecurity and uncertainty of postsocialist life was the primary terrain in which all residents of the town lived.

What does it mean to be a Muslim in Bazaar-Korgon? This chapter address that question. It starts, however, with a discussion not of religion but of the economy, society, and politics. For most residents, dealing with the economic, social, and political dislocations of the postsocialist period was their primary concern; interrogating religion was at best secondary. But there were some in the community for whom religion was of central importance—those who were "interested in Islam." The chapter moves to a discussion of such individuals and what kinds of debates their modes of understanding and living Islam sparked.

Small-Town Hardships

In 2004, Bazaar-Korgon was administratively classified as a village, despite the fact that approximately thirty thousand people inhabited the community. There were few paved roads. Most inhabitants did not having running water in their homes. There were only a handful of businesses, and they employed no more than thirty persons on average, with the exception of an ice-cream company with one hundred workers. Despite this village character, it was the capital of the *rayon* (an administrative unit or district).[5] Paid work was scarce. The vast majority of residents were either employed in the state sector (education, health care, and government offices), worked in the bazaar, or engaged in agricultural work. When the two collective farms were divided up after the Soviet breakup, nearly everyone received a piece of land, located just outside town, which today provides supplemental income either through the sale of crops or the rent and/or sale of the land. Moreover, the majority of people had small bits of land at their residences on which to grow fruit and vegetables for household consumption.

The older part of the town, at least according to local oral history, dates back more than two hundred years. Few families living there at the time of this research, however, could trace their lineage back to the early days of the community. Those who could claimed to know which cities in contemporary Uzbekistan their families had left in order to found and settle in Bazaar-Korgon. The population was approximately 80 percent Uzbek and 20 percent Kyrgyz. In terms of trading, social networks, and cultural linkages, residents had long looked to the urban centers of the south and west—contemporary Uzbekistan or Uzbek-dominated regions of Kyrgyzstan—rather than to the mountains of the north and east. This orientation remained in place after republican boundaries were drawn in the early twentieth century and the town of Bazaar-Korgon became part of the Kyrgyz Soviet Socialist Republic. Ties with Uzbekistan remained strong throughout the Soviet and early post-Soviet periods partly because of the highly porous border. The situation did not change until 1999, when Islam Karimov, the president of Uzbekistan, sealed the border following an assassination attempt by unknown assailants. The growing influence of the Islamic Movement of Uzbekistan (IMU), including their kidnappings of foreigners on the Kyrgyz-Tajik border and their desire to topple the Karimov regime, aggravated by what Uzbekistan saw as weak Kyrgyzstani antiterrorism efforts and ineffective border patrol, provided further impetus for Karimov to seal the border (Megoran 2002). After this closure, trading and social networks became more difficult to maintain.

Bazaar-Korgon is in the Fergana Valley, thirty kilometers east of the Uzbek border, twenty kilometers west of its oblast (province) capital, Jalal-Abad, and just off the main highway that connects Bishkek and Osh, Kyrgyzstan's largest and second-largest cities, respectively. While the town of Bazaar-Korgon is predominantly Uzbek, Bazaar-Korgon rayon is inversely dominated by Kyrgyz. The ethnic makeup of the rayon reflects the Kyrgyz-Uzbek ratio of the country. The Fergana Valley has been the site of major sedentary populations of Central Asia since antiquity. Contemporary Uzbeks assert the most forceful claim as primary descendants of these populations, despite the long-standing heterogeneity of the region's peoples (see Schoeberlein-Engel 1994; Finke 2014). Prior to Soviet modernization campaigns of the early twentieth century, which included a massive project of forced settlement, the contemporary Kyrgyz population was nomadic. During the Russian imperialist period and the Soviet era, Russians and then others from around the Soviet Union settled in Kyrgyzstan. Following the Soviet collapse, most of these newer residents fled. Only a handful of what once was a significant Slavic population in Bazaar-Korgon (approximately 10 percent of the total) from the 1970s to the early 1990s remained at the time of research. There are two official languages in Kyrgyzstan—Kyrgyz and Russian. Uzbek is not an official language, though it is the language of instruction in many schools of southern Kyrgyzstan. In Bazaar-Korgon, for example, four out of seven schools use Uzbek as a language of instruction and follow the curriculum used in Uzbekistan, though with the addition of courses in Kyrgyz language and the history of Kyrgyzstan. Kyrgyz residents of the north often note the heavy influence of the Uzbek language on the Kyrgyz spoken by southerners.

Ethnonational identity is an important issue in Kyrgyzstan, not least because of the sizable Uzbek population. During the Osh riots of 1990, 120 Uzbeks and 50 Kyrgyz were killed during three days of ethnic violence sparked by land disputes, the uneven distribution of power, and high levels of unemployment (Tishkov 1995, 134). In the first decade following the collapse of the Soviet Union, Uzbekistan seemed to prosper while Kyrgyzstan lay in misery. This differential led many Uzbeks in Kyrgyzstan to look longingly toward Uzbekistan. For many, Karimov typified the strong leader Central Asians thought they needed to pull them through the difficulties of the early post-Soviet period. The early economic success of Uzbekistan seemed to confirm this idea. Yet, by the turn of the millennium, the situation had been nearly reversed. Many Uzbeks in Kyrgyzstan began to perceive the Karimov administration as increasingly authoritarian. Moreover, they expressed satisfaction with the freedom they enjoyed in Kyrgyzstan to grow, sell, or manufacture what they wanted and when, in contrast to the centrally controlled Uzbek economy (see Liu 2012, 9). They saw Uzbeks across the border experience a sharp decrease in living standards as well as a curtailment of freedoms, including freedom of expression and conscience. The Andijan massacre of 2005, in which several hundred people were slaughtered by the Karimov government, confirmed what locals knew and human rights organizations had feared—the authoritarian regime would use any means to maintain control, including torture, kidnapping, arrest, and mass killings (Human Rights Watch 2005; International Crisis Group 2005). Many of those who fled the 2005 massacre landed in Bazaar-Korgon rayon.

For many Uzbeks at the turn of the millennium, Kyrgyzstan was a place of relative freedom. Those I spoke with in Bazaar-Korgon celebrated their independence, which their friends, families, and business partners in Uzbekistan did not have. Yet, when compared to Kyrgyz people in Kyrgyzstan, Uzbeks often felt less than equal, despite full citizenship and equal rights guaranteed by law (Khamidov 2002). Uzbeks and Kyrgyz were in agreement, however, concerning Kyrgyzstan's poor economic growth and the rampant corruption in politics and business. In March 2005, the Tulip Revolution took place, ousting President Askar Akaev, who had been in office since 1991. While many hoped the revolution would signal a changing political and economic environment, the cronyism and corruption of the former regime continued. Economic conditions, too, remained bleak (Sershen 2007), a persistent situation that by 2010 played a role in a second political upheaval. Tragically, massive ethnic violence followed quickly on the heels of these political shifts.[6] In June 2010, some 400 people were killed, nearly 2,000 were treated for injuries, and approximately 300,000 people were displaced, with about 111,000 fleeing to Uzbekistan during three days of violence in southern Kyrgyzstan (Kyrgyzstan Inquiry Commission 2011; Human Rights Watch 2010). Bazaar-Korgon was at the center of this violence (McBrien 2011, 2013). This tumult, however, was not even imagined in 2003–4 when I conducted my research.

At that time what was crucial for day-to-day living was economic survival and reorienting oneself within rapidly shifting economic and political environments (see Creed 2002). With few businesses or factories in town, work was found in one of three arenas—the field, the bazaar, or the government. For most, in order to maintain an average income that would feed and clothe a family, provide a comfortable home, and leave enough for small luxuries like televisions, radios, cell phones, and hosting guests at small parties, work in all these sectors had to be combined. When I asked an agricultural specialist from the rayon government what percentage of the population was involved in agricultural work, he replied, "Everyone."

His answer was not in jest. The land that had belonged to the collective farms had been divided among town residents regardless of whether they had worked there. The amount of land allotted was based on family size. The average allotment was between fifty and sixty-five *sotik*.[7] In theory everyone was to receive a piece. In practice the land was doled out more quickly to those close to power and those who had worked the land. Others had to fight for their parcels. Interestingly, some of these fights came a decade after the dissolution of the union. In the early 1990s, many professionals—teachers, doctors, and administrators (the majority of whom were Kyrgyz)—imagined that the economic downturn would be temporary. They were not farmers but professionals, they lived in apartments, and land seemed unimportant. Only after the reality of the economic situation set in did many of these people assert their right to the land parcels. One couple, for example, two physicians in their fifties, received their parcel in 2004. The land closer to town having already been given away, they received their fifty-five sotik (0.55 hectare) on an edge of town that was more than an hour's walk from their home.

Inconveniences like an hour's walk didn't stop residents from cultivating cash crops.[8] The parcels of land had become extremely important for income generation, and great effort was put into their cultivation. In the household surveys I conducted, I found that for those families who had one or two adults employed as schoolteachers, taxi drivers, bazaar merchants, or civil servants and bureaucrats, the revenue they received from their land still made up at least 50 percent of their total income for the year. These people were generally perceived by their neighbors as being average in economic terms. The rich, of whom there were few, found their money in the same places. They just had a bit more land—usually two hectares or more—had bigger, more successful stalls at the bazaar, or were higher-level bureaucrats. One of the most important means of additional income for household budgets was the money brought in by circular migration. Paid work was not only hard to find in town; its absence was a chronic national problem. Large numbers of Bazaar-Korgonians sought work abroad, primarily in Russia, though there were some from the town working in Turkey and the European Union as well. Residents who migrated to Russia worked primarily as manual laborers and merchants. This trend would dramatically increase over the next decade. In 2013, Kyrgyzstan was third in the World Bank's rankings of countries dependent on remittances, with one-fifth of its workforce employed as migrant laborers (*Economist* 2013).[9]

In 2004, the average Kyrgyz household was much smaller than an Uzbek one. This was partly because the Kyrgyz living in town had moved there relatively recently, leaving their extended families in their villages of origin. Their households consisted of the nuclear members alone, generally two parents and three children. However, extended family members regularly visited, and it wasn't uncommon to have a relative—particularly those needing extra care, like a small child or an elderly adult—staying for several months. Uzbek families, however, had generally lived in the town for a couple of generations; several nuclear families often occupied one piece of land. Among Kyrgyz and Uzbeks alike, the youngest son ideally lives with his parents until they die, upon which time he inherits their home and land. Thus, depending on the stage in the family cycle, one Uzbek household would likely consist of seven or more members—a married couple, their children, and the parents of the adult male. However, in the post-Soviet period, economic considerations meant that other adult sons frequently remained with their parents as well, building additional structures on the same piece of land for their families. This could mean upwards of fourteen people living together in a family compound (*havla*) (see Liu 2012, 125–47).

However, in these cases, each family tended to regulate household finances somewhat independently. The term "independently" is used very loosely. The youngest son and his wife generally had the responsibility for providing meals for themselves, their children, and his parents. Others in the compound were responsible for themselves. Similarly, each household financed its own clothes, transportation, and so on. But child care was shared, as were all sorts of material resources, such as washing machines, irons, and stoves. Labor was also pooled, as were any number of small, everyday necessities. Households were usually distinguished according to who ate together on a regular basis. The phrase *bir kazandan* (from one pot) was the term most often employed to indicate a separate household.

When asked what percentage of the town's population was poor, a middle-aged, low-level bureaucrat, who had been described as having an average income, looked at me, sighed, and said, "We are all poor." His first reaction should be taken seriously in at least one regard—as a comparative statement about the perception of economic and social decline following the collapse of socialism. After a bit more discussion concerning relative levels of poverty—having enough to eat, owning a television, and hosting parties being indicators of the "average" poor—the man guessed that perhaps 20 or 30 percent of the population was "very" or "really" poor. The only available documentation of poverty levels—a project proposal produced by the town government in 2002 for a poverty alleviation program—indicated a similar proportion (33 percent) of the population to be very poor.[10] The mayor was a bit more pessimistic; he guessed at least half the people lived in poverty. But what did poverty mean for these men and for the committee that prepared the report? What did real poverty mean for residents?

For Bazaar-Korgonians, real poverty meant selling household items like carpets and furniture in order to buy food. It meant replacing broken windows with thin sheets of plastic—only slightly thicker than a grocery bag—to keep the cold out. It meant not buying meat and only a limited number of in-season vegetables. Potatoes or pasta (*makaron*) once a day, with a bit of bread and tea for the other two meals, was the norm for the very poor. Real poverty meant owning two pairs of pants—one for the summer and one for the winter. And in the winter, if there was electricity, it meant using a tiny hot plate designed to boil water to heat a nearly bare room of some twenty square meters. That was real poverty. Those who lived with average means, however, did not always feel fortunate. While they might have had enough to eat, to host a few parties, and even to buy a few luxuries, there were many "essentials" of life they had given up or reduced their standards on. These included buying or building houses for their sons or hosting big wedding parties for their children. They had to find new ways to fulfill these social obligations.

Finding enough money for daily sustenance was not the only issue occupying residents' minds in the wake of socialism's failure; they were also discovering novel ways of coping with the overall economic collapse. In order to construct new buildings cheaply, people purchased old structures that had been abandoned by schools, businesses, and families and then recycled the building materials. Bazaar-Korgonians learned how to live in apartments without indoor plumbing and how to repair old machinery, cars, and electrical appliances when spare parts were no longer in production. Residents had to adjust to new means of obtaining the services, goods, and positions needed for every aspect of daily life, and that new means was money. As Alena Ledeneva (2006) argues, what was novel about the post-Soviet situation was not the use of personal networks to gain access to goods and services but rather the monetization of these connections. During the Soviet period, individuals used reciprocal exchanges and patron-client relationships to access goods, power, and resources. The post-Soviet context created the space and the need for profit maximization, and those in power—whether in the government, hospitals, or universities—used their positions for financial benefit.

Bazaar-Korgonians also discovered the business behind humanitarian agencies, foreign development programs, and NGOs. Learning to churn out grant proposals, small business plans, and educational programs in order to garner funds from foreign sources became an art and a business (see Boehm 1999; Mandel 2002). One afternoon the rayon education department visited a local school in order to "assess" it. The visit came on the same day that a group of foreign and national development workers were discussing a pertinent social issue with a group of secondary school students.[11] The head of the education department walked into the classroom, interrupted the discussion, and took the opportunity to praise the foreigners for helping Kyrgyzstan. He then told the students that the surest way to prepare a good future for themselves and their school would be through these foreigners. "Learn to write good proposals. Win grants. That is the key," he told them. Looking to the foreigners he asked, "Am I right?"

These were the new rules of life—the hazy roads of bribery, "democratically elected" but financially influenced power clusters, and foreign grants.[12] These were the matters—along with the daily conflicts, celebrations, loves, losses, disappointments, and triumphs of human interaction—that were central concerns for Muslims in Bazaar-Korgon, both those understood as "interested in Islam" and those who were not. Although religious institutions in other Muslim-majority societies have come to play a powerful role in public life by explicitly dealing with the kinds of difficulties faced by the Muslims of Bazaar-Korgon—especially poverty and lack of social services—the religious institutions that developed in the community up to 2004 contributed little in this way; they were primarily aimed at education.[13]

When residents of Bazaar-Korgon did talk about religion, what was often most prominent in their discussions was the apparent inevitability of violence due to an "Islamic threat." Bleak economic prospects and massive dissatisfaction with the economic and political state of the nation provide at least part of the impetus for the urban poor to take an interest in Islamist movements like Hizb ut-Tahrir (International Crisis Group 2003; Ilkhamov 2001; Khamidov 2002). The urban poor in the southern part of the country, where these movements were most active, were largely Uzbek youth who, because of their minority status, often felt even more alienated from political and economic opportunities than their Kyrgyz age cohorts. However, the membership of these groups was very limited (International Crisis Group 2003; McBrien and Pelkmans 2008). Most people who had "come close to Islam" had no political motivations or agendas.

The economic and political situation in Kyrgyzstan led to drastic attempts at political change, but none of them took a religious tone. The unfolding of the 2005 Tulip Revolution is instructive in this regard. Reports about the demonstrations and marches that culminated in the toppling of the Akaev regime did not make a single reference to religious symbolism or motivations.[14] Despite these observations and the fact that actual participation in politically motivated Islamist movements was small, if not insignificant, political and scholarly discourse remains occupied with a "growing Islamist threat" (e.g., Baran et al. 2006; Karagiannis 2006; Naumkin 2005). It seems that a rather paranoid and ungrounded fear of religiously inspired violent political action has captured the imaginations of politicians, scholars, and residents of the Fergana Valley—Bazaar-Korgon included. While the Uzbek regime utilized the discourse of antiterrorism to (violently) consolidate its power and eliminate any opposition (Fumagalli 2006), Kyrgyzstani government officials and elites deployed the discourse more as a means of demarcating acceptable and unacceptable interpretations of Islam, though there have been some reports of illegal imprisonment and violence (Khamidov 2013).

The Kyrgyzstani government's policies and actions regarding religious freedom and antiterrorism reflect not only internal concerns but also the various
pressures applied by the major international players in the region. The government has allowed an influx of Christian missionaries as a part of its democratic
stance, but by 2009 a new law had begun restricting the ability of these groups
to enter and operate in the country. At the same time, the government has been
pressured, by the Russian, US, Uzbek, and Chinese governments to take a much
tougher line in combating terrorism. These foreign powers tended to view the
rather weak Kyrgyzstani government and its perceived lax policies and procedures regarding terrorism as creating a perfect breeding ground for so-called
fundamentalism. Using various means of persuasion—for example, Uzbekistan's
withholding of natural resources, not to mention the massive numbers of rewards
and threats the United States can brandish—they have continued to push the
Kyrgyzstani state to further restrict and regulate the practice of Islam.

Discourses about terrorism or an Islamic threat inform and shape not only
the policies and actions of the Kyrgyzstani state and the various international
actors in Kyrgyzstan; they also have a real and present power in the daily life of
Kyrgyzstani citizens, including those in Bazaar-Korgon. The fear of a state that
acts erratically against its citizens under the aegis of antiterrorism efforts was
not the primary form in which these narratives exerted power, however. Rather,
what residents most feared was terrorists, extremism, or religion otherwise gone
awry. Bazaar-Korgonians suspected possible terrorists in their midst, and they
employed all the well-worn stereotypes known the world over to identify them.
These (anthropologically deconstructed) stereotypes of Islamic extremism took
on their own social life in town (see Tarlo 2005; Deeb 2009). Therefore, just as
my study into Muslim life in Bazaar-Korgon had to consider the actions and policies of state and international actors, these locally produced, global discourses
too became part of what co-constituted religion and the secular, as well as the
project of secularism, in Bazaar-Korgon.

Debating Muslimness

I ran into an acquaintance of mine, Eliar, a manual laborer in his mid-twenties,
on the road to the bazaar early one weekday morning in the spring of 2004.[15] We
walked together a ways. Despite Eliar's attempts to maintain a physical space of
separation—keeping a generous distance between us and averting his gaze from
mine—he nonetheless felt free in conversation; we were old acquaintances, and I
was friends with both his mother and his wife. Eliar was worried about a friend
of his who apparently was drinking too much and heading down the wrong path.
Eliar had asked his friend to meet him at the local cemetery one night later that
week. Eliar, accompanied by a few other young men of the same social circle,

hoped the confrontation, with the graveyard as a symbol of mortality, would compel his friend to give up his errant ways and come "close to Islam."

I never heard what happened with Eliar's plan. Perhaps the friend realized the intent of the gathering and did not come; it seemed a rather bold endeavor. In fact, I never came across a more confrontational mode of proselytizing in all my time in the town, except perhaps the few times interlocutors tried to convert me. There were regular proselytizing endeavors occurring in or originating in the town. Men, and occasionally women, both referred to as *davatchi*s, traveled to neighboring and sometimes distant villages to do exactly what Eliar tried with his friend—invite people to come closer to Islam.[16] But even if these activities involved similar kinds of calls, the men and women approached by the davatchis knew what kinds of meetings they were being invited to and had the chance to refuse. By contrast, Eliar's proposed meeting seemed more like a moral and religious ambush.

Eliar's story and the *davat* efforts were extreme examples of the religious encounters in Bazaar-Korgon in the post-Soviet period. They were part of a new public Islam that included (among other things) the individual and collective observance of rituals, such as prayer; the focused study of texts; the reinvigoration of scholarly life; bodily fashioning; the construction of buildings; and the development of institutions. Importantly, not only was there a diversification of ideas and practices that would be classified as "Islamic" or "Muslim" by those espousing or taking part in them, but the variety in practice and discourse led to debate over which ones were authentic.

While many in Bazaar-Korgon evaluated actions such as the recitation of prayers by female religious specialists during funeral rites (*ma'raka*), the participation in certain kinds of healing or divination practices, the mode of celebrating life-cycle events such as marriages or burials, the use of amulets and charms, or the appeal to ancestors and saints for protection as inherent and essential aspects of Muslimness, others considered these practices un-Islamic. This debate is an old one in Islam, and it existed in a limited form among Muslims in Central Asia—primarily the *ulama*—during the Soviet period. It is a discussion that within the social sciences has often been discussed in terms of "great" and "little" tradition, starting with Robert Redfield's (1960) initial use of the terms to describe and situate variances in culture between urban centers and dependent villages, but it is most well known with reference to Islam in Ernest Gellner's (1981) work.[17]

Throughout post-Soviet Central Asia, one of the most important features of this debate is the way ideas about proper or true Islam have been bound up with notions of Muslimness and ideas of nationhood. Two of the first postsocialist monographs on Islam in Central Asia dealt specifically with debates over Mus-

FIGURE 1.4. Shrine in Bazaar-Korgon. Photograph by the author, 2004.

limness: Bruce Privratsky's *Muslim Turkistan* (2001) and Maria Louw's *Everyday Islam in Post-Soviet Central Asia* (2007). Privratsky and Louw both focus their attention on the collective creation of Muslimness by exploring the role of domestic rituals, pilgrimage, healing, and sacred sites in the production and negotiation of this concept. Privratsky's (2001, 19–22) aim is to show the way that collective memory not only sustained a sense of Muslimness through the Soviet period but also helped Kazakhs relate their practices and notions of Muslimness to the locally labeled pure way (*taza jol*), a scripture-based interpretation of Islam they perceived to be lived only by the elders and religious specialists (75–76). Louw, on the other hand, actively focuses her analysis on the way that Bukharans create and negotiate the concept of Muslimness in order to deal with a traumatic post-socialist environment.

The theme of Muslimness remained central in the literature even as the critique of the concept of "great" and "little," or "orthodox" and "popular," religion continued. Johan Rasanayagam's (2006b) explication of the practice and imagery of healing in the Fergana Valley discusses the way this old debate between "great" and "little" traditions plays out in post-Soviet Uzbekistan. He demonstrates the linkages that connect the practices and practitioners of these seeming oppositional modes of understanding and living Islam and shows how the interaction informs contemporary constructions of Muslimness. Krisztina Kehl-Bodrogi (2006) also illuminates the struggle between these competing visions of Muslimness in her discussion of the holy site Ulli Pir, arguing that there is an even wider range of interpretations regarding shrine-based beliefs and practices than this simple dichotomy presents. In the case of Ulli Pir, she notes the varied significance attached to the shrine by "official religious staff, the traditional religious figures, and the pilgrims themselves," not to mention the secular and nationalist meanings attached to it and the general criticism canonical interpretations of Islam present (2006, 248). Finally, Irene Hilgers's (2009) posthumously published book on Muslimness in Uzbekistan examines the isomorphism of these two subject positions and discursive terrains. "Why do Uzbeks have to be Muslims?" the title of her book asks. Situating her work with reference to what she called the images of "static, unchanging Islam" held by "locals and Western observers alike" (2009, 2), she argued for an understanding of the dynamics of contemporary Uzbek Islam and explored, among other things, how "ethnic identification became tied to religious affiliation" (5).

The proximity, shared history, and contemporary religious and secular linkages between Uzbekistan, Kazakhstan, and Kyrgyzstan explain the similarities in the religious landscapes of these nation-states, especially in the shared territory of the Fergana Valley. But the divergent political system of the states, and the policies and actions of their governments, especially since 1999, have increased the gap between the shared experiences of Muslims in these regions. The most notable difference between Kyrgyzstan and Uzbekistan, for example, was that while freedom of conscience in Uzbekistan rapidly decreased and dissenting voices were eliminated, thus shrinking the possibility for and scope of debates like those described by Rasanayagam and Kehl-Bodrogi, the public sphere for debate and action in Kyrgyzstan has remained relatively open. This is also true when comparisons are made with neighboring western China, where similar debates occur but are much more constrained due to governmental regulation (see Waite 2006).

My own look at these debates addresses not only the way they constitute alternative notions or practices of Islam, or what is acceptable practice, but how they are intertwined with and therefore co-constitute broader conceptualizations of religion, the secular, and secularism that extend beyond the conversations of those who are actively trying to "come close to Islam." The crucial matter in this discussion is the redefinition of "Muslim" as a primarily if not exclusively religious category by some, rather than the ethnic-religious-national marker it has long been for many others. Along with the critique that those "close to religion" pose regarding the traditions and customs that form central elements of local forms of identification, their challenge to ethnonational identity, and by extension to the power of the state to define and regulate "the nation," partly explains why their public, apolitical actions have become politically charged. As Dale Eickelman and James Piscatori's (1996, 4) explication of similar struggles in other Muslim societies indicates, these processes are "political in part [not only] because they involve challenges to the limits of state authority but also because they involve a contest over people's understandings of and wishes for social order."

A return to the discussion of terminology is instructive. If Bazaar-Korgonians struggled to label "those interested in Islam," what about those who could not be said to have "turned and gone over to Islam"? To varying degrees and in different constellations, they found the new rituals, institutions, modes of dress, and conceptualizations of Islam created and sanctioned by those who had "gone to Islam" to be objectionable, not essential Muslim behavior, or threatening to their way of life, variously or multiply conceived as their family, culture, or nation. Importantly, these oppositional stances regularly led to disquiet about personal positioning in reference to Islam and Muslimness. Were they really Muslims? What did they mean with the term? The multiple definitions of Muslim in use prompted the feeling that there should be a qualifier or a descriptor before the term "Muslim"—as in, what *kind* of Muslim was this person or that? The problem for those who had not "gone to religion" was that they didn't know which word to use.

Those Who Have "Turned and Gone to Islam"

Many Bazaar-Korgonians found it difficult to position themselves in reference to the locally new interpretations and practices of Islam that were developing in the early 2000s. Residents of the town tried out and interacted with new rituals, institutions, objects, and modes of dress, to name a few elements of the emerging

Islamic landscape, in various ways and with varying reactions. Religious life in Bazaar-Korgon, as elsewhere in Kyrgyzstan, was heterogeneous (see Montgomery 2007). But common to the majority of the residents—those who would not be considered to have "turned and gone to religion"—was an unease with proliferating conceptualizations and practices of Islam that seemed to exclude older ideas and practices as sufficient qualities for being called a Muslim. A concomitant disquiet developed about their self-positioning, and their positioning of others, in reference to these practices and to the concept of Muslimness.

My own struggle in writing about this process comes precisely from the fact that there really was no vocabulary for talking about this process of differentiation—those who participated in what was beginning to be labeled "Islam" and "religion" (and those who kind of did) versus those who did not (or mostly did not). Yet, residents' need to self-identify and to differentiate was pressing. They talked about, debated, and tried to bring shape to the emerging categories and their boundaries but did so without an easy, readily available vocabulary. For example, the locally novel way certain women were wearing their headscarves did not have a name. It was spoken about with short descriptive phrases ("women who wear their headscarves like this") that included a gesture that mimicked the fold of the fabric and the way it surrounded the face. This phrase was used by people with varying opinions about the wearing of such a scarf, as well as by some women wearing it that way themselves.

In another case, those creating, sanctioning, and participating in a number of new practices and discourses that were associated with Islam, but were understood to be new to the area, foreign to the region, or prohibited or discouraged during the socialist era, could not be simply referred to by others in town. The most commonly heard phrases were that these were "people who had turned and gone to Islam" (*dinge burulup getkin adamdar*) or people who had "come close to Islam" (*dinge jakyn kelde*). But again, as in the case of the headscarf, these were descriptive phrases speakers were employing, and there was usually a struggle with how to identify these people—indicated through pauses, hesitations, and the necessity for lots of explanation. In short, there was no vocabulary to label these actors unless, of course, the speaker was labeling them as "terrorists" or "Wahhabis."

The demographic markers of the majority of those "close to Islam" reflected those of the largest portion of the town's population. They were Uzbek. There were as many males as females. They had received primary and secondary education; some had postsecondary technical and vocational training. Few had attended university. They were peasants, petty merchants and traders, seamstresses, cobblers, and the unemployed. Of course some were outliers relative to these indicators; a few were members of the "old" and the "new" rich Uzbek families in town—those running cotton-ginning plants, those with larger businesses, and those suspected of trafficking in drugs.[18]

There were also portions of the Kyrgyz population who could be classified as "close to" or "interested in" Islam. They were more likely to be newcomers to the community who had arrived after the collapse of the Soviet Union, when town life and the prospects of trading in the bazaar seemed potentially more profitable than remaining in the villages. Generally speaking, the highly educated, middle- to high-level administrators, teachers, and other white-collar workers were underrepresented among those with a recent interest in Islam. Likewise, while the ranks of those close to Islam include boys and young men (with youth being locally understood as lasting until the early to mid-thirties), middle-aged men in their mid-thirties to fifties were likewise underrepresented. What explains the demographic patterns of the newly pious in Bazaar-Korgon? Why was there an interest in Islam among semiurbanized, literate peasants (i.e., the Uzbeks) and not among the educated or highly educated white-collar elites (the Kyrgyz)?

In Kyrgyzstan, there is a persistent stereotype that Uzbeks are, and have been, by definition, more religious than Kyrgyz. The most widespread explanation for this "inherent" variance is that Islam came late to the Kyrgyz, "settled lightly" on them, and never took root among them because of their nomadic ways (see Liu 2012, 66). Concurrent with this explanation is the portrayal of the Kyrgyz as having mixed their pre-Islamic beliefs, rituals, and codes of conduct with Islamic ones, thus creating a less orthodox and, as some would argue, more tolerant system and national character.[19] The supposed "national characteristic" of Uzbeks as being "inherently" more Islamic is offered as an explanation for the increase in religious practice among Uzbeks in the post-Soviet period. Without the constraints of an atheist system, the standard argument implies, their religiosity revived. While a full exploration of these stereotypes was never the intent of this chapter, they are worth mentioning because I have encountered demographic patterns in Bazaar-Korgon that seem to confirm at least one of the stereotypes.

Without fully explaining these demographic patterns, the larger social context does provide some indicators as to why these stereotypes might hold some truth. In many ways, Bazaar-Korgon should be viewed as an Uzbek town. Its population is 80 percent Uzbek, it is thirty kilometers from the Uzbek border, and, despite stricter regulation of the border by the Uzbeks since 1999 (Megoran 2004), there is fairly free travel across it (see Megoran 2006). Regular contacts are maintained with friends, relatives, and business partners in Uzbekistan. Until the mid- to late 1970s, the population of Bazaar-Korgon was almost all Uzbek. It was administratively classified as a village, and the majority of its inhabitants were peasants (collective farm workers). In the late 1970s, however, it was decided that a new rayon would be created. The town of Bazaar-Korgon, the largest within the boundaries of the new rayon, became its administrative head. Significantly, because the new rayon was part of the Kyrgyz Soviet Socialist Republic and since the majority of its inhabitants were Kyrgyz, the state sent large numbers of Kyrgyz men and women to the predominantly Uzbek town of Bazaar-Korgon to staff the departments, offices, hospitals, and schools for the new rayon.[20]

Thus, the Uzbek peasants of Bazaar-Korgon were joined by Kyrgyz doctors, administrators, agricultural specialists, and other professionals; they were "educated cadres" who had come from all over the country and had been trained not only in Kyrgyzstan but also at various locations throughout the Soviet Union. They were sent to Bazaar-Korgon to create the new Soviet rayon and to modernize the town that already existed. As a result of these demographic changes, during the 1980s the population of Bazaar-Korgon was divided into three major groups: educated, white-collar Kyrgyz, Uzbek kolkhozniki, and Russians. The fact that those who "came close to Islam" are predominantly Uzbek rather than Kyrgyz is just as related to their socioeconomic class or position within the state apparatus as it is to their ethnicity. Recognition of this is crucial when considering the place and significance of Soviet ideals, and one's approbation of them, among the population of Bazaar-Korgon. The Kyrgyz who settled in the town in the 1970s and 1980s were more integrated into official state networks, more invested in socialist rhetoric, more open to "control" by officials, and—lest we forget—more likely to feel devoted to, and proud of, the goals of the Soviet Union.

Local elite and peasants differed in the way the two groups understood, appropriated, challenged, and worked with socialist concepts. This is especially true with regard to the keeping of certain Soviet-era regulated Islamic practices.[21] Peasants had greater space to maintain these practices because they were under less scrutiny by authorities and less invested in the rhetoric, practices, networks, and obligations necessary for success in new social and political environments. Peasants also had fewer incentives to abandon these practices. However, only the most private, individual practices—like prayer at home—could be maintained, which is why some have referred to religion in the Soviet period as "domesticated" (Dragadze 1993). Even when those born in the pre-Soviet or early Soviet years maintained certain practices, these same observances were rarely continued in subsequent generations. Among the life histories I collected, of those Uzbeks born in the 1930s and 1940s who continued to pray during the Soviet period, almost none of their children did.

By and large, only among those who claimed to have had family members who were Islamic specialists, scholars, or otherwise highly knowledgeable about Islam prior to the Soviet period was there continuation of the observances or practices targeted or discouraged in the atheist campaigns by succeeding gener-

FIGURE 1.5. School with Kyrgyz as language of instruction—part of the construction and modernization efforts of the early 1980s. Photograph by the author, 2004.

FIGURE 1.6. The erstwhile elite apartments in the Sai neighborhood. Photograph by the author, 2004.

ations in the Soviet period (see Babadjanov and Kamilov 2001; Ilkhamov 2001). Though rare and very few in terms of the overall population, these individuals and their families were important. The burgeoning interest in Islam during the 1990s and 2000s was directly facilitated by the men and women who had secretly received religious training from official and unofficial scholars and religious specialists—whether family members or otherwise. It was among these limited numbers of scholars and authorities that Islamic thought and practice developed and persisted over the Soviet period. And it was they who taught, guided, and advised those who, in the post-Soviet period, became "interested in Islam" (*dinge kyzyktuu bölüp kaluu*) and those who ultimately experienced a sustained transformation.

Rather than being inherently characteristic of the "nation," as is often locally argued, various kinds of participation in certain Islamic rituals, bodily performances, and discursive practices can be understood as related to socioeconomic class, the maintenance of familial ties, and relative proximity and attachment to Soviet ideals and power centers.[22] The fact that Uzbeks mostly occupy a lower socioeconomic strata than the Kyrgyz raises another type of question. The relation of material constraints to religious belief is a contentious topic. Ever since Marx proffered the notion that religion serves as an opiate for the masses (Marx [1844] 2002, 170–81)—assuaging their suffering, pacifying their revolutionary potential, and legitimating the power of capitalists—social scientists have been intrigued by the role of material, social, or political malaise in religious belief and practice. Biographies of those interested in Islam in Bazaar-Korgon indeed show that Islam has been a comfort for them in times of trouble. Moreover, the demographic data I have gathered demonstrates that religiosity was higher among the lower strata of society, a pattern that would seem to confirm a basic reading of Marx.[23] But what the above depiction of Bazaar-Korgon's population also shows is that difficult material circumstances by no means dictate a turn to religion; the majority of the poor did not turn to Islam (*dinge burlup getkin*). And while I claim that Uzbeks were more likely than Kyrgyz to alter their lives so that their actions and discourses more closely mirrored an ideal type prescribed by local variants of scripturalist Islam, this is still, at best, only a partial answer; not all Uzbeks of the town "went to religion" (*dinge getkin*).

Public Islam

In some ways, the public Islam I observed in Kyrgyzstan in the early 2000s mirrored the general post-Soviet public flourishing of religion, but it also reflected the burgeoning of Islam seen worldwide in the 1980s and 1990s. Unlike descriptions of those who were part of the so-called "Islamic resurgence" elsewhere, however, those who have become "interested in Islam" in Kyrgyzstan are demographically distinct. While "new veiling," for example, has often begun in capital cities and universities (Brenner 1996; Göle 1996; White 2002), newly veiled women in Kyrgyzstan in the early 2000s were largely absent from Bishkek's universities and public spaces, though the piety movements in Almaty just a few years later seem to have reflected the urban, academic trend (see Schwab 2011, 2012, 2014). Instead they were found in southern cities and small towns predominantly populated by Uzbeks. The newly veiled rarely had more than a high school education and tended to be lower middle class or lower class, in contrast to the middle-class character of piety movements elsewhere.

One important similarity can be drawn, however, between those who became "interested in Islam" in Bazaar-Korgon and those who were involved in piety movements elsewhere, like Robert Hefner's "newly pious" (2005), Ayse Saktanber's "conscious Muslims" (2002), or the Egyptian women of Saba Mahmood's study (2005): they were not involved in politics. Hefner (2005, 21), for example, argues that "most of the newly pious were primarily interested in just what they claimed to be: religious study, heightened public devotion, expressing a Muslim identity, and ensuring that public arenas were subject to ethical regulation. The key symbols of the resurgence were similarly pietistic: reciting the Quran, keeping the fast, wearing the veil, avoiding alcohol, giving alms." Significantly, however, he notes that "in its early years, the resurgence was a profoundly *public* event, but not one that was especially *political* in any formal sense of the word" (21; original emphasis).

This is important to note because there is another powerful trope often employed in analysis of Islam in Central Asia—that of political Islam and the Muslim extremist. Central Asia, Morgan Liu (2012, 16) has astutely noted, is "an overdetermined yet understudied region," a description particularly true when considering the place of Islam and politics in the region. The assumed desire for political action on behalf of those who might be "too religious" motivates much of the political science, media framing, and local fears of Islam in Central Asia (see Montgomery 2014). Fears of Muslim extremism are often seen as a recent arrival, a part of the post-9/11 landscape. But notions of the fanatical Muslim "other" have a much longer history in the region. At the end of the nineteenth century, Russian authorities held typically imperialist and orientalist notions of the Central Asian Muslim population (Geraci 1997). They were perceived of as undeveloped and waiting for help from imperial Russia. At the same time, Islam was seen as a destabilizing force and was assumed to be fanatical at its heart. According to Adeeb Khalid (1998, 51), "Russia as progress stood in contrast to Central Asia as fanaticism and barbarity, much of which was seen to reside in Islam. 'Fanaticism' came to be seen as the defining characteristic of Central Asians." Russian fears about political subversion and their "abiding prejudice

against Muslim religious piety" (Brower 1997, 119) led to a two-pronged campaign against Islam—political, to control a population, and cultural, to civilize
the fanatic "other" (Khalid 1998, 50–52). British conceptions of Islam in the
region at the same time were strikingly similar (Meyer 2002, 11).

The orientalized view of Central Asian Muslims prevalent in the early Soviet
era was likewise remarkably reminiscent of that of the late imperial period
(Northrop 2004). For example, Douglas Northrop (2004, 40) notes that "in
the eyes of these early Bolshevik observers, much of the explanation for these
problems lay in the paramount importance of religion in Central Asian life.
Primitive, 'barbaric' practices could thus be ascribed straightforwardly to Islam."
Moreover, the concomitant need to civilize and modernize the "backward" Muslim populations and to subdue their fanatic nature under political rule was also
a part of early Soviet campaigns in Central Asia (Bräker 1994; Lorenz 1994;
Northrop 2004). There was always an ambiguity in Moscow's perception of its
Muslim periphery, however, and over the course of the Soviet era Central Asia
was, at times, positively evaluated and displayed. In the 1950s, for example, as
Will Myer (2002, 12–19) asserts, Central Asia and its Muslim population were a
source of tremendous pride for the Soviet authorities, who showcased the area as
a model for socialist modernization. The hope of Soviet authorities was that this
demonstration of socialist achievements in Muslim societies would win other
Muslim populations to the side of the second world in the Cold War.

During the Cold War era, the idea that Muslim unity could be a destabilizing
force pervaded Western academic writings on politics in the region. Myer (2002)
argues that this notion was rooted in a Euro-American view of Central Asia as a
Soviet colony. The conclusion drawn was that just as colonial uprisings had led
to the collapse of Western European empires, Central Asian Muslims too would
rise up to unsettle the Soviet Union. Links between the Muslim populations of
Central Asia and those on the other side of the Iron Curtain were thought to
facilitate such uprisings (Akiner 1993; Myer 2002). Although these predictions
about the demise of the Soviet Union turned out to be false and Central Asians
remained the strongest supporters of the Soviet Union even as it began to collapse, the threat of Muslim insurrection in the region somehow remained. As
Shirin Akiner (1993) has argued, "old suspicions die hard. After the collapse of
the Soviet Union in December 1991 a new fear emerged: that of Central Asia as
a key link in a Muslim fundamentalist 'arc of instability'" (quoted in Myer 2002,
236–37). More recent US policies and pronouncements in the region—as well
as those of the Central Asian governments themselves—made as a part of the
"war on terror" demonstrate the contemporary saliency of the perceived threat of
unity among "radical" Muslims. Equally illustrative of the centrality of this ex-
planatory framework are popular, widely read works on the region, such as those

produced by Ahmed Rashid (1994, 2002) with inflammatory titles like *Jihad: The Rise of Militant Islam in Central Asia* (2002).

Hefner's (2005) analysis of Muslim politics in Indonesia stresses the public but nonpolitical nature of the newly pious and their actions, a point that can also be made about "those interested in Islam" in Bazaar-Korgon but one that is often overlooked, missed, or ignored by residents, Kyrgyzstani politicians, local and foreign media, and outside observers, academics, and officials. Politicized Islam and its supposed threats are the primary concern for most who are examining Islam in the region. For Hefner's newly pious, publicity came in the form of Islamic associations utilized for public participation. Those "interested in Islam" in Bazaar-Korgon have not created religious institutions outside of mosques and home-based study groups (davat). Moreover, they have not articulated a political agenda or critiqued the form of governance. Although they may critique the government's functioning or a particular administration, they do so without reference to Islamic discourses as the bases for their appraisals or proposed solutions. They have, however, criticized mainstream modes of religiosity and widespread conceptions of Muslimness in town, making their presence in the community and the propagation of their ideas controversial despite the absence of a political agenda.

The discourses and actions of those who had "turned and gone to Islam" in Bazaar-Korgon, though not avowedly political, have nonetheless had highly political consequences (see Mahmood 2011, xi). The most startling impact they have had in town is their implicit and explicit contestation of Muslimness, a concept (along with other intertwined notions, such as Islam specifically and religion more generally) that was not open for public debate during the mid- to late Soviet period. While some of their acts and beliefs are visible and accessible to wide portions of the community and are thus "public," others are viewed or heard by smaller portions of the community. Following Dale Eickelman and Armando Salvatore's (2004) reading of John Dewey, I argue that even those actions, or the articulation and propagation of certain beliefs that occur in private or semiprivate locations, become public because of their wider reverberations in communal life. "In drawing attention to the communicative and interconnected aspects of social life that we call the public sphere," Eickelman and Salvatore (2004, 16) write, "Dewey shows how acts become public when their consequences, even if initiated in private, indirectly affect the welfare of many others."

Applying these insights to the context of Bazaar-Korgon, I argue that the rearticulations of Muslimness challenged definitions central to individual and collective processes of identification, including the collective imagination of Islam and of "the nation." Moreover, in undermining the supposed tie between ethnic and religious affiliation by asserting that Muslimness was inherently

FIGURE 1.7. Cars parked near the rayon Friday mosque during prayer time. Photograph by the author, 2004.

about belief and not belonging, they undermined local notions of religion and its place in modern social and political life. Those "interested in Islam," individually and collectively, sought to address communal issues formerly attended to by state agencies and actors. These acts and beliefs were concomitantly political because they took up the constitution of communal life, the values that underlay it, and the day-to-day maintenance of collective living. In some instances this involved challenging or questioning the authority and role of the state. In these ways, I understand the religious process of Bazaar-Korgon as "public Islam." Significantly, however, incorporating the insights Salvatore (2006, 2007) provided regarding the Casanova-Asad debate and those made by Chris Hann (1996) on the dichotomy of state-society, as well as recent interventions by Hussein Ali Agrama (2014) on the ambiguity at the heart of secular power, I assert that public Islam occurs both in reaction to and in cooperation with the actors, policies, and foundational concepts of the secular Kyrgyzstani government.

In this respect Kyrgyzstani citizens are quite privileged among Central Asians because they are afforded perhaps the largest degree of freedom regarding religious belief, expression, and organization. Relatively open policies and practices have allowed public Islam to play a constructive role in society—and not just for those who have "gone to Islam." Despite the constraints global, national, and local discourses on Islamic extremism place on the development of public Islam, tentative steps toward the formation of Muslim publics have been taken in Bazaar-Korgon. They emerge through Islamically motivated social action, actual—or imagined—links with Muslims from outside the region, and the rearticulating of key norms in Islamically textured language. These publics also indicate that while secular political actors have played, until now, the dominant role in shaping local conceptions and programs of modernity, those interested in Islam are offering alternative visions and enactments that have challenged the status quo. It is this meeting—the contestations and creative intertwinements of what came before and what was emerging in these religious scapes, especially the idea of religion itself—that forms this book's central focus.

CHAPTER 2

LISTENING TO THE WEDDING SPEAKER

Autumn 2003 was a particularly busy wedding season in Bazaar-Korgon. The fresh fruits and vegetables needed for wedding parties were plentiful and at the lowest prices of the year. Cash crops had just been harvested, the sale of which provided the funds needed to finance the weddings. The number of weddings was particularly high that year because Ramadan began at the end of October. No one would marry during the month of fasting and not many wanted a winter wedding, so all the autumn weddings were crammed into September and October. It was easy to tell when there was a wedding nearby; one could hear the trumpeting of horns that marked the commencement and conclusion of various stages of the day's events. The rush to marry before Ramadan meant that the days and nights of September and October 2003 were filled with the cacophony of competing horns.

The climax of wedding celebrations in Bazaar-Korgon was the evening party. The celebration was typically held outside in the courtyard of the groom's parents' home. Party lights were strung about, interwoven in the grapevines hanging overhead. A head table covered with chocolates, alcoholic beverages, and floral arrangements dominated the courtyard. The bride and groom, with their witnesses beside them, sat at the table. The bride wore a "European-style" (*evromoda*) wed-

FIGURE 2.1. Horns being played during a wedding ceremony. Photograph by the author, 2004.

FIGURE 2.2. Bride and groom presentation at the evening party of a wedding ceremony. Photograph by the author, 2004.

ding dress, rented from a local shop. Her hair would have been carefully styled and perhaps even colored with metallic-flecked spray; her makeup was most likely professionally done. The bride's witness wore her best dress and had done her hair and makeup similar to the bride's. The groom and his friend donned suits and Uzbek hats (*doppa*). Behind the party hung a large backboard colorfully painted with the words *kosh kelingniz* (welcome) and bedecked with blinking lights.

Evening wedding parties nearly always included a DJ who played music and orchestrated the toasts, the exchange of gifts, and dances. Several tables would be in the center of the yard. Guests, generally friends of the bride and groom, sat at the tables and ate. During the festivities, members of the opposite sex watched and flirted with one another, guests consumed alcohol, and the occasional fight broke out. Gossip was circulated at these events. The evening wedding parties were among the most popular social events in town.

However, in the late 1990s and early 2000s, some residents of Bazaar-Korgon began holding a different sort of wedding, one that either eliminated altogether the evening party described above or dramatically altered it. Organizers of these "new weddings" explained their alteration of the ceremony as an Islamically motivated act. They claimed that the environment and structure of the "typical" wedding party, as well as the actions of guests, were inappropriate for Muslims. Thus, they sought to reform the weddings in order to make them more Islamic.

The new weddings took various forms, with the most basic version being one in which the organizers eliminated the evening party, along with other presumably offending elements. Other organizers of the new weddings, however, did not find it sufficient to simply cut the "non-Muslim" elements out of the celebration. In addition to eliminating these practices, they revamped several portions of the wedding ceremony, most notably the evening wedding party. At these events there was no music, dancing, or alcohol. The sexes were strictly segregated, and the bride was hidden away. There were often two head tables. The groom sat at one. At the other was the wedding speaker. The wedding speaker, an Islamic preacher typically from outside the community, was invited to the wedding to deliver a religious message that called on the guests to observe more closely the ways of Islam. The addition of the speaker turned the celebration into an event directed at transforming the beliefs and practices of the wedding guests.

The altered wedding parties presented a new, and very public, forum for sharing and acquiring information about Islam in the town. They thus became sites for learning about alternative interpretations of Islam and (possibly) exploring the lifestyle suggested by these interpretations. However, the evening wedding party was not universally embraced by the community. The ideas expressed in the message delivered at the evening party were contested by some. Moreover, the form in which the teachings were presented was also disputed. Opponents argued that this type of "propaganda" should not be promoted during rites of passage.

This chapter focuses on the reactions of community members to the new wedding parties. It suggests that while the responses to the parties were varied, patterns of response emerged along generational lines. Similarity of response appeared among age cohorts largely because of their shared ideas about the category of religion. The new weddings had become sites where the concepts and the boundaries between what was "truly" religion and what was not were contested. Thus, while for the young the wedding could more easily be a site of exploration, the middle-aged were more often confronted by the implicit and explicit ways the weddings challenged their ideas of religion. They therefore had more reserved and sometimes outright hostile opinions of the events. Reactions to the new weddings in Bazaar-Korgon were likewise strongly related to discourses developed over the long Soviet period.

New Weddings

Weddings among Uzbeks in Bazaar-Korgon were lengthy affairs, with meals, exchanging of gifts, and the performance of many rituals before, during, and after the wedding day. On the wedding day elaborate meals were prepared and nearly all members of the social networks of the respective families were invited to partake. The bride and groom typically participated in a civil ceremony. During this event they signed the necessary documents at the *rayon* registration office and toured local sites of interest with friends and relatives of their age cohort, a process referred to as ZAGS.[1] The couple also had a small ritual at the bride's parents' home with an imam or *moldo* officiating.[2] In the evening, a large party (described in the introduction to this chapter) would be held at the groom's parents' home.

Although there was some variation in the way the new weddings were held, they all aimed to eliminate the supposedly sinful elements of the "normal" weddings held in town, such as the drinking of alcohol, dancing, the mixing of the sexes, and the public display of the bride. Many organizers of the new weddings simply eliminated the evening wedding party, as it was the part perceived to contain the most objectionable elements. In addition, many did away with the Western-style wedding dress, as well as the ZAGS.

By eliminating the evening wedding party, the organizers of these events removed the one aspect of the event that was most gender integrated, thereby producing a wedding that was more strongly gender segregated. One of the strongest criticisms leveled at contemporary weddings was that men and women mixed

Figure 2.3. Bride and groom returning from ZAGS, which is the acronym of the civil registry office and the shorthand term for the wedding-day tour. Photograph by the author, 2003.

together during the party. It was not only perceived as an offense in and of itself, but it was also thought that such an arrangement might lead to other sins. Since the other aspects of the wedding (i.e., the meals and the *nikoh/nike*) were already highly gender segregated, dropping the party quickly produced a ceremony celebrated in gender-segregated spheres.[3] Moreover, eliminating the evening party also removed the practice of displaying the bride, an aspect of the ceremony that violated the gender norms promoted by the new wedding organizers.

Those participating in or adopting this new style of wedding presented it as an event in accordance with Islam. Moreover, they portrayed the changes as being introduced for Islamic reasons, similar to comparable alterations in weddings in Tajikistan (Roche and Hohmann 2011). A discussion of the terms used in reference to new weddings is illustrative. At the time of this research, there was not a fully established way of referring to these new weddings in Bazaar-Korgon. When it was necessary to make a distinction, one or two main adjectives would be chosen to describe which type of wedding it was. More precisely, an "average" wedding party was never referred to as anything other than a "wedding party" (*toi*). However, when the wedding was of the new variety, adjectives were applied to the word *wedding*. The adjectives used, *sunnati* and *ibodat*, signified the overtly

FIGURE 2.4. The signing of the marriage documents at ZAGS, or the civil registry. Photograph by the author, 2004.

FIGURE 2.5. The nikoh (Uzbek) or nike (Kyrgyz), the portion of a wedding ceremony conducted by a religious specialist. Photograph by the author, 2004.

Islamic nature of the events and thus explicitly contrasted these weddings with others that, by implication, were not so Islamic.[4]

A young woman explained, "We call it a sunnati wedding [sunnati toi]. *Sunna* means 'the things the prophet did.' In this type of wedding we try to honor the things the prophet said and did." She went on to say that other words, such as ibodat, could also be used to denote this type of wedding. She emphasized that because an ibodat wedding followed the ways of the prophet, it was, by implication a "correct" Muslim wedding. She further indicated that the bridal couple were also people who tried to live according to the prescriptions of the prophet Mohammad. A young man, who himself had married in the new style, was a bit more forthright with his comparison. "You've been around town, you've seen the way we have weddings? If I speak truthfully," he said, "the weddings here in our town are not in accordance with our religion." That is why, he explained, he had decided to have a sunnati wedding, a wedding "according to teachings of our prophet."

The transformations of wedding ceremonies in other settings have been interpreted as indicators of changes in economy (Yalçin-Heckmann 2001), gender roles and family structure (Tapper 1985), or broader shifts in culture (Kligman 1988, 24). The alteration of weddings in Bazaar-Korgon by simply cutting the evening party could likewise be partly explained in economic terms. The costs of the evening wedding party represented a large percentage of the total expenditure for the set of events, rituals, and exchanges involved in Uzbek weddings. By excising the evening festivities, those holding the most simple form of the new wedding saved money while justifying the excision in moral and religious terms, rather than economic.[5] Likewise, an analysis of the ceremonies could be made in terms of altered gender roles.

However, even if the alteration of weddings that simply cut the evening party could be partly explained in these ways, it would be difficult to similarly interpret other varieties of the new wedding party. In these cases, wedding organizers transformed the parties into morally acceptable events during which Islamic ideas were openly propagated. They removed the alcohol and dancing and in their place invited an Islamic preacher to deliver a message to the wedding guests. The organizers used this semipublic event as a forum for the transmission of religious knowledge and for proselytizing. Whatever else may have been involved, the organizers of these weddings made it clear that their understanding of Islam had motivated the change and shaped the new form of the event.

The Wedding Speaker

On a cold March evening in the outskirts of Bazaar-Korgon, guests made their way to the house where a new-style wedding party was to be held. They approached the courtyard surrounding the house in gender- and largely age-segregated groups. When they passed through the door, the male guests entered the courtyard, milled around, and talked to friends and acquaintances. Women made their way toward the main house, where they passed behind large pieces of cloth that hung near the house and in front of the porch. Once behind the cloth the women were concealed from view. However, small holes in the material enabled women to sneak a look at those gathered in the yard. Tables and benches lined the inner area of the courtyard. In front was a platform with a low table.

The table was decked with food and drinks, and behind it hung colorful tapestries and carpets. A few men sat at the table. The groom, hardly distinguishable from the other guests, walked up to the center table and greeted the men, taking more time to talk with the man in his forties who sat in the middle. After a few minutes, the groom took his seat at his table nearby. The crowd grew silent, and those not already seated crowded around, filling every available space in the yard and even spilling onto the street. The man at the center of the head table took the microphone and began to speak. He welcomed the guests and pronounced blessings for the groom and his new bride. He gave advice about how the new couple should live. He continued to talk. As time passed his voice grew louder and more impassioned, urging the listeners to follow the true path.

His voice waxed and waned, guiding the ear and the emotions of the listeners. He talked for more than ninety minutes. The wedding speaker focused his message on the primacy of prayer in a Muslim's life. He challenged the listeners by saying that all their good deeds, all their best intentions would not be counted if they did not pray:

> But this [heaven] is not a daydream . . . the place is promised by Allah. Thanks to what? Thanks to performing *namaz*.[6] If namaz is not performed on time . . . if you fast during Ramadan, if your wealth has increased and you give alms [*zakat*], if your way is open and you go on hajj . . . if you help in the construction of a mosque, or if you give charity, in the end . . . the good deeds that are done by people, as Islam says, as our religion explains, as our parents show, if you do the good deeds, the benefits, the merits will not be written in your book until you perform namaz.

He emphasized the need to pray the full five times a day and to begin immediately. He directly challenged the notions that it was acceptable to save up the day's prayers and do them at the end of the day, or that the listeners could wait until their old age to begin their prayers. He told them that Allah wanted the prayers of young, strong men. Again and again he referred to the shortness and unpredictability of life, urging the listeners to begin their duties now lest they be punished for their irresponsibility in the afterlife. He also emphasized that praying and good deeds must be augmented by the act of reminding others of their religious duties:

> Whether one is knowledgeable or not, whether old or young, no matter who the person is, the task is given to each man and woman to call one another back to the right way. Thus . . . if we intend to perform namaz, get ready for namaz, and get ready for goodness, we should call the people next to us to walk in Allah's, in God's religion. If you yourself don't smoke, don't drink, don't follow the bad way, but your fellow next to you is a drinker, or a smoker, or a thief . . . it is your obligation to call the one next to you to back away from that way.

There was a small break in his talk and the guests were served *ash* (rice pilaf). Afterward the talk began again. When he finished, young men came forward to ask questions. Others, including the women who sat hidden behind the tapestries and sheets, passed small pieces of paper forward with their inquiries.

The questions varied. One asked who implements the punishment for those who don't perform namaz. Another wanted to know about the legal schools of Islam and why there "had become so many." One man asked about marriage and how many wives are allowed. This query led the wedding speaker into a discussion of gender roles, female dress and behavior, men's obligations to the women in their family, and the correct conduct and meaning of a wedding. Although he did not discuss the idea of wedding speakers, he did explicitly condemn the practice of displaying the bride, noting that when a man takes a wife, she belongs to him and should not be paraded and shown to others. Another guest inquired whether it was right or wrong to celebrate Noruz.[7] Although the wedding speaker did not expressly forbid celebration of the holiday, he strongly advised against doing so, noting that in the Shari'a the only holidays mentioned were the two *hayit*s and Fridays.[8] He also indicated which elements in these annual celebrations were sinful and why they should be avoided.

There were also a number of questions regarding Hizb ut-Tahrir and Wahhabism, which ultimately led to a heated debate between the wedding speaker and a member of Hizb ut-Tahrir who was present at the wedding. The discussion began with a debate over which legal school should be adhered to, whether a Muslim should adhere to only one school or could borrow from all, and ultimately whether the writings of the legal schools should be considered at all. A sharp disagreement on these points between the wedding speaker and the member of Hizb ut-Tahrir led to an argument over who was more knowledgeable about Islam and what type of knowledge was in fact important.

An analysis of the full message of this particular wedding speaker compared with the messages of other speakers would provide interesting and important insight into the range of Islamic ideas circulating in Bazaar-Korgon and how these

FIGURE 2.6. Men at a wedding party. Photograph by the author, 2003.

(varying) ideas interact with one another.[9] This endeavor is, however, beyond the scope of this chapter. Nevertheless, a short summary of the wedding speaker's message is provided here to give an indication of the themes being addressed during these wedding parties and to offer a look at reactions to them. The wedding speaker's own message focused heavily on the necessity of performing particular rituals, with the keeping of namaz signaled as the foundational practice for a Muslim's life. He emphasized the need for Muslims to act, through prayer and by encouraging others to do the same, and not simply to assume that being born Muslim and doing "good deeds" made one a good Muslim. He explicitly criticized the notion that the performance of the specified rituals was for the old and encouraged the young to take up their duties. His emphasis on these issues speaks to what he saw as the major shortcomings of the Muslims in the area, namely, the lack of ritual observance in their lives. The questions asked by the attendees show what things concerned those attending the wedding. Several questions explicitly sought to ascertain whether or not local practices that were presumed to be part of "Muslim life" were in fact in accordance with Islam (e.g., weddings, Noruz, and marriage and its responsibilities). Together, the speaker's message and the guests' questions show a preoccupation with the examination of widespread ideas about "proper" Muslim behavior, the comparison of these ideas with the teachings of the Islamic texts, and the encouragement to live according to the "true" way.[10] This "true" way in many cases meant that listeners should change their beliefs about Muslimness and Islam and realign their lives to fit the "new" ideas. What they were being asked to leave behind were the customary beliefs that proper Muslim behavior consisted, in essence, of the marking of life-cycle events, the observance of "Muslim" holidays, and religious devotion late in life.

Situating New Weddings

The messages delivered by wedding speakers at the new evening parties provided an innovative way for residents of Bazaar-Korgon to learn about Islam and to explore alternative ways of being a Muslim. Moreover, the forum was a highly interactive and stimulating one. Wedding guests often commented on how exciting or appealing a certain speaker had been. In fact, certain wedding speakers, such as Kadirbek, a teacher from Andijan, Uzbekistan, had become locally famous.

Perhaps partly for this reason, the new evening wedding parties in Bazaar-Korgon were popular events, especially among the youth. This counterintuitive situation becomes easier to understand when the new weddings are viewed in a broader context. Not everyone shared the opinion of the "new wedding" organizers that other forms of weddings were unacceptable. The majority of weddings in town were still held in the typical fashion that incorporated drinking and dancing at the evening party. Thus, the popularity of the new weddings, especially among the youth, did not necessarily indicate endorsement of replacing the party with a religious event. Rather, the weddings were popular because they were an additional element, one that provided a place where people could encounter new ideas and explore their interest in Islam. At the same time, attending a new wedding did not necessitate acceptance (to whatever degree) of either the form of the wedding or the ideas being expounded at the event.

Although for some the wedding was an exciting site for exploration, for others it was far more challenging. As the example of the wedding speech excerpted above illustrates, the messages entailed a rethinking of the essence of Islam and Muslimness. As a result, some residents of the town experienced the wedding as a challenge to their sense of themselves as Muslim. Opponents of the new weddings claimed that the parties were a deformation of "our culture" and an affront to "our way of life." This was especially true for middle-aged and elderly residents whose formative years were during the Soviet period and who largely held to a late Soviet-era notion of religion. Whether or not these age cohorts had changed their practices or beliefs since the end of the socialist period, they nearly all experienced some form of negative reaction to the new weddings. A closer look at some of the residents of Bazaar-Korgon who came into contact with the new weddings—whether first- or secondhand—will illustrate the varied reactions the events provoked.

Experiencing New Weddings

Exploring

Nigora, a twenty-year-old woman, was studying *zaochno* in her fourth year of university.[11] She had been performing namaz for nearly two years, though with one considerable break. Several members of her immediate and extended family also prayed and were very involved in "learning more about Islam." Nigora herself had also become interested in learning more and had regularly been listening to tape recordings of local Islamic leaders' talks that her older sister passed on to her. She had begun to consider seriously taking up the *hijab* and had been talking to young women who wore that form of veil.[12]

Nigora had been invited to a new wedding party in Bazaar-Korgon by a friend. She'd never been to one before, though she had heard quite a bit about them. She didn't know the bride or the groom and thus was a bit nervous about going. Nevertheless, she was so eager to see the wedding for herself, and especially to hear the wedding speaker, the famous Kadirbek, that she decided to join her friend. Nigora prepared for the evening. Had she been going to any other wedding, the preparation would have come as second nature. She would have chosen her most fashionable outfit, perhaps a skirt but maybe pants, carefully coiffed her hair, and perhaps even applied a bit of makeup. But Nigora found herself in a slightly uncertain position the afternoon of the wedding. She had no idea what to wear. She guessed that a long skirt and a long-sleeved shirt would be in order, but what about her head? Unmarried girls her age did not wear headscarves. But considering the company she was going with (her friend had been wearing the hijab for the last year) and imagining what the event would be like, Nigora took one of her mother's largest and nicest scarves, draped it over her head, and pinned it carefully under her chin.

A few days later, when Nigora related the events of the evening, she was glowing with excitement over what she'd seen and heard. She said she had learned so much from Kadirbek about "how we [Muslims] are supposed to live." What was different about this event, she explained, was the variety of topics addressed. She said that when she listened to tapes or talked to others about Islam, there was usually one major theme discussed. But at the wedding attendees were allowed to ask the speaker a range of questions, and thus she got to hear opinions about many different topics. She thought that was very exciting and interesting. She also could not believe how many young people were there: "Before if there was some kind of Islamic teaching, only old people would go. But there were so many young people there [at the wedding party]." She said she was definitely going to go to another wedding like it and would even consider having her own wedding in that fashion when the time came.

The highly gendered space of the wedding was also a new experience for Nigora.[13] She commented that on a day-to-day basis she saw young men and talked to them. She also said that when she was in the bazaar it never bothered her when she saw men, even if they ran into her in the crowded rows of the market. At the wedding, however, she felt very different. At one point a man peeked around the curtain looking for someone. His gaze passed over Nigora. "I bowed my head and lowered my eyes. I felt so embarrassed and ashamed to be seen by him. It was really strange. Then, after the wedding was over, we left the house, went out on the street, and men and women were mixing again. I didn't feel strange at all. But at the wedding, when that man looked at us, I did." I asked her about her clothes, whether she had made the right decision about what to wear. She flushed, covered her mouth with her hands, and laughed a bit. "It was so shameful," she said. Apparently many young women her age were there wearing normal dresses with only modest head covering or none at all. Even the older women veiled in the most common fashion—a simple scarf over the head tied at the nape of the neck and often revealing hair. Luckily Nigora knew only one or two of the young women at the wedding. Still, she was embarrassed. She guessed they would be talking about her inconsistency in dress styles—jeans at the bazaar and hijab at wedding parties.

Sherzod was a seventeen-year-old youth whose family had a long history of living in Bazaar-Korgon. He was a high school student and the second of four children. His elder sister attended university in the provincial capital about forty-five minutes away, and his younger siblings lived at home with him, his parents, and his maternal aunt. His father, Ibrahim, fifty-six, had been a foreman at a local plant in town but had resigned in the early 1990s after disagreements with the management. The plant, like most in the town, closed down not long afterward. His father remained unemployed. The family subsisted on the produce of their garden, money received from relatives who rented their land outside of town, assistance from Ibrahim's older brother, and a small business they ran selling candy, snacks, and school items (notebooks, pens, etc.). Their business was successful because of its location—their house was adjacent to a large school.

Sherzod explained that he was very interested in Islam. When he was fourteen and fifteen he performed namaz but had stopped for a while; he said he wanted to begin again. Many of his friends were also interested in learning more about Islam and had been attending home-based study groups in town. He had been attending the mosque on Fridays for a while but had recently stopped because his father forbade him from going. In a separate discussion, his father had told me he thought prayer was fine but that his son should do it at home like he and his father before him had done. Ibrahim said he also wanted to protect his son from religious zealots, so-called Wahhabis, so he no longer allowed his son to attend the mosque. He was afraid of the kinds of things they would teach his son, and he feared that his son would ultimately become one of them.

Sherzod had a good relationship with his father and respected him very much. He said he understood his father's reasoning, as he himself was worried about "extremists." However, Sherzod felt confident that he could discern the difference between what was good and what was extreme. He said that some of his friends were interested in and involved with groups like Hizb ut-Tahrir but that he strongly disagreed with them. Thus, though he knew his father would object if he were aware of what Sherzod was doing, Sherzod often attended the new weddings with the express purpose of hearing the wedding speaker. For Sherzod, attending the new wedding party was a way to explore his interest in Islam while circumventing his father's injunctions against participation in religious events.

Like Nigora, Sherzod was particularly drawn to the weddings when Kadirbek was speaking. "Whenever Kadirbek is speaking, we always go," Sherzod remarked. "My friends and I always listen for news about when he will be in town." Sherzod said he knew that some people, like his father, might perceive Kadirbek as one of the "extremists," but Sherzod thought they were wrong. Kadirbek, he said, was just teaching "real Islam." For Sherzod, the wedding was one of the few chances he had to hear Islamic messages and participate in this kind of Islamic life.

Rejecting

Nurlan, a schoolteacher in his early fifties, threw a party to celebrate his birthday. There had been a "new wedding" not long before Nurlan's birthday party, and during the evening he and one of his close friends, Bakyt, began discussing the wedding. Bakyt, also in his early fifties, opposed the new wedding parties. He referred to the messages being taught as "propaganda." From other interviews I had conducted with Bakyt and his family I learned that Bakyt was not opposed to all the ideas espoused by those holding the new wedding parties or preaching at them. For example, Bakyt was against veiling for women but valued prayer. He did not perform namaz himself, but his wife had recently begun and his daughter had prayed and studied Arabic for several years at their neighborhood mosque. Bakyt's difficulty with the ideas being taught by people like the wedding speaker was their claim that the practices were mandatory for all Muslims and that these practices were defined as "proper" Muslim behavior. Bakyt viewed the teaching at the weddings, which again he labeled "propaganda," as a form of coercion.

But, despite his criticism of the content of the messages delivered at the weddings, Bakyt's discussion with Nurlan focused on the form of the wedding, which he said was the biggest problem with it. "A wedding is not the proper forum for the spreading of propaganda," he said. "He [the wedding speaker] is trying to do away with Kyrgyz and Uzbek wedding traditions." Nurlan, on the other hand, was largely concerned with the content of the wedding. He immediately accused the speaker of being a member of Hizb ut-Tahrir. Bakyt tried to correct his friend's misunderstanding by explaining that in fact the particular speaker who gave the message at the wedding in question was a Wahhabi and that the two were different things. Nurlan was not interested in such a fine distinction. He said that he was certain that in any case the man was an extremist and dangerous, and thus the new wedding party was a bad idea.

Doubting

Nozima was a fifty-five-year-old schoolteacher who had been performing namaz and fasting during Ramadan for ten years, though she had long wanted to pray. But, she said, "You know, such things were not allowed [during the Soviet period]." She was considered a devout woman by many of her neighbors and colleagues, though she would hardly label herself as such. She saw herself as a very open-minded, educated woman. She encouraged her children to be the same and gave them considerable freedom in a society dominated by the control of elders. One of her daughters had chosen to wear the hijab. Another routinely wore pants, makeup, and a baseball cap. She found both routes valuable and acceptable. She had never been to a new wedding, though some of her children had. She learned about the weddings from them.

When I talked to her about the evening parties, she said it was good that people had a chance to learn about Islam. She thought the forum for asking questions was particularly "great." She herself often had many questions and regularly read books about Islam. As a schoolteacher and the daughter of a scholar, she was very supportive of the pursuit of knowledge, and she found the pursuit of religious knowledge to be of even greater worth. So at first she endorsed the weddings. However, as her daughters told her about them in more detail, she began to wonder about the ideas being presented.

Some of the teachings of the wedding speaker seemed odd to her. When certain practices were deemed un-Islamic and the wedding guests were told not to participate in them (e.g., the discussion of Noruz in the wedding message presented in this chapter), Nozima was a bit nonplussed. She wondered why someone would consider such practices "un-Islamic." "They are Uzbek traditions," she said.

Reflections

The new weddings organized in Bazaar-Korgon were a means for transmitting alternative ideas of Islam in town. As such, for those who were interested, the events provided a site for learning about, and exploring, certain religious interpretations. But not everyone in the community found the events, or the alternative ideas, so exciting. Nor were all so willing to explore new notions of Islam and Muslimness. The weddings thus provoked a variety of reactions.

The youth saw the events as a way to learn more about Islam.[14] The weddings were a forum in which the young could seek direct advice on matters of personal conduct. The events were also exciting and stimulating. They offered a chance to interact with others who were also "interested in Islam." In addition, the large number of young persons at the event confirmed that interest and involvement in religion were no longer just for the old. If their parents disagreed with their burgeoning interest, the sight of others of a like mind helped bolster their own confidence in their belief and interests. Moreover, as the example of Sherzod demonstrated, the weddings provided a way for the young to pursue their interest in Islam even when their parents disagreed.

The evening wedding party was also a way for the guests to explore certain Islamic teachings and modes of living without necessarily having to accept them. Nigora's experiences were particularly telling. In wearing the hijab and experiencing more complete forms of gender segregation than what she was used to, she got a small glimpse of what "other" Muslims' lives might be like. At the same time, her experiences did not involve any kind of commitment. This was partly because there was no face-to-face involvement between the wedding speaker and the guests. Moreover, because attendance at the event was open, some guests came to the event knowing few or none of the others present, as was the case with Nigora. This meant there may have been little pressure to follow the teachings. This absence of pressure to commit stands in contrast to the other main forum for Islamic education in town—the small home-based study groups. These small groups led by a teacher formed tight units. In these groups greater religious and social coercion could be brought to bear on members to conform to the teachings of the group.

Attending an evening wedding party was largely free of commitment. There was no requirement to "come again," and the lack of membership in a specified social group gave attendees freedom from social pressure. This was not so different from the kind of learning experienced by listening to recordings. However, as Nigora noted, one of the attractions of the evening party was its interactive nature, in which guests could pose their questions to the speaker. Attendees received guidance about matters of everyday life—gender relations, dress codes, morality, and so on. Moreover, it was a "live" event with an exciting atmosphere. It was no coincidence that Nigora and Sherzod were both drawn not only to the new type of wedding itself but also to the particular speaker, Kadirbek. The role of a charismatic teacher should not be underestimated in evaluating the attraction of these events for the youth.

It is interesting to note that the youth never discussed the fact that the messages were being delivered at a wedding. The use of this type of event to deliver a message about Islam seemed unimportant. What was important to them was simply the chance to hear the message and ask their questions. Only when Nigora remarked that she might consider having such a wedding herself was the form of the event explicitly discussed. Even then, Nigora did not give a good indication as to why she would like to have a "new wedding" other than the fact that she had very much liked the one she had attended.

For other community members, largely middle-aged and elderly residents, the new evening wedding parties were more threatening than inspiring. Many, like Nurlan and Ibrahim, were against the teachings promoted at the events. Reflecting the general views on excessive religiosity that people held during the late-Soviet period, they saw the high degree of religious observance of those involved in the weddings as worrisome, problematic, and a marker of "extremism." Moreover, they disagreed with the admonishments of the speakers, claiming that it simply was not necessary to comply with their teachings in order to be a good Muslim.

The teachings of the wedding speaker represented alternative interpretations of Islam that were gaining currency in the town and thus threatened customary ways of living Islam. Although people like Nurlan and Ibrahim may have genuinely been frightened of some nebulous threat supposedly posed by "extremists" and "Wahhabis," the more salient threat they felt may have been to their sense of self and way of life. Ibrahim emphasized that his son would do well to adhere to the manner of piety practiced by himself and his father. He attempted to shield his son from influences that may have led him down a different path, breaking with the custom and practice of his own family.

Bakyt's reactions to the new wedding party, though at times directed at larger, abstract notions like "culture" and "religion," were grounded in ideas similar to those of Ibrahim. They both felt the wedding formed an (implicit) critique on their "way of life," though how that way of life was perceived—in reference to family or the nation, for example—differed. The ideas about Islam espoused by the wedding speaker were threatening to Bakyt, Nurlan, and Ibrahim partly because their understanding of "way of life" was tied up with notions of proper Muslim behavior. Nancy Tapper (1991, 143) has argued that changes in wedding ceremonies in a Turkish town were linked to the way that "townspeople use[d] wedding ceremonials to create and reflect social status and personal identity." In Bazaar-Korgon, however, the changes in wedding parties reflected, created, and were read as shifts in definitions of Muslimness, Kyrgyzness/Uzbekness, and the category of religion. The new weddings themselves, for Bakyt and Nurlan, for example, were direct proof of the threat posed by "new" interpretations of Islam; they were concrete examples of how these interpretations would undermine the most basic ideas, practices, and institutions of their Kyrgyzness. And while Gerald Creed (2002, 70) observed in Bulgaria that the "depoliticization of culture may have contributed to ritual's declining appeal or political utility," in the Central Asian case—where ethnonational/religious culture remained highly politicized, especially in light of the threats posed to it by varying articulations of Muslimness—ritual remained important as a field where this contest played out.[15]

A simple analysis of the reactions presented here might reveal that those "interested" in Islam or those who practiced Islam more like the mode endorsed by the wedding speaker were the people who supported the event, while others were more skeptical or antagonistic. Yet the reaction of Nozima highlights the fact that this easy dichotomy does not completely hold. A woman esteemed for her piety, she endorsed the event as a legitimate means of learning about Islam. Moreover, she generally supported the preaching of the wedding speakers. Nevertheless, she found some of their teachings quite odd, especially when they criticized certain practices she valued as Islamic. Her ambiguous position reveals that while she had much in common with those "interested" in religion and who saw the weddings as a means of learning and exploring, she also shared ideas with those who found the new wedding parties troubling and threatening to an established way of life.

Thus, reactions to the weddings often had as much to do with understandings of the category "religion" as they did with opinions about certain interpretations of Islam and the practices prescribed by these interpretations. A pattern that emerges is that those who criticized the new weddings tended to be of the same age cohort. Nozima was intrigued by and supportive of the weddings for many of the same reasons as the young. But where she differed from them and fell more in line with her contemporaries was in her reaction to the implied renegotiation of the boundaries and definitions of concepts like religion and culture. For Nozima, being Muslim and being Uzbek were synonymous. Regardless of the fact that she differed from her peers in her practice of particular rituals, she felt the same tension they did when it came to negotiating these notions. Nozima, like her peers, had grown up in the Soviet period, and her ideas regarding these concepts were shaped by Soviet modernization programs that had inadvertently strengthened the bond between being Muslim and being Uzbek, to the extent that they were inextricable and the only publicly allowed variant of religion.

In her work on consumption in Russia, Caroline Humphrey (2002, 41) has likewise noted that differences in attitudes and ideas were directly linked to age and, thus, attachment to Soviet ideals: "the extreme compression of historical changes into a few years has polarized the population; this has occurred most notably by generation, separating those people whose attitudes were formed by the Soviet regime from those who came to adulthood after . . . the mid-1980s." The sharing of these late Soviet-era conceptualizations had a profound effect on how residents in town reacted to the new wedding parties. In addition, certain age cohorts also similarly experienced the weddings as an implicit threat to their way of life and perhaps ultimately the legitimacy of their control of and authority over their children and community. That is why, despite variation in belief and practice, patterns of response to the new wedding parties fell (generally) along generational lines.

CHAPTER 3

LIVING AND LEARNING ISLAM

The Friday mosque of Bazaar-Korgon *rayon* officially opened in the year 2000. The project, which took six years to complete, was led by Tajideen Satvoldiev, the first head imam of the rayon (*rayondun imam-khatiby*) in the post-Soviet period. Teacher of many of the young generation of Islamic authorities and guide to the newly pious, he was revered by them as a highly knowledgeable scholar and an example of proper Muslim conduct. Tajideen was equally respected by those in the community inclined toward different interpretations of Islam. While neither partaking of his religious instruction nor necessarily agreeing with all of his points of view, they nonetheless lauded his "pure" character and his contribution to the community. Despite being widely respected, not long after the mosque opened Tajideen stepped down as head imam. The official documents of resignation cited poor health as the motivating factor. Local human rights groups and foreign media, however, indicated that he was accused of being a Wahhabi and forced out of the position.[1]

In this chapter I trace, in part, how interest in and particular modes of living Islam became so widespread in southern Kyrgyzstan in the early post-Soviet period. I argue that they were linked to and grew out of Islam as it was practiced and understood by a network of religious scholars in the late Soviet period. To demonstrate this growth, I explore the networks of Islamic education in Bazaar-Korgon, focusing on home-based study groups and their leaders. I pay particular attention to the life story of Tajideen.[2] Born in 1955, he was trained during the late Soviet period. His biography—from his youth as a member of the underground *ulama* of the Soviet period to his adult role as leader of the post-Soviet religious community—indicates that Islamic authorities in the Fergana Valley, of which Bazaar-Korgon is part, have long been actively involved in strategic power plays—with each other, with society, and with the government—and have been creatively attempting to interpret Islam and live properly as Muslims. I argue that it was men and women like him who not only kept teaching Islam when socialism ended but also expanded their activities when a new political and economic environment facilitated a growing interest in Islam.

Contemporary Islam in Kyrgyzstan and the manner and modes of its transmission are, to some extent, congruent with both pre-Soviet enactments and conceptualizations of Islam as well as contemporary international Islamist currents. However, while home-based study groups grew out of long-term local traditions of Islamic scholarship, they also built upon the needs, views, institutions, and actions of religious actors in the Soviet period. Similarly, as these groups continue to constitute an important base of religious knowledge transmission in the post-Soviet period, their forms adjust to new needs, possibilities, and contexts, the most salient of which are contemporary capitalism, the (long-term) globalization of certain nonpolitical Islamic movements, and anti-terrorism rhetoric.

I thus show how contemporary religious education is linked to and mirrors its various regional religious antecedents, as well as how it is equally related to spatially "other" (sometimes nonreligious) actors, contexts, and institutions. In short, I argue that in order to understand the origin of contemporary public Islam in southern Kyrgyzstan, broader frames of view and comparisons must be employed, including those that take into account the nation-state, capitalist markets, and the structuring power of discourses on Islamic extremism. Contemporary public Islam in Kyrgyzstan is immediately traceable to the lived Islam of the late Soviet period. It likewise resonates so clearly with other spatial-temporal instances because it is part of a long, lived tradition—Islam—with a history of texts, rituals, bodily practices, debates, and institutional forms (see Asad 1986), because it is situated in the wider modern project of nation-states and secularism (Kandiyoti 2002, 2009; Khalid 2006; McBrien 2009), and because it is now more thoroughly a part of global capitalist currents.

Religious Authority in Post-Soviet Kyrgyzstan

In 1993 Tajideen was approached by a group of elders (*aksakals*) and asked to become the imam of Bazaar-Korgon rayon's Friday mosque. At that time, it was

FIGURE 3.1. The "old" mosque. Photograph by the author, 2004.

an old structure located somewhat away from the town center in the quarter of
the former Komsomol State Farm. Tajideen said he was a bit surprised at their
request. But he acknowledged that one of the reasons they asked him was because
they believed he would be able to develop the land in the center of town that had
been given to them by the district government: "I didn't have a relationship with
them [aksakals]. I knew all of them, and we greeted each other in the street. Why
I was elected? I am not sure. But the main reason is that for two years there had
been a goal of building something on the land they had in the town center. But
it was never begun. [The aksakals] said, 'This teacher [*damla*] has a lot of friends,
he gets along well with people, he is active. If we elect him, [his friends] will help
him reach our goal.'"

Tajideen accepted their request and was made imam. Already an important teacher, his influence widened. He taught two subsequent imams of Friday
mosques—one of whom took over his post as head imam—as well as many of the
young men who were becoming known in their neighborhoods as knowledgeable
about Islam.

Tajideen was selected by local elders who singled him out not only for his
"religious" qualifications but also, and more importantly, for his social ones. He
had developed both types of connections in the Soviet period in his dual roles
as an "unofficial" religious authority and Soviet manager. Tajideen's biography

provides a starting point for understanding the contemporary roles of imams in the religious life of Bazaar-Korgon and understanding the adequacy of academic categorizations of religious leadership.

During the Soviet period, the Spiritual Directorate of Muslims of Central Asia and Kazakhstan (SADUM) coordinated and directed religious affairs of Muslims. The mufti was the head of the directorate, with a *qazi* administering each of the five republics. When the Soviet Union collapsed, the newly independent republics nationalized the formerly regional spiritual authorities, mirroring them in form. The Spiritual Board of Muslims in Kyrgyzstan (DUMK) was established in 1996, with a mufti as its head and a qazi directing the affairs of each oblast. In the post-Soviet period, the *muftiate* had under its purview a department of fatwa (ruling on Islamic law) and a department of publications that together seek to produce and regulate acceptable Muslim doctrine and practice in the country. Just as in the Soviet period, the Spiritual Board of Muslims in Kyrgyzstan is a hierarchical administrative apparatus that, while independent from the government, is nonetheless supervised by the State Committee of Religious Affairs. Importantly, however, unlike the Soviet state—whose strength and legitimacy afforded it considerable control over the spiritual board of its time— the Kyrgyzstani government is weak and its legitimacy is constantly contested, reducing its influence over the spiritual directorate.

A qazi in Kyrgyzstan is charged with supervising the imams of his oblast, appointing new imams, evaluating the religious knowledge of the imams, and regulating religious publications and education in his area. There are no religious courts in Kyrgyzstan, and the qazi of each oblast does not perform any legal tasks. Under the qazi are head imams (*rayondun/shaardyn imam-khatiby*), who are the religious authorities for the rayons and large cities. Under these rayon heads are imams (*imam-khatiby*) who officiate over other Friday mosques in towns or villages. There is, for example, one other Friday mosque in Bazaar-Korgon in addition to the one over which the rayon head imam presides. Finally, there are the imams of the small mosques of cities, towns, and villages that are used on a daily basis.

The head imam of Bazaar-Korgon rayon officiates over the area from the administrative center of the district, the town of Bazaar-Korgon. He is also the head of the central mosque of the rayon, which is likewise located in the town. On average, eight hundred to one thousand males attend this mosque every Friday.[3] The rayon head imam has the responsibility of overseeing all religious matters in the area, including the publication of religious materials, the regulation of religious proselytizing (*davat*), the regulation of madrasa, and the selection and supervision of imams. As of 2004, there were 101 mosques and thus 101 imams in the rayon.[4] The head imam recites the Friday prayers at the rayon mosque and

FIGURE 3.2. The groundskeeper and his grandson inside the Bazaar-Korgon rayon
Friday mosque. Photograph by the author, 2004.

delivers a weekly message. His position is not paid, though like other religious
specialists in town he receives remuneration for providing services to community
members (e.g., the reciting of prayers, performing wedding ceremonies, etc). The
day-to-day religious affairs of the villages and the neighborhoods of towns are
primarily left up to the local imams. However, the proximity of the mosques and
imams in the town of Bazaar-Korgon to the head imam and Friday mosque of
the rayon means that they are more heavily influenced by the rayon head imam.

In 2004, there were twenty-eight mosques in the town of Bazaar-Korgon and
at least one construction proposal on the table. Since the population of the town
is roughly thirty thousand, there is nearly one mosque for every one thousand
inhabitants or one mosque for every five hundred males in town. The number
should be reduced even more to account for young boys who do not attend the
mosque. But the rough figure of one mosque for every five hundred male inhabitants gives a close enough estimation of the mosque saturation in town. As
already mentioned, there are two Friday mosques in Bazaar-Korgon—the larger
rayon mosque and a smaller one originally constructed in the early twentieth
century.[5]

Despite the fact that the religious leadership is organized hierarchically and
in many ways designed from the top down, local actors retain a high degree of

agency in choosing leaders and influencing the local structures, as the story of Tajideen's selection demonstrates. For those with a vested interest (whether that be religious or otherwise) in who leads the Islamic community and what these teachers do and say, in Bazaar-Korgon there is plenty of room for local influence in the process. Because the imams are quite influential, the selection of a leader also implies an endorsement of the kind of Islam to be widely taught in the town.

According to the constitution of the Spiritual Board of Muslims in Kyrgyzstan, an imam is appointed by the qazi of the oblast. In reality, however, the process is far more rooted in local action. To begin with, an imam can be appointed only if there is a mosque to which he should be attached. Mosque construction in Bazaar-Korgon has been accomplished primarily through locally led initiatives. Small communities based on neighborhoods and informal networks decide to build a mosque. The process often needs help and leadership (in the form of outside donors, local "experts," and religious authorities) and thus does escape the control of locals. But the initiative and the final product remain in the hands of the neighborhood.[6]

Local community members often select an imam themselves, usually from within their own ranks. If a suitable candidate is available, he is suggested to the rayon head imam. The head imam then presents the candidate to the qazi, who "appoints" the man as imam. Every two to three years the *qaziate* (the office of the qazi) gives an exam to test the knowledge of the imams. However, as Tajideen lamented, the tests are often for show, as the majority of imams are unable to pass. Tajideen was hopeful, though, that with the new opportunities for Islamic education—both within and outside of Kyrgyzstan—there would be a greater pool of knowledgeable candidates to choose from in the future. Only if no real candidate for the position exists in the community does the qazi actually appoint an imam over a mosque. Even then, he selects based on the advice of the rayon head imam, who in turns searches for someone from a neighborhood near the mosque.

From a local perspective, the muftiate appears of relatively little importance regarding the appointment and regulation of religious authorities. The leaders are viewed as locally chosen, rather than appointed, and their "localness"—being from the community and a part of its networks—helps validate their authority. Yet, for others in Bazaar-Korgon who may not attend the mosque or davat groups, or who may not individually seek the advice and/or assistance of religious authorities, the legitimacy of these leaders is validated by their connection to the national hierarchical structure—the Spiritual Board of Muslims in Kyrgyzstan (the DUMK). Despite seeing connection to, and thus regulation by, the DUMK as an essential element in the validation of authority, there is still an underlying notion that the leaders are legitimate because they are local. In this reading, however, the meaning of "local" has shifted from the town to the nation. Religious authorities are perceived of as legitimate by people because they conform to "local"—that is, national—conceptions and practices of Islam as defined and regulated by the DUMK. Thus, they are not foreign "radicals" attempting to corrupt "local" forms of Islam.

Since independence, the Kyrgyzstani government has attempted to control definitions of Muslimness to ensure that "tolerant," "democratic," and "moderate" interpretations of Islam are practiced in its borders. In doing so, it promotes a vision of Muslimness consonant with that of the Soviet era, which was in essence an element of national identity. The indirect regulation of religious authorities, Islamic doctrine, missionary endeavors, religious publications, and religious meetings by the state through its unofficial influence over the muftiate ensures, for those in Bazaar-Korgon who have begun to distance themselves from those who have "gone to Islam," that Islam in their town remains of the benevolent variety. For these residents the regulation of religious authorities fortifies the borders around proper Muslimness, which, in their conception, is an ethnonational/religious identity. Thus, while it may be irrelevant to them who a particular imam is, his "locality"—that is, his endorsement of proper notions of Muslimness as it relates to ethnonational identity—is assured by the nature of state approbation of his role. Furthermore, the regulation ensures that "local"— that is, Kyrgyz or Uzbek—Islam is not contaminated by supposedly "radical" foreign influences.

Tajideen

I first met Tajideen early in the fall of 2003 not long after I began my research in Bazaar-Korgon. From the beginning of my research I was interested in understanding the ways religion was constructed, contested, and experienced by a wide spectrum of the town's population, and I therefore worked with interlocutors from the various social categories that one might distinguish in town—Uzbek and Kyrgyz; men and women; older and younger generations; those "close to Islam," those not, and those in between; and current and former elites, as well as those on the margins of political, social, and economic power. When I started my research on public Islam in Bazaar-Korgon, my first self-appointed goal was to trace the construction of the Friday mosque in the center of town. I imagined that understanding the history of perhaps the most visible symbol of contemporary public Islam would begin to lay bare some of the contours of the religious field and its situation in a new political, legal, and economic environment. I started my queries simply. "Who built the mosque?" I asked. Time and time again, Tajideen was named. I began collecting more information, about the mosque and also about Tajideen. The stories, and opinions, about him were legion.

FIGURE 3.3. Men milling around the mosque after prayer. Photograph by the author, 2003.

Like many religious leaders in the town, Tajideen knew about my research before I ever met him. He was told about my work by one of his students with whom I was acquainted. At my behest, the student asked if I could speak with him. He agreed and asked me to meet him outside the Friday mosque after prayers. He said he would answer my questions. I was accompanied to this meeting by a close friend—a woman in her early sixties, esteemed in town for her education, her honesty, her business acumen, and, increasingly, her piety. She had long ago enthusiastically agreed to help me in my work as needed, but in this case her willingness to assist was equally rooted in her desire to meet and speak with Tajideen.

She, Tajideen, and I spoke briefly in front of the mosque that day, surrounded by the hundreds of men leaving after prayers. After greeting Tajideen, she began by introducing herself, which inevitably included a discussion that continued until the two could place one another in common social and professional networks. She introduced me and laid before Tajideen a sketch of my life—my history in the town, my connections to various residents, my work at a local school, my academic credentials, my own family networks in the United States and Europe, her summation of my character, and my research aims. After this, Tajideen turned and greeted me himself. At his request, I reiterated the goal of my research project and the specific aims I had in meeting with him. Tajideen agreed to be interviewed. We made an appointment to meet at his home the following week.

Initially—as at that time my comprehension of Uzbek was still limited—a female interlocutor of mine, who was known by Tajideen, served as a translator (between Uzbek and Kyrgyz), facilitating my interview of him. He could understand my spoken Kyrgyz well, and as time progressed and my proficiency in Uzbek grew, my informal interpreter's linguistic assistance was no longer necessary, though she nonetheless accompanied me to the meetings. During five conversations (two to three hours each) over the course of my fieldwork, Tajideen shared his life story with me. Imperfect as his account may be, my use of his narrative nonetheless offers a situated account of a complex history of religious scholarship and leadership, analyzed through the viewpoint of one specific scholar.

Born in 1955 in Bazaar-Korgon, Tajideen was the son of a collective farmer. During his childhood, a paternal aunt who was an *otinbuva* (Uzbek: a female religious specialist) and, in his words, highly knowledgeable about Islam lived with his family. She taught him and his siblings about religion. His genealogy reveals a line of religious specialists, healers, and one ancestor with the title of *supi* (Sufi). Tajideen says his own interest in religion began in high school. At that time he began secretly studying Arabic and Farsi (Persian) in the homes of local Muslim teachers. Following high school he went to Frunze (now Bishkek) in an attempt to secure a position at the madrasa in Bukhara. Unsuccessful in gaining entrance and frustrated with his situation in Bazaar-Korgon, Tajideen left his home secretly and traveled to Leninabad (now Dushanbe) in the Tajik SSR. While there, he found a teacher who continued his religious education—Mullah Abdirashid Qadi. Tajideen was in Dushanbe for three months.

Tajideen recounts that Abdirashid felt if would be better if Tajideen were near his family, so he recommended him to another teacher in Margilan, a city closer to his native Bazaar-Korgon. The teacher was Mullah Hakimjon Imam, a prominent Fergana Valley scholar. While at Hakimjon's home, Tajideen says he was mainly taught by Hakimjon's apprentice. There, along with studying Islamic law and thought, he learned Arabic. He studied in Margilan for two years. Tajideen then moved to Tashkent, where he studied secretly for a year before moving to Andijan. In Andijan he studied with Imam Djamoldin, who had been trained in the Bukhara madrasa. Djamoldin was subsequently given a position as imam in Samarkand. Tajideen followed him and remained there until 1978, when he returned to Bazaar-Korgon. His teacher, Djamoldin, went back to Andijan.

When Tajideen first left home in 1971, his parents had been saddened by his departure and his choice of vocation; his father had wanted his son to join him in farming. Although they eventually accepted and supported his desire to study, their impatience with his long absence grew and in 1978 they insisted he return

home and be married. Tajideen agreed begrudgingly. He married later that year
and settled in Bazaar-Korgon. Following his marriage, his knowledge of Islam, as
he put it, became "dormant," and his own heavy investment in Islamic education
ceased for some time as he worked to provide for his growing family. Nevertheless, in the 1980s he did secretly give Arabic lessons at home to young boys. He
taught them the Arabic alphabet and how to pray, and he taught the best students Quranic recitation. This effort continued into the 1990s. He estimates that
during these two decades he held classes an average of six times a week, with each
class having approximately ten boys. During the 1980s, Tajideen worked first as
a security guard for the police and later as a foreman for a large bread factory
in town. While employed at the bread factory, he traveled quite extensively on
tourist trips organized by the government. In 1984 he visited Czechoslovakia, in
1987, India, and in 1989, Syria.

The academic literature on religious authorities in Central Asia produced
during the Soviet era (e.g., Bennigsen and Lemercier-Quelquejay 1979; Bennigsen and Wimbush 1985) and even thereafter (e.g., Makarov and Mukhametshin 2003) suggested the official religious leadership to be little more than
agents of the Soviet authorities and lacking in societal legitimacy. It regarded real religious life as maintained by unofficial religious leaders—those not
part of the Spiritual Directorate of Muslims of Central Asia and Kazakhstan
(SADUM)—who were not only completely separate from but inimical to the
official religious leadership. This official/unofficial dichotomy structured most
academic interpretations of Islamic leadership in the region. The unofficial religious leadership was believed to comprise underground scholars, as well as
other religiously knowledgeable men and women, who "preserved" Islam from
Soviet attacks and who, being respected by local communities, led the secret
and/or parallel forms of religious life. While it was certainly true that SADUM
was created by Soviet authorities and often worked in collusion with them and
while there was much criticism of SADUM and its members on the part of the
unofficial religious scholars, the dichotomized and rather antagonistic view of
official/unofficial religious leadership obscures the connections between the people and ideas glossed over by labels like "official" and "unofficial."[7] Attempts to
regulate Islamic knowledge and Muslim practice, as well as efforts to maintain
or gain power on the part of multiple parties, created a much more complex set
of relationships than this dichotomy presumes. In addition, the relationship of
these religious authorities to Soviet authority was more complicated than simple
acquiescence or resistance.

Mark Saroyan (1993) mounted one of the first critiques of the bifurcated categories of "official" and "unofficial." Such a separation, he argues, was based on
notions of power that simplistically juxtaposed state and society. Saroyan chal-

lenges the paradigm that characterized boards of religious authorities as mere mouthpieces of the state that were largely disconnected from so-called ordinary Muslims. Instead, he argues that the official religious leadership—who drew their legitimacy from their position as representatives of the Muslim community, as experts on Islamic knowledge, and as Soviet citizens—were involved in an on-going series of negotiations between a variety actors in positions of social and po-litical power; they were likewise important mediators between those with power and other Muslims in less-than-powerful political, social, or religious positions. "Thus," Saroyan claims (1997, 34), "the Muslim clergy can be seen as engaged in a creative process of constructing new forms of identity and religious organi-zation in order to situate and establish itself and its community in a complex set of constantly changing power relationships." Saroyan focuses on how Muslim leaders constructed new forms of institutions and "identity," but his insight into the complex connections and power struggles in which the Soviet-era ulama were engaged can be applied more broadly.

More recent historical research has begun to uncover the variety of Mus-lim experience and discourse that existed over the long Soviet period, including the ways religious and secular lives, authorities, ideas, and practices were inter-twined.[8] Stéphane Dudoignon's (2011) insightful research into "religious person-nel" of the Tajik SSR during the latter half of the Soviet period (1955–91), for example, describes not only the intellectual and spiritual lives of these religious figures but also the wider debates they and their contemporaries were engaged in at the time. Dudoignon sketches an environment in which Islamic authorities in the broadest sense—registered or not, Sufi or otherwise—were in constant nego-tiation and deliberation with each other and with civil authorities. This interac-tion, he argues, consisted "of a large variety of attitudes[,] including permanent negotiation at least during varied periods of lesser repression of religious practice" (2011, 69).

A major part of Eren Tasar's (2010) thoughtful and thorough investigation into the postwar institutionalization of Central Asian Islam focuses on the role unregistered religious authorities played in this process. For Tasar, the unofficial religious figures are seen as complicating and sometimes frustrating SADUM's efforts at regulating Soviet Muslim life. He also describes their relationship to official leaders, however, as ambiguous, a situation in which "registered and un-registered imams could maintain vibrant and symbiotic relationships" (2010, 41), and he argues that in some ways they complemented the muftiate rather than serving as its competition (524). Tasar describes the official leaders themselves, often seen as nothing more than spokespersons of the state, as engaged in a thoughtful attempt to understand, live, and teach Islam from within Soviet athe-ism. He argues that the leading ulama of SADUM attempted to "convince both state and society that the Central Asian population could be fully Soviet and Muslim without undermining either source of affiliation" (7).

Similarly, the intellectual biography of Tajideen is important in that it reveals the complexity of the relationships that linked the so-called official and unofficial religious teachers and leaders. It demonstrates that the struggles involved in religious life went beyond rather simple dichotomies of the state and its "official" Islam versus the "real, underground" Muslims. The webs of relationship were much more dense, overlapping, and tangled and the struggles far less straightforward. First trained by his aunt and later by underground scholars, Tajideen wanted to continue his religious education by attending the madrasa in Tashkent, which was hardly a logical choice if the institute had been perceived as wholly illegitimate. Most certainly the intent of the Soviet authorities was to control and further regulate the ideas of Muslims through these institutes. At the same time, the institutes were the last remaining religious centers of higher education—places where religious leaders sought to continue a certain tradition of scholarship and, in light of new experiences, policies, discourses, and frames of reference, where they attempted to work out the nature of Muslim life in a particular political setting. For some, this may have been an attempt to intellectually meld Islam and socialism, while for others it may have been an attempt to help Muslims find an appropriate way to live a "proper" Muslim life under Soviet rule, and still others may have found studying or teaching at these institutes to have been a means of survival or a road to power.[9]

According to Tajideen, he was not allowed to officially study in Tashkent because he was too young, a fact he tried to conceal from authorities but that eventually prohibited his admission to the madrasa. Frustrated with this turn of events, he continued his study in other ways—entering a *hujra*, a home-based form of Islamic education not approved by the state. Yet, even then, he was not wholly disconnected from the official religious hierarchy, for as his biography reveals he later studied under an officially trained imam. While certainly there must have been intellectual disputes between official and unofficial religious authorities and within each of those categories as well, there was nonetheless cooperation, dialogue, and tutelage. Tajideen's biography is by no means the only or most noteworthy one to reveal these interconnections. Muhammadjan (Mawlawi) Hindustani, for example, who was one of the most prominent Fergana Valley scholars, "played an important role as intermediary between the demographically limited 'registered' religious personnel of the Tajik SSR and a wider variety of 'non-registered' protagonists of the religious field" (Dudoignon 2011, 68). Muhammadjan Hindustani was a part of Tajideen's own intellectual lineage.

Tajideen's biography is also important for what it shows about the relationship between unofficial religious authorities and the local systems of Soviet governance. Despite his religious observances, study, and role as a teacher—all of which, in retrospect, would qualify him as a "real, underground" religious Muslim—he was also linked to official religious authorities and obviously integrated into the Soviet system. To put it bluntly, Tajideen was a Soviet.[10] After all, he had risen to the level of foreman in a bread factory and traveled abroad, which was no small feat for a man from Bazaar-Korgon, especially considering how rare and highly coveted such trips were. In order to establish the networks, perform the favors, and incur the debts that must have been needed to secure his places in these organized trips, Tajideen's involvement in local power networks could not have been a mere ruse used to disguise his religious activities.

In fact it was his networks—both within the religious communities and with influential members of the district and town governments—that later motivated town elders to choose Tajideen as the first district head imam of the post-Soviet period. Tajideen's life story thus complicates not only the overly dualistic categories of "official" and "unofficial" as they were applied to Soviet-era religious leaders but also conceptions of the "hidden" resistance and Soviet antireligious policies and discourse. Not only could one be Muslim and Soviet, but competencies, networks, and knowledge from one domain were utilized in others and often helped one succeed. Similarly, Svetlana Peshkova's (2014, 81) work on home-based Islamic education in post-Soviet Uzbekistan details the story of a female teacher whose success in gaining, teaching, and impacting students was, like Tajideen's, partly rooted in her status as a social leader during the Soviet period.[11]

The term "official" might be an accurate label to describe the category of Soviet-era scholars who belonged to the SADUM, or spiritual directorate. They were official in the sense that they were approved of by the state. However, when "official" is placed as a counterpoint to "unofficial" in most academic analysis on that era, the term assumes, asserts, and (re)creates a conceptualization of what these scholars were. "Official" is read as completely illegitimate in the eyes of the people, as a fixed and unchanging group of scholars, as puppets of the state having little more than hostile contact with "unofficial" religious authorities, or as being genuinely uninterested in Islamic doctrine or the spiritual lives of the Muslims under their jurisdiction. This conceptualization of "official" is inadequate, overly simplified, and at times false. Within the little space that existed, Muslim religious authorities—both official and unofficial—remained actively engaged in debating and constructing Muslim life in Soviet Central Asia.

Schisms and Labels

Tajideen's scholarly biography is exceptional. As part of the underground religious leaders and educational networks of the Soviet period, he was connected directly to some of the most influential scholars of the period and one of their most important debates in the late Soviet era, what Bakhtiyar Babadjanov and Muzaffar Kamilov (2001) have called the Great Schism. This debate and the way it has been mobilized in political struggles have left a lasting impact on perceptions of Islam in the region, including the consolidation of the discourse about "Wahhabis" in Central Asia and the perceived threat of Islam. The debate centered on the propriety of certain rituals and practices, with one camp accusing the other of allowing cultural accretions to replace true Islamic practice, while the accused claimed that their opponents were guilty of innovation. But the argument was equally about the proper relation of religious authorities to the regulations and institutions of Soviet governmental control. The debate did not remain solely a discussion between religious authorities, however. For their own reasons, Soviet leaders became interested in some of the practices under dispute. What resulted was an alignment of Soviet leaders, some official ulama, and unofficial, reform-minded ulama. Their collusion amounted to a strategic alliance of parties whose ultimate goals were in fact highly divergent.

After World War II, especially under Khrushchev, Soviet authorities initiated another series of campaigns against Islam in Central Asia, targeting certain practices the leadership saw as "vestiges" of religious practice. Simultaneously, the idea of an Islam free of the aberrations of shrine worship and certain "domestic practices" became important among certain elements of the religious leadership (Babadjanov 2004, 170; Saroyan 1997). This idea sparked debate among the ulama, official and otherwise, in which it was argued that at least some of these domestic forms were in fact sanctioned by the Hanafi school. Muhammadjan (Mawlawi) Hindustani, one of the most important scholars of the Soviet period, and his students were at the center of these debates.[12]

Hindustani was one of the few ulama who survived the antireligious campaigns and purges of the 1920s and 1930s. While he interpreted his actions during these years as an effort to preserve Islam, his students, looking back from the mid-Soviet period, judged his behavior as overly accommodating to the Soviet regime, and they criticized him for not having taken a stronger stance during these early antireligious campaigns. They also accused him of having condoned the persistence of certain cultural traditions among Muslims—and the association of these practices with Muslimness—despite the "un-Islamic" nature of them. These traditions included "improperly" conducted life-cycle rituals, shrine visitation and saint veneration, or the wearing of amulets and charms, for example. Hindustani was similarly reprimanded for such behavior by his elder, Qazi Abd al-Rasid, and also for his close associations with Sufi leaders and for the fact that he made room for "'secular' (*duniyawi*) issues in his teaching, marking a break with the strict pietism of the SADUM" (Dudoignon 2011, 61). Hindustani, on the other hand, criticized his students for innovation in rituals and deviance from Hanafi interpretations of the Quran, hadiths, and so on. The most prominent of these students were Rahmatullah 'Alloma and 'Abduvali-Qori. One of their former teachers, and most likely one of Hindustani's own students—though he later denied it—was Hakimjon, Tajideen's teacher for two years.[13]

These opponents of Hindustani—or reformers, as Nazif Shahrani (2005) has referred to them—rejected nearly all of the so-called domestic forms of Islam in Central Asia.[14] Moreover, as Dudoignon (2011, 61) argues, they positioned themselves against "the Qaziyyat on the central question of pietism" despite the fact that many of them had studied with Qazi al-Rasid. Because of the convergence of Soviet aims to eliminate the vestiges of Islamic practices and the reformers' desire to reform Central Asian Islam, Soviet authorities allowed these religious authorities greater freedom to spread their ideas, hoping that their teachings would help curb the practice of the masses (Babadzhanov 1999). While the ultimate goals of the three parties—the reformers, portions of the official ulama, and Soviet authorities—remained divergent, the manner through which they attempted to fulfill their aims—the elimination of "domestic" Islam—had momentarily converged, allowing their unlikely alliance.

However, this uneasy coalition did not last long. As the ideals of reformers became clearer and their numbers of adherents grew, the Soviet authorities saw them as a political threat. They interpreted the purified form of Islam they had been backing to be far more subversive than the "domestic" forms endorsed by Hindustani. They discontinued their tacit support of the reformers, and the relationship between them took another turn, one that would affect the religious landscape of the area for decades to come. Jettisoning their alliance with the reformers, Soviet authorities began recasting them as politically threatening. In the 1970s, those in political and religious power also began using the term "Wahhabi" as a way to label Muslims whom they perceived to have deviant points of view. Actual Wahhabi ideas from Saudi Arabia may have been among the ideas used by the reformers, though they most likely had indigenous roots as well. Babadjanov and Kamilov (2001) speculated that the term "Wahhabi" was first used by Hindustani to label his own students whose theological ideas had veered from his and who had criticized local Islamic practices that the scholar validated. Whatever the provenance of the term, it stuck as a pejorative label for Muslims whom state and religious authorities considered deviant or threatening. As I have argued elsewhere (McBrien 2006), the term was successfully associated with the reformers' understanding and practice of Islam such that even if not referred to directly in state-level and media discourses, the label was explicitly used with reference to these practices at the local level by average Muslims unaware of these historical processes and scholarly debates.

Although these early reformers found followers, many Central Asians held negative views about them because the reformers directly criticized their main modes of religious expression as un-Islamic. Moreover, the general population viewed the so-called Wahhabis with suspicion because of their emphasis on practices that had been negatively stereotyped as "extreme" during the early Soviet period. A large number of the ulama, both official and unofficial, were equally against the ideas of the Wahhabis because some of them held divergent views on the validity and use of the four Islamic legal schools. Moreover, it is plausible that the Soviet leadership, in light of its experiences in Afghanistan and its fear of a Muslim population unified under the banner of Islam, employed the term itself and solidified the equation of "Wahhabi" with "extremist." Thus, from many fronts the reformers (whether actual Wahhabis or not) were viewed with suspicion and perceived as a threat, though for different reasons and from different angles. Nevertheless, the common usage of the term "Wahhabi" solidified its place in the Central Asian lexicon.[15]

Tajideen never articulated a position regarding the split among Soviet-era Fergana Valley ulama. He studied under a scholar—Hakimjon—who has been linked to the strongest reformist movements in the area, and in recounting his biography he made no repudiation of this scholar or his teachings. Yet, Tajideen himself appeared to be less inclined toward certain reform-minded impulses in the area than was his former teacher. For example, when I asked him whether he accepted or rejected practices like the wearing of amulets, he responded that he respected Muslims whose beliefs and practices varied from his own. Small variances in the observances of rituals—like prayer—were also unimportant, he said.

After telling an extensive story in which two prophets debated the ritual performance of a shepherd, Tajideen explained to me that one prophet told the other, "The important thing is that he [the shepherd] believes in God with his heart." Tajideen concluded the story by saying, "So what I want to say is that even if we wear amulets [*koz munchik*], we do it with some kind of hope that God will keep us from evil things." If the intention of an act is good—as long as it does not go against the unity of God (*shirk*)—he said he respects that act. Counter to this, when I asked several of Tajideen's students—young men in their mid- to late twenties—similar questions, they articulated positions at odds with Tajideen's and more clearly in line with reformist trends. One young man claimed that "we should rely on God to protect us, not on amulets [*köz monchok*]." Tajideen's students likewise strongly disagreed with shrine visitation and the veneration of saints on the same grounds. Yet, it was Tajideen—whose views sound much closer to what many would interpret as a Sufi-inspired interpretation—who would later be removed from office on grounds that he was a Wahhabi (McBrien 2006).

The regional use of the term "Wahhabi" and the association of this label with potentially subversive Muslims and their supposedly politically threatening visions of Islam have melded with contemporary international discourse of a similar nature, though the labels "terrorist" and "extremist" are more often employed in that context.[16] This fusion of terms and these modes of interpretation have permeated foreign and local perceptions and interpretations of the Central Asian landscape. A lack of investigation into and little evidence for the religious and political actions and discourses of Central Asians—especially the concrete and varied positions taken by religious scholars and leaders—have created a situation in which apolitical religious movements, like those represented by Tajideen and the home-based study groups, are often read as politically subversive and potentially violent.

Nazif Shahrani's (2005) and Martha Brill Olcott's (2007) classification of the two groups involved in what has been called the Great Schism into the categories of "traditionalist" (among whom was Hindustani) and "reformists" (his opponents) is certainly more helpful than the continued employment of terms like "Wahhabi"; it overcomes the normative labeling involved in any invocation of this term.[17] It also illustrates the commonalities between this dispute and similar ones among ulama of other parts of the Muslim world, especially the move to "purify" Islam. But these terms likewise form an overly dichotomist reading of the ulama engaged in the debates, a reading in which any critical attempt at assuring proper Islamic practice and discourse, or any contact with a scholar favoring such, lands the scholar in the reformist category. This is trend is in need of change because it is intellectually problematic. More importantly, however, a change is imperative because the contemporary works looking at Soviet-era home-based schools, the biographies of Islamic scholars, and reformist-oriented leanings among the ulama (i.e., the criticism of certain practices and discourse as un-Islamic) often do so in efforts to describe, as Olcott (2007) did, the "roots of radical Islam."

The fact that there exists a tradition of criticism of local Muslim discourses and practices by ulama who would self-identify as Hanafi but who might distance themselves from those they label as "traditional," "Salafi," "reformist," or "Wahhabi" is ignored, as is the way this diversity in interpretation has carried over until today. Contemporary debates over orthodoxy are much more diverse than these labels allow, they are not always connected to violent political aims, and, even when they attempt to "rid" Islam of what they view as "unorthodox" notions and practices, they are not necessarily Salafi, though certainly some are. Moreover, even when religious teachers and leaders have studied with self-proclaimed reformists, Salafis or Wahhabis, they do not necessarily become Salafis (or anything else) themselves, as Tajideen's biography—and the leanings of his teachers and students—shows.

FIGURE 3.4. Bazaar Korgon. Photograph by the author, 2004.

Beyond congruent discourses—like those about Wahhabis or reformers—
institutional forms in places like Bazaar-Korgon that are consonant with what
is understood to be the basis of so-called radical Islam lend further weight to
"evidence" that it exists. Among these the most popular indicator is the "terrorist
cell." In the post-Soviet era, the institutional form through which residents of
the town have come to learn about textual interpretations of Islam and to seek
guidance in proper conduct is the small home-based study group, referred to in
town as davat. In form—small, private, informal, and unregistered—and content—Islamic education—they resemble the "cell" so many inside and outside
Kyrgyzstan fear. On the other hand, davat is also consonant with local historical
forms (the hujra) and contemporary forms of sociability (*gap*). Led by male and
female religious specialists trained in the Soviet period, these study groups were
the main means through which interest in textual Islam was stimulated and
transmitted in the post-Soviet era.

In Bazaar-Korgon the term "davat" encompasses more than just home-based
schools. As in other contexts, davat (Arabic: *da'wa*) indicates a general calling
to Islam. This call has been carried out not only in home-based schools but also
through local missionizing efforts—a form that simultaneously mirrors contemporary international varieties (da'wa), especially those of the Tablighi Jamaat.[18]
Yet the similarities with any of the four congruous forms (the cell, the hujra,

the gap, or da'wa) should not be overstated; a consonant institutional form does not mean an equivalent function or set of effects. Today's davat are no longer the secret enclaves of religious learning they once were, even if some opponents in town suspect them to be secret terrorist cells. Moreover, though they mirror international movements to "call" others to Islam (da'wa), they do so in a locally specific way.

Home Schools and the Transmission of Religious Knowledge

Seventeen women sat quietly on a glassed-in terrace on a sunny afternoon. They were waiting for her arrival. The group usually gathered every week for lessons at Amina's house. Amina would read from the Quran, hadiths, and other religious texts that had been passed down through her family, as well as new ones obtained since the collapse of the Soviet Union.[19] She gave an exegesis of the texts, telling supplemental illustrative stories. The women practiced their recitations of the Quran and sought advice regarding proper Muslim behavior and good conduct in troubling circumstances. But things were different today, quiet. The group was waiting for the arrival of a religious specialist invited for the day's davat. She had not arrived, so, following the women's recitations from the Quran, Amina decided to continue with the lesson as usual and began by reading a text. Amina paused when one of the young girls living at her home called her. The women looked at the windows and began to chatter excitedly to one another. "She's here, she's here," they said. Amina rose and walked to the entrance of her compound (havla) to greet two women. One was dressed in blue, with a headscarf fastened beneath her chin. She removed the small piece of fabric that covered her nose and mouth. The other woman, completely swathed in black, lifted the long cloth that hung over her face, body, and upper legs, revealing her face and another black dress and headscarf beneath. After greeting Amina, they walked to the terrace and sat down in places of honor. Rakhima, the woman in black, took off her gloves. She began her own lesson—teaching the women and taking their questions.

The davat group's excitement that day was due to the special appearance of Rakhima, one of the most revered female religious specialists in Bazaar-Korgon. She is one of the few women in town who completely covers her body—including her entire face and hands. Rakhima began dressing in this way whenever she leaves the home back in the early 1980s, when she married. It was something she had considered for some time, she said, and the moment of her marriage seemed the right time to start. It was a big decision to make in the Soviet period, one that forced her to leave home at the oddest of hours and travel only by car so she would not be noticed.

Rakhima was the granddaughter of a famous *atincha* (female religious specialist) from Suzak, a neighboring community. Rakhima said that she never intended to be a teacher; people just started coming to her. By the time I met her, she was the leader of a study group for other female religious specialists and teacher to several young girls who lived, or regularly visited, her home. She was often invited to teach at other home-study groups. Humble, but nonetheless aware of her fame, Rakhima offered a tentative explanation: "Perhaps it is because of my grandmother. Maybe her good name has been passed on to me." Rakhima may be right. When the Soviet Union collapsed, those wishing to pray, to learn about Islam, or to have information about particular practices or ideas went to the locally available religious scholars, those who had been trained in secret hujras or at home.[20]

Tajideen's story and the davat groups indicate the ways in which knowledge of textual interpretations of Islam were transmitted in Bazaar-Korgon. Local religious authorities like Tajideen, Rakhima, and Amina, trained by the "official" and "unofficial" ulama of the Soviet period, were well positioned to teach and guide those in the post-Soviet period with an interest in Islam. It was these Muslim leaders who facilitated the growth of public Islam in Bazaar-Korgon early in the independence era and took initial leadership of it. They taught an Islam that anchored its legitimacy in texts, but their diverging opinions reveal a finely textured field of varying interpretations, all of which were local and yet none of which can be seen as disconnected from a long history of debate among Muslims the world over about the nature of Islamic orthodoxy.

Like Rakhima, Amina was born into what she called "an Islamic family." She lived and studied with a locally famous female religious specialist (otinbuva) in Andijan for five years in the late 1970s. After marrying a man from Bazaar-Korgon, she moved there and began teaching her own pupils, who lived with her. In the post-Soviet period she continued this practice but also began conducting weekly lessons for older girls and women. In the mid-1990s she began covering not only her head when she left home but her lower face as well. She was a respected and well-liked teacher among women in the community even if she lacked the fame of Rakhima. It is not surprising that of the ten biographies I collected of locally influential male and female religious specialists (*moldo*, atincha, otinbuva), teachers (damla), and imams, who were instructing large numbers of students and were well connected in the networks of "those who had turned and gone to Islam" (*dinge burulup getkin adamdar*), all had, like Amina and Rakhima, reached maturity in the Soviet period and all were either from religious families and/or had studied Islam either secretly or officially in the Soviet period.

These men and women estimated that on average they taught approximately fifty students a week. And while it is not clear how many study groups were in town, I personally attended and heard of enough of them to feel certain that they were popular, numerous, and in nearly every neighborhood.[21] Most of the younger generation—those thirty years of age and younger—whose influence and status as "close to religion" or "knowledgeable" individuals was growing, traced at least part of their own religious and scholarly history to the older generation referenced above and, in some cases, to their teachers as well. This genealogy of scholars—from the Soviet period to the adult leaders of the post-Soviet community like Rakhima, Amina, and Tajideen, and finally to the rising young scholars, leaders, and specialists of the early 2000s—indicates that much of the "return of religion" to the region was facilitated by local actors.[22] The primary means was through davat—home-based Islamic instruction.

Similar to da'wa movements worldwide, davat in Kyrgyzstan entails calling others to a version of Islam that includes proselytizing and efforts aimed at what Michael Peletz (2005, 245) called in the Malaysian case "making Muslims better Muslims." However, unlike the Malaysian context Peletz explored, there are no davat organizations as such. Moreover, davat groups in Kyrgyzstan do not participate in politics and do not make efforts at providing social services, except for religious education. In Kyrgyzstan, the term "davat" has two connotations. First, it denotes proselytizing efforts. Men and on occasion women hold davat meetings, either in their own town or in other villages, towns, or cities. They invite residents of the area to attend these meetings, where sermons are given. Additionally, men and women engage individuals in discussions about Islam and its—according to them—true nature. In both cases, listeners are invited to come "close to Islam" (*dinge jakyn*). While the imams and qazis authorize these endeavors, they are not the ones who carry them out.[23]

Second, davat is used in reference to home-based study groups where one gives or attends davat. Men and women elect to hold or attend these regular study group meetings. In these meetings—like the ones led by Tajideen, Rakhima, and Amina—members usually begin by learning the Arabic script and the pronunciation of Arabic words. From there they learn to recite the Quran—though they rarely ever learn to understand the Arabic. In addition to this, the teacher spends time instructing students on proper Muslim conduct and the basics of Islamic doctrines and practices. This is usually done through textual exegesis and the use of instruction manuals that illustrate proper performance of rituals, including prayer. Most students own their own copy of the Quran, though the type and condition vary with the income of the student. Teachers use a variety of texts, with no standardization from group to group. This form of davat is the most common type of religious education in Bazaar-Korgon, the only other option being lessons at the madrasa, which, in 2004, was unavailable to women.[24]

These davat groups in Bazaar-Korgon are quite similar to home-based Islamic education throughout Central Asia, like the women's and youth groups in Uzbekistan examined by Svetlana Peshkova (2014) and in Tajikistan by Manja

Stephan (2010), and those in nearby Jalal-Abad, Kyrgyzstan, studied by Noor Borbieva (2012). Much like the group studied by Peshkova, the davat groups in Bazaar-Korgon used Uzbek or Kyrgyz for the language of instruction; Arabic was used only when Quranic recitations and the Arabic alphabet were taught. The lessons usually began with study of the alphabet and learning to recite simple, short *suras*, while the majority of the time was spent discussing proper Muslim conduct and concrete situations that occurred in the women's lives. Some groups, taught by the most learned, like Rakhima, paid more careful attention to texts and textual interpretation. Unlike the home school that Peshkova (2014) studies, however, the davat meetings in Bazaar-Korgon had much less of a classroom feel. There was no blackboard, for example, though certainly the teachers sat at the front of the table, simultaneously occupying the "space" of a teacher but also the seat of the most respected guest. Lessons were given at low tables set up exactly how they would be for meals, and they were often ready for tea—covered with basic bread, fruit, and snacks. Unlike those groups studied by Stephan (2010), however, the home-based education was not a place largely populated by adolescents. Although there were certainly students of high school age being taught independently by a religious specialist and sometimes as members of davat groups, this was not typically a part of local adolescent behavior nor a strategy regularly utilized by parents for upbringing or socialization, as seen in Dushanbe (Stephan 2010). When adolescents did study with religious specialists, however, they often went to live with them for a period of time.

Some davat groups were open to outsiders, the membership being based around everyone's desire to study with or receive advice from a particular teacher. Other groups were based on gaps, which are small groups of Uzbek men or women who meet together, usually on a monthly basis, to share a meal, socialize, and support one another. These study groups tended to be closed to people outside the social circles of the gap groups. Gap social groups were typically made up of classmates, neighbors, or age cohorts otherwise connected. Deniz Kandiyoti and Nadira Azimova (2004, 336) have shown how these groups provide a variety of functions, from financial to spiritual, arguing that in the case of women's gaps women experience as a "seamless totality" the "economic, social, and religious components of ritual and associational life." Despite this general picture of gaps as groups that meet a variety of women's needs, not the least of which is the "enactment of communal belonging and solidarity" (337), in some cases male and female groups have been transformed into overtly Islamic study groups whose nearly exclusive purpose is to gain knowledge of textual Islam and to seek advice about proper Muslim living.[25]

If enough members of a preexisting gap group are interested, they invite a local teacher (damla), imam, or religious specialist (atincha or otinbuva) to regularly meet with their gap. Study groups are formed in other ways as well. Sometimes teachers have enough individual students—usually young students still in primary or secondary school—that they form a group from among them. They may also open up meetings initially conducted with two or three individuals to include others. The study groups usually meet on a weekly basis. While many of the groups are made up of youth and young adults (up to about thirty-five years of age), there were also groups formed for older men and women. A significant portion of all davat groups are run by current—and former—imams, as well as those around them (their assistants, students, teachers, and wives). The groups and their leaders are not part of any other organization, institution, or movement. Strictly speaking, the groups do not fall under the control or regulation of the spiritual board. Their teachers are not, for example, appointed or trained by the board nor are their materials provided by or tightly regulated by the spiritual authority. However, it is the task of imams to check up on any study group or religious gathering to ensure that neither the teacher nor what is being taught falls outside the boundaries set by the muftiate. Additionally, leaders of neighborhood committees (*mahalla komitet*)—voluntary associations that work in conjunction with the town government—are similarly asked by the town government to be aware of anything "suspicious" in religious gatherings.

Suspicion of religious gatherings or religious activities—or religion in general—is rampant in Bazaar-Korgon, and the fact that one of the primary modes of contemporary Islamic training is congruent in form with the "secret" hujra of the Soviet era and the internationally known "terrorist cell" adds weight to local and foreign arguments that characterize these as sites of subversive, nefarious activity. While it is intriguing and important to untangle the ways in which these transnational discourses on religious extremism inform local religious landscapes, it is dangerous to use these discourses to insinuate more than a congruity in form between davat study groups and so-called "terrorist cells" or hujras.[26] This would be false on at least two accounts. First, davat study groups are just as easily related to a number of other institutions. As I have argued, these home-based groups are analogous in form to local modes of male/female sociability, as well as to institutions through which knowledge of Islamic texts and precepts was transmitted, debated, and developed secretly during the Soviet period. The form can likewise be related to "traditional" modes of Islamic education prevalent in the region in the past (Khalid 1998) and to contemporary study groups popular among pious Muslims in places such as Indonesia (Rinaldo 2008), Bangladesh (Huq 2008), Egypt (Mahmood 2005; Hirschkind 2006), or Sri Lanka (Haniffa 2008). And finally, when these groups are understood in the context of a broader local conception of davat, they can be seen as similar in function and form to global Islamic missionizing efforts.

Second, having the same type of institutional form does not mean having the same function, aim, or meaning. In each of the comparisons above there is both overlap and divergence. The study groups, in contrast to gaps, have become nearly exclusively about gaining and spreading knowledge of Islam—with legitimacy grounded in texts—and proper Muslim conduct; in contrast to hujras, they are not legally prohibited institutions. They diverge from "traditional" modes of education by the means through which they impart and conceive of knowledge, as well as in their relationship and residential patterns between teacher and students. Unlike many of the study groups seen throughout the Muslim-majority world, these groups are not linked to political parties or organizations; their students have usually received no more than a secondary school education and are of lower-middle-class and lower-class backgrounds. Moreover, the study groups did not begin in the capital city but in smaller urban areas, with the exception of those that started in Osh, the country's second-largest city.

These are obviously merely some of the differences (and some of the most obvious ones) between davat study groups and similar forms. Tracing the full range of convergences and divergences as well as the singularities of what is going on in these Kyrgyzstani groups opens up a fruitful research field. I have merely attempted to show that it was through them that knowledge of Islamic texts and proper Muslim conduct was transmitted. I also suggest simply that these groups based their authority and claims to legitimacy in an appeal to text. Nevertheless, despite this similar epistemological basis, all sorts of varying interpretations arose, including what various actors (including academics writing about them) would call Salafi, "traditional" Hanafi, critical Hanafi, reformist, modernist, Sufi, Wahhabi, extremist, or inauthentic.

Fissures in the Community

When the group of elders originally approached Tajideen and asked him to become the imam of the rayon, one of their hopes was that he would be able to develop the land in the center of town that the rayon government had allocated to them. The land was located on the hill overlooking the bazaar, near the rayon government offices. Initially, the elders wanted to build a madrasa on the land. There was already a Friday mosque operating at the time. However, it was a fifteen-minute walk from the center of town; in Tajideen's words, it was "in the corner." Tajideen argued that the rayon's Friday mosque should be more centrally located. His push for the mosque project was also influenced by his trips abroad:

> The permission to build a mosque had been given in 1991, but nobody had taken
> the responsibility [to build it]. So in 1993 I was the imam and decided to do some-
> thing useful for the people; I had the idea of building a mosque. I had traveled a
> lot since 1982. I went to the Czech Republic and Poland. Later I was in India and

Syria. I went to the Arab republics when I went on hajj [in 1991]. I saw beautiful mosques along the main roads. I saw women and men coming to pray *namaz*. I was kind of jealous. I thought, "Why don't we have buildings like that?" I thought about our mosques. They were little, dark, cold. I thought about our mosques and wondered why we didn't have any with domes like those in Bukhara or Samarkand.

The aksakals were skeptical that enough support could be raised for the project. Tajideen, however, mobilizing his relationships with contractors and builders in Uzbekistan, as well as his "foreign friends," convinced the aksakals. Construction began that year.

It was largely as a result of Tajideen's networks that the construction of the rayon mosque was so successful. Local connections with a well-positioned official in the district government smoothed over legal hassles. Other local networks secured the bulk of materials needed for the project. Contractors and architects in Uzbekistan (whom he knew through a relative in Tashkent) provided the technical capability. Perhaps most importantly, large amounts of economic assistance came from Saudi Arabia and Turkey, through individuals he had met on hajj.

Tajideen's strong leadership and vision for the mosque also won him support in the community. When questioned about the construction of the mosque, Tajideen always emphasized first and foremost the involvement of the local community. He explained with pride how people gave whatever they could to help realize the dream—money, food for workers, construction materials, or labor. In fact, nearly every neighborhood in the community took "ownership" of a few meters of the mosque construction (whether literally with physical labor or through donations of materials or money). Contribution to the construction was widespread in the community, even among those who today do not attend it or who would not be seen as "close to Islam." Those who helped in the project were proud of their involvement and of the outcome. Nevertheless, the role of the community is not foremost in people's minds when they discuss its construction. When asked the question, "Who built the mosque?" most people reply "Tajideen." When pushed a bit more, they sometimes also referred to the "sponsors from Arabistan."

In addition to the construction of the mosque, there was planning for a relandscaping of the grounds and the erection of a large minaret. The mosque was completed in 1999, and the foundation for the minaret lay ready for its construction when controversy surrounding Tajideen began. A group of men opposed Tajideen's leadership and mounted a movement to oust him from his position as head imam. Those who described the events hypothesize that the opposition was dissatisfied with Tajideen's alleged combination of business with his pilgrimage to Mecca. Others argued that those against Tajideen had started the moves to oust him on the premise that he had embezzled money or goods from the mosque project. Another tale insisted that he had sold local girls in Saudi Arabia.

At the same time that the moves against Tajideen began, a native Bazaar-Korgonian, Rahimjon, who had been trained in the Bukharan madrasa during the Soviet period and who had worked for many years in Bukhara as an imam, returned with his family to live in town. He positioned himself, or was positioned by others, to replace Tajideen. The religious community surrounding the mosque split in their support of the men. Those against Tajideen sent written protests to the qazi in Jalal-Abad. They laid out various allegations against him and supported Rahimjon on the basis that his education was more "formal" than Tajideen's. As the opposition grew, the nature of the claims shifted and allegations that Tajideen was a Wahhabi were made to government and religious authorities at the rayon and oblast levels. The main force behind these accusations, Tolombai, was a relative of Tajideen. Tolombai was a well-known builder in town and the constructor/owner of the teahouse adjacent to the mosque. Nevertheless, despite Tolombai's attempts to participate in the design and construction of the mosque, he was not included in the project.[27] His bitterness over the slight was still apparent a decade later.

Still unable to obtain Tajideen's removal, his opponents mobilized their connections in the rayon government, convincing a rayon official to put pressure on the qazi in Jalal-Abad to remove Tajideen from his position.[28] In the end, Tajideen himself decided to step down. The official report cited "poor health" as the reason for his resignation. When he spoke about the matter with me, he refused to discuss the movement against him, never openly mentioning it and never directly accusing anyone of attempting to remove him from his post.[29] He said merely that he had grown tired of the gossip and infighting; he felt there was too much injustice. In short, he says, he became displeased with the work. Askar Jamilov, a local human rights activist, reported that petitions signed by residents had been sent to the qazi immediately following Tajideen's removal. They asked for his reinstatement. The efforts were to no avail. Rahimjon, the Bukhara-trained imam, replaced Tajideen as rayon head imam.

Rahimjon did not last long in his position. After one and a half years he was removed from office and replaced with Toktosun, the imam at the time of research. Toktosun himself had been a student of Tajideen's and was the assistant imam from 1992 until 2000. The circumstances surrounding Rahimjon's removal are even less clear. Some indicated that the qazi had removed him from office because he was supposedly linked to Hizb ut-Tahrir. Other residents claim that it was in fact his son, who oddly disappeared from town for a few years, who was involved with Hizb ut-Tahrir. They say the blame was misplaced on the father. Meanwhile, under Rahimjon and Toktosun, the construction of the minaret,

FIGURE 3.5. The Bazaar-Korgon rayon Friday mosque being prepared for a visit from the president of Kyrgyzstan. Photograph by the author, 2004.

which ceased when Tajideen was removed, did not resume and no further work on the grounds' renovation was done.[30] Despite all the gossip swirling around Tajideen and his removal from office, he remained one of the most respected men in town. He was lauded for his pure, kind, and true character, for his religious knowledge, and for his ability to do something concrete for the community—the construction of the mosque.

While the opposition's specific grievances against Tajideen remain opaque, the means they employed to oust him are clear. Unable to obtain his removal from office themselves, the opposition cast him in such a light as to force the hand of secular authorities and his religious superiors. By branding him a Wahhabi and gathering either sufficient "evidence" or enough powerful support to back their claim, they levied a charge that could not be ignored in the contemporary political environment.

Peter Mandaville (2007) argues that while the contemporary pluralization of Islamic religious knowledge and authority is often linked with the process of globalization, they are in fact not new in kind but rather only in degree, that is, in their extent and intensity. The unprecedented scope of pluralization has had important impacts on the politicization of Islam, he argues: "With discourses about 'authentic Islam' or 'true Muslims' increasingly framed in terms of how one responds and positions oneself in relation to various geopolitical agents (e.g. the United States, al-Qaeda) and events (e.g. American military action in Afghanistan and Iraq), the articulation of 'Islamic' positions and viewpoints are easily ensnared within a discursive field defined in geopolitical terms. That is to say that claims and pronouncements as to what Islam is and is not tend to function today simultaneously as statements of geopolitical and geocultural affiliation" (2007, 112).

If Mandaville's analysis is powerful in reference to Muslim minorities in Europe and the United States and the way their articulation of Muslimness must necessarily be in dialogue with specific national and international political conversations, it is nonetheless so in a different context, one where the political agents and events against which one is positioned are more broad than concrete. In Bazaar-Korgon when one speaks of Muslimness, it may not be in direct dialogue or with specific reference to, for example, the discourses on military action in specific incursions like Afghanistan, but it is certainly within broad frames of "moderate" Islam and the dangers of religious extremism. When residents criticize home-based study groups, they appear to do so with ideas of the malevolent, incendiary capacities of secret, cell-like activities, notions produced as much by current geopolitical events as by the experiences and discourses of the Soviet era. And when they speak of "good Islam," they do so in reference to a national ideal of moderate religious belief and practice, threatened by extreme foreign voices. These views have been created and melded because Bazaar-Korgon has never been isolated—extraregional discourses, institutions, and actions have long been part of everyday life, even if these international forces were not always the ones imagined. These views ultimately made possible Tajideen's removal.

In this chapter I have argued that the increasing numbers of people practicing and showing interest in certain interpretations of Islam in southern Kyrgyzstan have been taught and guided by religious authorities who were largely trained during the Soviet period. Although the transmission and development of religious knowledge were severely curbed during the Soviet era—to varying degrees and through various means—such activity continued in a muted form; religious authorities engaged directly with the very real impact of Soviet ideology, institutions, and life on Muslim thought and practice. This combination of active preservation and transformation, both occurring through strategic interactions with state power, brought about a very specific set of conceptions regarding Muslim life in the post-Soviet era that can be seen neither as a "reversion" to or "revival" of pre-Soviet ideas nor as an import from foreign sources, though they certainly share notions and practices with interpretations of Islam from the pre-Soviet era and from contemporary non–Central Asia locales. The most pertinent influences ·

on the contemporary religious landscapes in southern Kyrgyzstan are, I argue, the local religious scholars and leaders who experienced the late Soviet era.

Nevertheless, Islam in Kyrgyzstan has always been linked to, influenced by, and simultaneously created by global movements, but in a manner much more complex than has been acknowledged. Whether we consider the religious authorities' long-term connections with legal and philosophical texts and scholars throughout the Muslim world, long-term discourse about Islamic extremism, or, more recently, media-enhanced connections to ideas in places like Saudi Arabia, Pakistan, or Europe, we see a history of connectedness. In the first two decades of the post-Soviet era, the primary institutional forms through which residents of the town have learned about textual interpretations of Islam and sought guidance in proper conduct are consonant with local historical forms (the hujra) and contemporary forms of sociability (the gap), and these forms simultaneously mirror contemporary international varieties (davat). The discourse on Wahhabis that underpinned Tajideen's removal carried weight because of long-standing local discourse on religious extremism in the Soviet era, as well as contemporary global discourses about it. The religious authorities who survived the purges of the 1920s and 1930s had been connected, in one way or another, to a local modernizing movement, the Jadids, that was based on and linked to similar movements throughout the Muslim world of the late nineteenth and early twentieth centuries.[31] These authorities were most likely also connected to intellectual traditions more interested in protecting Islam from religious or secular modernization and who sought to bring Islam back to what they defined as its original sources (Olcott 2007, 5–9). Most of these authorities did not survive the early antireligious campaigns, but questions of the modernization of Islam continued in other, very different ways, one of which was through the official religious hierarchy and its members' positions as religious leaders within one of the original global movements—international socialism. The socialist movements of the late nineteenth and early twentieth centuries cannot be easily compared to the state structures of the Soviet Union in all its forms over its seventy-year span. But the point in noting this connection, and the way the whole network of (official and unofficial) religious authorities was linked together and worked, in concert and contestation, to live out and conceive of Islam in that environment, is to rethink how the "religious revival" has been interpreted in the literature on Central Asian religious authorities and religious knowledge in Muslim Central Asia.

CHAPTER 4

MUKADAS'S STRUGGLE

In the autumn of 2003, after protracted consideration, Mukadas Kadirova, age twenty-five, altered her mode of public dress. She changed the way she fastened her headscarf, pinning it securely under her chin so that it completely covered her hair and neck. She no longer bared her arms, and she started wearing skirts that revealed only her feet. Mukadas deliberated for so long not because she felt uncertain about a Muslim woman's obligations or because she lacked the desire to adhere to them. Her hesitation resulted from the possible consequences of her actions. Would she be perceived as a religious extremist? Would she be permitted to teach? How would her family react? And, perhaps most importantly, would she still be a modern woman?

Mukadas's worries are not particularly remarkable; they resonate with the contemporary experience of many Muslim women. The history of the veil as an antimodern symbol has been well documented (e.g., Ahmed 1992). Through critical ethnographies, anthropologists have challenged one-dimensional, orientalist readings of the headscarf, demonstrating its subaltern uses as a sign of protest (McLeod 1991), a means of creating an alternative modernity (Brenner 1996), or an element of pious self-fashioning (Mahmood 2005). Others have examined the veil in its role as Islamic fashion (Moors and Tarlo 2007) or political chic (White 1999). Nevertheless, the headscarf's ubiquitous antimodern image remains.[1] Mukadas's dilemma is tied to this globalized interpretation.

To analyze Mukadas's struggle as a challenge to narratives of modernity, gender, and Islam is, quite frankly, theoretically redundant. Yet, the redundancy itself is intriguing, because Mukadas is not from one of the regions—Europe or the "Muslim majority world"—that have figured prominently in such analyses. I present Mukadas's struggle not to critique once more these familiar "modernist" narratives. Rather, Mukadas's dilemma is interesting because it shows that she and other Bazaar-Korgonians read her decision to veil through these same discourses. The similarity reveals not only the effects of contemporary globalization but also those of a longer history of global interconnectedness as it unfolded in Central Asia over the twentieth century. In part it demonstrates congruencies between Western and Soviet modernization campaigns and their concomitant ideas of the modern.

However, it is equally significant that Mukadas's problematic is not identical to that of Muslim women in other countries. The dilemmas faced by Mukadas shows the erosion of the Soviet normative order, the rising influence of alternative orders in local and national communities, and the continued saliency of some Soviet-era notions—most notably, negative discourses about the veil and ideas about "proper" religion. When Mukadas contemplated veiling, she perceived herself as fully modern, even as she watched the modernity of her society crumble. The economic and social decay of the post-Soviet period precluded the institutional enactment of either Soviet norms or the new capitalist, consumption-oriented vision of modernity. Mukadas's decision to veil thus involved a reevaluation of her vision of modernity, as well as a creative attempt to overcome the material and social constraints impeding her decision. The distinctiveness of Mukadas's struggle suggests that even as modernity is multiple in its political and cultural forms (Eisenstadt 2000a, 2000b), individuals can experience these multiple modalities simultaneously; while modernity has often been understood as something experienced either as a present state or a desired future, Mukadas's dilemma demonstrates that the experience can likewise include a longing for a modern past. This chapter describes her struggle to provide insight into the lives of those in Bazaar-Korgon who had "turned and gone to Islam," to highlight the dilemmas they faced, and to situate their stories in a broader spatiotemporal story of modernization and (public) Islam.

The Soviet Modern

Mukadas is the second eldest child of Zeba Osmonalieva and Ulugbek Kadirov. Zeba, born in 1950 in the city of Osh, was the daughter of an illiterate mother and a father who was a history professor. Zeba was partly raised by her grandmother, who regularly took her to pray at the nearby pilgrimage site of Suleiman's Mountain when she was a young child.[2] Nevertheless, Zeba's teenage and adult years were devoid of similar experience, and she gave little thought to such matters, she said. She was, however, very occupied with studying and "advancing" herself.

Ulugbek was from Bazaar-Korgon and an artist of mixed Uzbek-Tatar origins. He met Zeba at a summer camp in his home region when both were working as youth leaders. After that summer, Zeba continued her university studies while Ulugbek traveled extensively throughout the Soviet Union and painted. Following his return to Bazaar-Korgon, he and Zeba married. She began teaching in Bazaar-Korgon. Between 1974 and 1985 their five daughters—Muyassar, Mukadas, Delnura, Delfuza, and Shasta—were born. At that time Bazaar-Korgon was a small agricultural town of around fifteen thousand inhabitants with some industry. Zeba and Ulugbek were part of the town's intelligentsia, and they taught their daughters to appreciate the arts and education.

While the Kadirova girls were growing up, the town of Bazaar-Korgon underwent an administrative reclassification that necessitated its modernization. The transformation of small towns like Bazaar-Korgon was part of a more widespread urbanization across the Soviet and an example of postwar projects of Soviet modernization (e.g., Kalinovsky forthcoming; Harris 2013; Collier 2011). These ventures altered the physical landscape and continued to industrialize and urbanize the Soviet Union. But they also affected the spaces where people lived and, as Stephen Collier (2011, 5) argues, linked residents to "urban need fulfillment" and the cities to "national mechanisms of economic coordination and circuits of resource flow." Soviet modernity was experienced more modestly by Bazaar-Korgonians; it meant the provision of infrastructure for everyday conveniences like running water, telephones, and electricity. But it nonetheless tied them into cooperative projects of construction and continued to stoke the collective fantasies of modernity. While a communist utopia was never realized, the decades of socialist campaigns wrought changes producing what has been called one of the "original alternative modernities" (Eisenstadt 2000a, 11).[3] Certainly one of its distinct features was the collective as the site and means of transformation or, as Collier (2011, 21) puts it, "collective life as a space of total planning."

While Bazaar-Korgonians indexed material alterations as the "arrival of modernity," it was just as much social and ideational changes engendered, if not planned, by Soviet projects that gave rise to Mukadas's struggle and that locate her dilemma as part of the larger story of modernity. As explained in the introduction, tied up with modernization campaigns, in the Soviet Union as well as elsewhere, is the political project of secularism (Asad 2003), an endeavor in which states have attempted to "construct categories of the secular and the religious in terms of which modern living is required to take place" (2003, 14). The atheism campaigns of the Soviet Union were among the most extreme examples of this kind of categorical transformation. Many of the features categorized as incompatible with modern living in Soviet Central Asia, like the veil, were congruent with those found in liberal modern projects. But, as discussed in the introduction, categories of religion and the secular had unique contours in Soviet secularism. Muslimness had become intrinsically tied up with national belonging. This remained the allowable category of religion, even if it was simultaneously thought of as antiquated, traditional, and something that would eventually be overcome. But again, this was a sense of Muslimness that excluded certain Islamic observances and labeled them as unmodern. The veil was one of the most targeted; evaluations of it were radically altered.

Notwithstanding this creation of particular identities and their centrality in everyday life, as well as the antireligious campaigns and other brutalities of the early Soviet period, by the middle to late Soviet period Central Asians nonetheless were conceiving of themselves as Soviets; they largely supported the union, its visions, and programs (see Ro'i 2000, 430). Bruce Grant (1995) has argued similarly with regard to one of the Soviet Union's small ethnic groups, the Nivkh. Despite all the contradictions of the Soviet experience and the reified dualisms of public political discourse—traditional/modern, local/federal, Nivkh/Soviet— these oppositions were less distinct at the local level. As Grant (1995, 159) claims, "most Nivkhi thought of themselves as Soviets first and Nivkhi second; a good number of others, especially younger people, thought of themselves as Soviets only." This feeling of being Soviet may be one of the most important differences between residents of the Soviet Union and the inhabitants of many places colonized by Western powers. A colonizer/colonized dichotomy did not exist in Central Asia. By the middle to late Soviet period, the Soviet Union was not perceived by Central Asians themselves as a colonial endeavor. They were Soviets and they were modern people, even if these identities were built upon seeming contradictions—like an "atheist" Muslim—and even if the veil came to be understood nearly universally as an indication of backward, radical, or suspect behavior.

This feeling of being Soviet was at least partly due to measurable and observable changes that Central Asians had witnessed in their lives and the discursive politics promoting them. These projects were promoted as routes to personal and societal advancement; tangible technological and infrastructural accomplishments lent credibility to the rhetoric of modernization. As Deniz Kandiyoti (2002, 295) has argued, if we compare the Middle East and Central Asia through the rubric of postcolonialism, one of the most striking differences is "the diffusion of the fruits of Soviet development to the lower strata of society [that] separates Central Asian societies from those of the Middle East."

While parallels can be seen in Ataturk's modernizing campaigns and the creation of Turkish citizens or, to a lesser degree, in long-term reforms in Egypt, the exceptionality of the Soviet campaigns—their militant intensity and long duration, along with the closed nature of the Soviet Union—suggests limits to this comparison. If in the 1950s in Turkey Islamic groups were already vying for power during a brief period of political pluralism (Göle 1996, 20) and the 1970s witnessed a worldwide Islamic resurgence, it was not until the 1990s that a similar space for political opposition was even imaginable in the former Soviet republics of Central Asia. In fact, even when the union collapsed, the leaders of the five Central Asian republics were among the last to accept its demise, and it was not until the turn of the millennium that a Central Asian "Islamic revival" became palpable in public spaces. Even since then, in Kyrgyzstan Islamist groups have been absent from the political scene. Certainly some of the post-Soviet changes were welcomed. The material wealth of capitalism enticed many, and religious freedom was widely celebrated. But as post-Soviet realities set in, former Soviet Muslims' relationship to both their Soviet past and capitalist present became much more complex.

Post-Soviet Changes

Mukadas was thirteen years old when the Soviet Union collapsed. When asked about the changes in the early years, she first recalled how expensive everything had become. Others in her community around her age remembered waiting in line for hours to acquire scarce resources. While they had similarly queued for items during the Soviet era, the difference was the dearth of even the most basic items, such as bread. Mukadas remembers things were particularly difficult for her father. As an artist, he had received regular payment for his work. Such payments ended with the demise of the Soviet Union, and the ensuing economic crisis meant that there was no private demand for his paintings. Mukadas's father did not survive the collapse of the union. He died in 1994 under mysterious circumstances. Despite the double shock and hardship of personal loss and societal collapse, Mukadas's mother worked out a modicum of economic success trading gold jewelry. The girls thrived in the seemingly inhospitable environment and grew up to be well-liked and respected young women.

Mukadas talked of her father often. Although in the years just preceding his death there had been friction between them—mostly as a result of Mukadas's burgeoning independence—she remembered her father tenderly. Mukadas recounted how he taught her about the nature of life and how she should live it. She talked very pointedly about wanting to be a cultured person, to better herself, and to be intelligent and well read. She was pleased with the freedoms of the post-Soviet period, especially freedom of conscience. She said that only since the end of the Soviet Union were people learning to think for themselves, rather than listening to the dictates of others.

Mukadas's positive evaluation of the post-Soviet period arose primarily from her satisfaction with the change—with the dwindling of certain unsavory elements of the Soviet Union—and was not necessarily an endorsement of the new forms of political, economic, societal, and moral organization that had replaced those of the Soviet era. Her actual encounter with the realities of postsocialist life provoked more disillusionment and disappointment than celebration. Dreams and values nurtured in the Soviet period were accompanied by institutional arrangements that could bring them to fruition. One could embrace socialist ideals of modernity even if they were never fully attainable. As Frances Pine (1996, 133–34) argues, criticism during the socialist period focused not on socialist ideals but on the incompleteness of specific projects. There was a sense that some dreams could be reached—for example, the education and employment of women, along with their full participation in society—and that the system could be changed to make the implementation of these ideals more complete. However, when these same dreams and values were set in the radically new context that we may loosely term "capitalism," the possibility of their fulfillment was largely curtailed. A deficit of jobs, absence of child care, lack of money, and limited access to "quality goods" meant Mukadas was constantly frustrated by the mismatch of her dreams and realities.

She was equally disappointed by the hollowness of "Western" modernity. Actually lived socialist modernity was characterized by infrastructural improvement, scientific advancement, a certain ethos of community and communal effort to create a new, superior society, and, importantly, a set of values—gender equality, mass literacy, economic equality, and meaningful work for all—that were, if only partly, attainable. Postsocialist modernity, by contrast, was not about lived experiences and values—it was almost exclusively about dreams. These were dreams of Western consumption and material standards of living that did not fit the logics of Soviet life and were rather unattainable in the economic realities of postsocialist life. Thus, while hopes for a prosperous "modern" future abounded, they were coeval with nostalgia for an equally modern, if different, past (Pine and Bridger 1998).

The material prosperity that Western forms of modernity promised—but often failed to deliver—was not the only source of unease in the post-Soviet period. In the early 1990s Kyrgyzstan elected for "shock therapy," enacting not only radical economic transformations to hasten its "transition" to capitalism but also political ones—including freedom of conscience—to accelerate its passage to democracy. This shift resulted in the growth of multiple religious communities. While Christian and Muslim missionaries from outside the country certainly

FIGURE 4.1. Working woman without headscarf. Photograph by the author, 2004.

FIGURE 4.2. Working woman without headscarf. Photograph by the author, 2009.

FIGURE 4.3. The variety of ways to wear a headscarf (or not). Photograph by the author, 2003.

took advantage of Kyrgyzstan's liberal policies, in places like Bazaar-Korgon the local religious scholars and leaders facilitated the expansion of Islam more directly. Media—first in the form of printed material and cassette tapes, but television as well later on—also facilitated engagement with global ideas about and practices of Islam, as well as alternative ideas about religion.

In most of the Muslim world, recent instances of widespread veiling have been preceded or accompanied by Islamist projects ensuring that women's veiling is embedded within larger political struggles (Göle 1996; Mahmood 2005; Saktanber 2002; White 2002). But in the case of Bazaar-Korgon, and Kyrgyzstan more generally, women's veiling became politically charged despite women's lack of (formal) political involvement and the absence of Islamist movements. The political consequences of their actions can be understood then only in reference to alternative narratives of Muslimness and modernity (see Mahmood 2005). As the number of newly pious in the community increased, their alternative visions, articulations, and representations of Muslimness sparked public debates not only over religious observance and doctrine but also over wider notions of religion and politics. Changing modes of veiling and the increased public visibility of these new forms played a prominent role in these discussions. By wearing headscarves and dresses that more fully covered their bodies, women like Mukadas presented

FIGURE 4.4. Women who "wear their headscarves like this." Photograph by the author, 2004.

FIGURE 4.5. A woman who does not "wear her headscarf like this." Photograph by the author, 2004.

a challenge to community members who read their actions as reversals of one of the biggest triumphs of Soviet modernizing campaigns—women's emancipation.

Although most married women in Bazaar-Korgon wear a headscarf—usually tied at the nape of the neck with some hair revealed at the top—the covering is considered an aspect of age, familial, and social roles, not of particularly pious commitments. Many professional women choose to forgo head covering altogether. The mode of veiling known outside the region as *hijab*—in which the hair and neck are covered but the entire face is revealed—is the most common and most rapidly spreading form among those interested in Islam. The term "hijab," however, was not locally used for such headscarves in 2004, not even by the women who wore them. Instead, people talked about women who had "closed their headscarves" (*jooluk japty*). More commonly they spoke of women who "wear their headscarves like this" (*jooluk mynday salynyp jüröt*). As they said the phrase, they would trace an oval with two fingers around their faces, beginning at the forehead, following the curve of their face, and meeting just below the chin. Normally the hijab is combined with a long-sleeved, loose-fitting dress bought or made either in Bazaar-Korgon or in one of the nearby cities. Although the new style is usually locally produced, the manner in which it is worn, the kinds of colors, fabrics, and clothing combinations that are chosen, and the fact that only young women (under age forty) wear it raises eyebrows in the community. Women who cover their bodies as fully as those wearing hijab but who do so in "local" styles generally do so out of pious conviction as well, yet they draw little attention in public and are not stigmatized in discussions critical of emerging public expression of religiosity. When people in town talk about women who have "turned and gone to Islam" (*dinge burulup getkin*) or who have come "close to Islam" (*dinge jakyn*), they never indicate women wearing veils in anything other than hijab styles.

When a young woman wears a hijab, she is automatically assumed to take part in a locally new cluster of religious practices—attending religious study groups, learning to recite the Quran, and praying regularly. For example, not long after she began wearing the hijab, Mukadas met a small neighborhood group of girls who asked her if she could recite the Quran. When she replied that she could not, the girls responded with shock, "But you wear your headscarf like this!" For many community members, the hijab is a conspicuous form of head covering because of its style as well as the religious commitments assumed to have inspired its wearer. While a certain degree of religious commitment is acceptable, wearing the hijab, perceived as part of being "close to Islam," challenges the boundaries around what is permissible and what is not. This is related to what, for many, the veil symbolized.

Women choosing to veil, like Mukadas, are therefore forced to situate their decisions not only in terms of their commitments as Muslims and to God but with reference to what Annelies Moors (2009, 195) has called the veil's "burden of representation." Just as in the European cases studied by Moors, women in Bazaar-Korgon are constrained by what, in discourses of modernity, the veil has come to represent. In Mukadas's case, her decision to veil was burdened by Soviet-era notions that had cast the veil as a symbol of excessive religious fervor and part of the curvature of religion that had been targeted in the antireligious campaigns and delegitimized as acceptable religion. It was also read as an indicator of the reversal of women's emancipation and thus the failure of Soviet modernizing campaigns. Both of these evaluations were reinvigorated by congruent global scripts in the region as a part of the post-9/11 so-called "War on Terror."

Constraints on Veiling

In the early morning hours of a hot June day, I walked with three young Uzbek women across Bazaar-Korgon. Each of us wore a headscarf. It was unusual for the girls to do so, as young, unmarried women their age did not normally cover their heads. However, because we wore our scarves in a style typical around the town—tied simply at the nape of our necks—no one took notice of us along the way. Twenty minutes later we arrived at a house where we were to meet a few young women who would take us to a religious study group. We had been invited to attend this women's *davat* gathering in the Sai area but did not know the specific location. All of the women wore hijabs. A few added a piece of fabric to cover their nose, mouth and chin as well (*niqab*). Before leaving the gated compound (*havla*), one of the oldest of the women broke us up into groups of two or three, each of which had someone who knew the way to the meeting. The groups left one at a time, with a few minutes between groups. I asked a young woman in my group why we had been divided. She told me that the women did not want to draw extra attention to themselves. It was hard enough wearing the hijab or niqab in the community, she said, let alone traveling in large groups with similarly dressed women. They didn't want to arouse the suspicion of the neighbors. They didn't want people to know where they were going.

Alterations in bodily appearance were one of the "indicators" most frequently referenced when Bazaar-Korgonians wished to demonstrate that someone had "turned and gone to Islam." The forms of dress adopted were perceived of as foreign and as signs of extremism. The number of women altering their form of dress from the norm in Bazaar-Korgon was greater than the number of men. Indeed, the husbands of most of the women I knew who wore the hijab looked like "average" men in town. Perhaps that is why men having a differentiated bodily appearance drew even more attention than women. I had a discussion with the four children, ages thirteen to twenty, of a family one afternoon about their lives and the life of their neighborhood. The children's parents both regularly prayed *namaz* and fasted during Ramadan. Their mother wished to make the pilgrimage to Mecca, but because the head of the household was out of work, the family could barely get by let alone finance the hajj. All the children were interested in learning more about Islam, and the eldest two had been praying off and on for the previous few years.

We were discussing their neighborhood mosque and who in their area attended it. The boys, who did not attend themselves, guessed that somewhere between ten and twenty men went daily. At least one of the regular attendees, they said, was a member of Hizb ut-Tahrir. He lived around the corner from the family. I asked the boys how they knew the man was a member. Abror began describing the man—his beard and his white, tuniclike shirt. Abror's younger sister chimed in: "even their two-and-a-half-year-old daughter wears a headscarf like this!" and she traced a circle around her face, starting at her forehead and closing tightly under her chin. I pushed them further, asking whether there was any other way they knew. Had the man himself admitted that he was a member? Abror reiterated his comments about the man's clothing. Whether or not there were other untold "signs" that led Abror and his siblings to their conclusion about their neighbor (or whether they were simply reiterating the opinion of others), their comments show that they were convinced that referencing his bodily appearance and clothing should be enough to substantiate their claims and convince me of the man's membership in the group.

The discussion of women's bodily fashioning occurred more frequently in the community. More covered forms of veiling—like those worn by Mukadas—were one of the most common traits that signified to many that a certain person was an extremist. In Bazaar-Korgon, the tropes of religious extremism were part of the discourse residents utilized as they dealt with the expansion of Islam, the proliferation of a plurality of religious voices, and the effects these changes had on their community and on themselves.[4] The association has multiple roots. First, the hijab is locally understood to be an "Arab" form of dress (see Brenner 1996, 674) and is often associated with "Wahhabis." The term "Wahhabi" became synonymous with "extremist" in the late 1970s and early 1980s.[5] But more recent global deployments of the term have given it new salience, as already discussed. On the local level, residents of Bazaar-Korgon have become convinced that there must be "extremists" in their midst. As they gossiped about this supposed threat, they often speculated on who might be a "terrorist," with the hijab often taken as a sign of someone's radicalization (McBrien 2006).

Contemporary stereotypes surrounding the veil carry weight precisely because they are consonant with Soviet-era notions in which the veil had come to symbolize the apparent oppressive, backward, and fanatical nature of Islam. It also indicates a departure from the norms and practices of gender equality established during the Soviet era, making it doubly problematic. The veil thus signaled a retreat from Soviet modernity. Female interlocutors, especially those in their forties and fifties, often told me that women who "wear their headscarves like this" were backward and unmodern. They suggested that these women had been coerced into the practice. Men likewise questioned the women's motives for veiling, wondering why they would have given up their independence.

There is yet another reason why the veil was particularly troublesome for many residents. As a part of a cluster of practices and discourses associated with "those interested in Islam," it was read as a challenge to local definitions of Muslimness and to the category of religion crafted during Soviet secularism. Nazgul, a teacher in her fifties, made this link as we discussed religion. She often found my questions about religious matters ridiculous. In a fit of frustration one day she said, "We are atheists. Yes, we are Muslims, but let me explain—we are all Muslim people, Kazakhs, Kyrgyz, Uzbeks, Turkmen, Tajiks, Tatars. . . . We were born Muslims. That's it." On another occasion I met her sitting outside her home with two of her neighbors with whom I was also acquainted. We began talking, and Nazgul, in a slightly better mood, said, more patiently, "Look, we are atheists, but of course we all believe in God. We always did. I do. Now we are free. We build mosques, people pray, that's good. But those, those who wear scarves like this [she traces an oval around her face, starting at her forehead and closing tightly under her chin] and keep their women at home, they are bad. They are Wahhabis."

In the first instance Nazgul indicates that it was enough to be born a Muslim in order to deserve that appellation, even if one was an atheist, a term that for Nazgul seems to indicate a (political) subject position. Religion here is about ethnonational belonging, which is a birthright. Her second remark reveals that tied up with this is a certain kind of practice—belief in God, the construction of mosques, and prayer. For her these all fell into the realm of good Muslim behavior and acceptable religion, largely consonant with what was understood locally as part of Muslimness in the late Soviet period. She drew the line at the issue of gender and dress. She perceived women's veiling not only as an unacceptable practice but as a clear sign that someone was a Wahhabi, an extremist. In Nazgul's replies we see the intertwining of various discourses on acceptable versus unacceptable religion and the way they were complexly intertwined with images of the veil. She approbates Soviet-era notions that religion is about national belonging and endorses regional Soviet-era and global post–Soviet-era ideas that equate "excessive" religious commitment with religious extremism.

Community perception of women who wore alternative forms of the veil and related clothing was not the only thing that delayed women from changing their mode of dress. The vast majority of women choosing to wear the hijab were relatively young. They wanted to set themselves apart from older women who veiled more fully. They were also keenly interested in fashion and beauty, especially given all the newly available consumer products and images in the post-Soviet period. Yet, for those wishing to wear the hijab, there were not many options available. Some young women had clothes made by local seamstresses. Even then, the selection of fabric in town was limited. Others traveled to nearby cities to search for garments that would meet their desires. But the garments they found were often deemed unattractive. Finding something that covered them, and was beautiful, was a great challenge. One unique solution was to "import" veils. Women who went on the hajj occasionally brought back scarves and other clothing for their family, friends, and acquaintances. But the number of women doing this was small. No traders in the bazaar catered to these women's needs, and foreign traders had yet to capitalize on such a niche market.

While those "interested in Islam" may not have been able to overcome all the stereotypes surrounding the hijab, their attempts at beautiful, fashionable veiling at least challenged some. Beautiful veiling for young women went against the grain concerning local aesthetics of the veil and its role in women's life cycle. These young women attempted to reconfigure the veil not as "tradition" from the pre-Soviet past but as contemporary and in line with new visions of modernity. In their search for beauty and fashion, they often employed images of Western modernity that they were seeking to blend with their religious devotion. Perhaps an even greater challenge to young women's veiling was poverty: most women simply did not have the resources they needed to wear the kind of clothing they desired. This dilemma was particularly intense for women who chose to wear the hijab just after marriage. Their wish to dress in this way meant that they had to give up their trousseau (*sep*). The garments that came as a part of the sep were not designed for hijab-wearing women.

Mukadas herself, for example, struggled with the veil and her image of herself as modern. This meant rethinking not only the (post) Soviet relationship between modernity and religion but also recent capitalism-fueled notions linking beauty, novelty, and consumption. One way of overcoming some of the veil's local antimodern stereotypes, for Mukadas, could be found in veiling beautifully. But capitalism turned out to be harsher than expected, and Mukadas's poverty thwarted her attempts in this regard, too. Economic constraints were the downside of the new capitalist modernity. Post-Soviet life, in a sense, forced Kyrgyzstani citizens to face aspects of the dark side of Western modernity while simultaneously being flooded with its promises and desires. This disjuncture in many ways stimulated longing for the Soviet era—for its perceived security, morality, and stability.[6] Post-Soviet citizens were nostalgic, but not blindly so. They had not forgotten the negative aspects of the Soviet system. But for many, the balance between good and bad seemed a bit better then than now.

FIGURE 4.6. The clothing in a trousseau (*sep*) that a bride receives from her family at marriage is not suitable for a woman who "wears her headscarf like this." Photograph by the author, 2004.

Kyrgyzstani citizens' relationship to both Soviet and post-Soviet modernity was mixed; neither modality was fully embraced or rejected. It is perhaps better to speak of a realignment of cultural and material frameworks, a process that became all the more complex for those Muslims who, in the post-Soviet period, decided to draw "close to Islam." Recent ethnographies of the "Islamic resurgence" have portrayed these movements as articulating strong criticism of Western, secular-liberal projects and thereby launching various alternative discourses and projects of modernity, in many cases through and by veiling women (e.g., Brenner 1996; Göle 1996; Mahmood 2005). These accounts depict a bifurcated discourse in which veiled women see Western projects and norms as inimical to Islamic principles. What is perhaps most striking about the post-Soviet Central Asian case is the more ambivalent relationship with the West. The concern of Muslims in the region has been focused on what Westernization would do to Soviet structures and values rather than Islamic ones. Westernization, and its form of secularism, was in fact viewed by those concerned with religion of any sort partly as an improvement because of the space provided for religious expression, even if, morally, economically, and socially, Westernization soon exhibited its downsides. Yet these were still measured against an imagined Soviet past rather than an Islamic one. Western secularism sustained and supported Soviet-era narratives about women's agency and modernity but in an institutional environment that allowed relatively greater freedom for religious expression. Soviet-era accomplishments, institutions, and values often became the basis of comparison and debate, with Western secularism playing a more ambiguous role in these discussions.

Mukadas Kadirova's Story

There was a black-and-white photograph at the Kadirova home that showed a young woman standing on Red Square, the onion domes of Saint Basil's Cathedral behind her. Her hair was braided, and she had on a small square hat (*doppa*). She wore a smart dress of Uzbek *atlas* (silk) that fell just above her knees. She smiled. The Kadirova sisters loved to look at that photograph of their mother. Through it they could imagine their mother as a young girl—someone like themselves. But they also commented on how different their mother's youth had been—more opportunities to travel and an easier life with more hope for the future. Their lives were different. The older ones in particular had been steeped in the discourse of becoming intelligent, modern people who were part of the great Soviet project. But these were dreams that they, unlike their mother, were unable to realize. Taught by their parents that education was the key to a fruitful, modern life, the sisters witnessed the depreciation of these values in the post-Soviet era.

Even though the rhetoric of communist modernity was never an accurate reflection of the realities of Soviet life, Soviet citizens were active participants in creating and sustaining the rhetoric and largely felt part of the overarching effort. The dreams and values of the Kadirova sisters started in the Soviet era.

Even after the collapse, their ideas, visions, and hopes were nurtured by family, teachers, and community members who had grown up during socialist times (see Lampland 2002). And yet, though links to the past are durable, the way people evaluate bygone eras changes in shifting environments and new situations. Pine (1996, 133) argues that many of the positive achievements of the socialist states, especially with regard to gender equality, were not recognized until after the collapse, when the experience with "actually existing capitalism" cast new light on former socialist realities. Thus, in some cases, reevaluation shores up and even strengthens notions created and sustained in a social and political environment that no longer exists. Furthermore, such notions can even be reinvigorated in the new environment when old and new rhetorics align. For example, the role of education in individual and societal advancement is central to both Soviet and Western discourses. Western campaigns on educational reform and massive foreign funding for study abroad programs consolidated the Soviet/post-Soviet value of education. Unfortunately, the promises of education, partly fulfilled in the Soviet years, are unattainable in contemporary Kyrgyzstan.

Three out of five of the Kadirova sisters attended university. Despite their training—Mukadas in education, Delnura in border control, and Delfuza in art—only one found employment in her chosen field. Delfuza's study of art seemed rather hopeless from the outset. Mukadas worked as a teacher for one year before leaving to have her first child. She never returned to work, partly because child-care systems had broken down. Delnura's failure to secure work as a border guard shows another odd twist of the post-Soviet period. Ironically, while Mukadas herself lauded the independence period for allowing people to think critically and independently, the education system became even more riddled with corruption than during Soviet times. Everything could be bought for a price in post-Soviet universities—admission, grades, exam results, even diplomas. This continued into the job market such that, while Delnura was still able to earn her degree the old-fashioned way—by studying—she could not pay the bribes necessary to secure work as a border guard or customs officer. Delnura pursued an alternative dream. In partnership with another young woman, she opened a small clothing stall in the bazaar. Delfuza and Shasta helped out as well. In the first few months of business they never made a profit.

In addition to their wish for fulfilling, well-paid work, the sisters longed for love, good husbands, kind mothers-in-law, and nice homes. They all wanted children. Mukadas had some of these desired things. Unlike most of her age cohort, she had married for love—with the full consent of her mother. However, her marital life had not been easy. Her husband and her in-laws were considerably less well educated than her own family. They were also quite poor. The differences between her natal and marital families, combined with a mother-in-law whom Mukadas described as unkind and critical and who looked unsympathetically on her less-than-robust constitution, made for a difficult home life for her.

The difficulties Mukadas faced at home were, in the end, a major impetus in her religious awakening. In 2002, she dreamed about troubles she was having with her mother-in-law and husband. In the dream, she explained, the trials in her home life manifested themselves in the form of a snake that, coiled around her body, was constricting and killing her. She called on God to rescue her from the snake, and he instructed her that she must pray and come "close to Islam" to find relief. She took the dream literally and began praying five times daily. Around the same time, her husband also had a self-described awakening. He also began to pray and attend a Quranic study group, in which he learned to recite the Quran and received religious instruction. Mukadas likewise had begun to learn more about Islam by visiting a female religious specialist (*atincha*).

One afternoon in the early autumn of 2003, Mukadas and I sat in her mother's small orchard and talked. She told me she was considering wearing the hijab. Her husband had brought up the subject some months before. Mukadas told him she was not ready at that moment. However, she agreed to think about it. She had been considering it for some time and decided that she was nearly ready to do it. She felt sure that it was her duty before God and her responsibility as a Muslim woman. At the same time she was unsure of herself because, as she explained, she wanted to be a modern woman. She considered herself different from many other young women who attended Islamic study groups: "They finished ninth form and after that they stayed at home. They go to the atincha and return home. That's it. They don't think, they don't question. But I am modern, I am educated."

Mukadas decided to wear the hijab, though she postponed her veiling until late autumn. It would be easier, she explained, because in autumn and winter one wore long sleeves and thus she would not have to buy new clothes. She would only have to change the way she pinned her scarf. Mukadas's husband was pleased with her decision, as were her mother-in-law, her mother, and two of her sisters. All three girls had become "interested in Islam" (*dinge kyzyktuu bölüp kaluu*). The three sisters had prayed the five-times-daily namaz when they were younger. Mukadas had returned to the practice in 2002 and Delfuza in 2003. Shasta was learning how to pray namaz from Delfuza. Mukadas's husband often brought home locally produced audio recordings of religious teachings from the bazaar, and the sisters all listened to and discussed them. When Mukadas decided to wear the hijab, Delfuza and Shasta went shopping with her, offering advice on which scarf to buy and how best to style it. Delnura, however, was upset with her decision. Delnura told her sister, "What matters is what you believe on the inside, and how you treat others. That is more important than what you wear on the outside. Veiling is for old women. We are modern," she said.

As the winter wore on, Mukadas doubted the attractiveness of the new scarf and took to wearing an older pink one that she thought suited her better. Her sisters and mother chided her that it was out of fashion. Mukadas, hurt by their comments, said she was angered at their focus on "things." She argued that clothes and other material objects were not important. She said that God teaches people to look at others and be thankful for what they have: "When we think about religious knowledge, we should look ahead to those who have more than us so that we may strive to have what they do. When we think about the things of this world, we should look behind to those who have less so that we are thankful for what we have and so that we may share with them, through *zakot* [alms]."

Although Mukadas had thought through many of the potential consequences of her changed mode of dress and was certain of the correctness of her decision, she nonetheless felt the tensions of competing visions and desires. She wanted to veil, but to do so fashionably and with good-quality clothes. She was motivated by her appreciation of beauty and a desire to participate in the attractive features of the new consumerist environment. Her wish to overcome Soviet-era notions that marked more fully covered forms of veiling as being for the old informed her wish to veil fashionably as well. However, her poverty, the dearth of locally available goods, and her own interpretation of the overly consumption-oriented attitudes of her family as being incongruent with proper Muslim behavior counteracted her own desires for beauty.

One afternoon in late spring, I opened the door to the small, sunny room to see four of the five Kadirova sisters preening in front of the mirror. Delfuza was telling her sisters about the *eskicha* girls she'd met while she'd been in Osh.[7] She described the beautiful headscarves and dresses the eskicha girls wore, demonstrating the ways they tied, pinned, folded, and fastened their scarves. The sisters were excited; they took turns experimenting with the veiling styles Delfuza demonstrated. As Delfuza helped her older sister Mukadas with one particularly complicated arrangement, she complemented Mukadas on her new headscarf and dress. Mukadas had just purchased what would be her spring and summer attire in a town nearby. It had cost her dearly, and she still felt uncertain about the purchase. Seeing her sister's delight in her dress, Mukadas went to the other room, took the garment off, and let her sister try it on. As Delfuza and her other sisters arranged the dress and coordinated scarf, Mukadas stood beside me and sighed. "Fashion comes last to Bazaar-Korgon," she observed.

At that moment, as they preened before the mirror, the girls' minds were on fashion and the most stylish ways to wear the veil. Of the four sisters experimenting with veiling styles, only one, Mukadas, actually wore a headscarf. Yet the lure of "dress-up"—of imagining how one would look, and be, if she were another, of searching for new ways to look beautiful—had tempted them all, even Delnura. Mukadas was certainly concerned with how the veil made her look. It must be beautiful, but it must properly cover her. The dual role of her new clothing expressed two of Mukadas's desires—to be lovely and obedient. But, as Mukadas's comment about fashion in Bazaar-Korgon revealed, there were many restraints on becoming a fashionable, pious young woman.

The Fruit of Devotion

As the weather became warmer, Mukadas contemplated her new spring outfit. Despite her sisters' validation concerning the beauty of her new clothes, Mukadas waited almost two weeks before wearing the brightly colored outfit in public. It was quite different from anything she had worn before, she said. She explained that the new form of dress made her decision to wear the hijab more tangible and final. It set her apart more demonstrably from other women in town. She was nervous. The dress and hijab did indeed draw more attention to her, and she began to hear people whispering about her as she walked about town. She went to an atincha with her difficulties and was advised to count them as tests from God.

One afternoon she had a particularly unsettling experience. As she was walking through the bazaar, a woman approached her, stared her in the face, and said, "I hate women who cover themselves." Mukadas walked away. She ignored the woman and went to see her husband, who worked in the bazaar: "When I told him what had happened, I felt very happy. I knew it was a test from God. The woman only said what she did for one of two reasons. One, she wanted to cover herself and knew she could not. Two, she really liked my clothes, thought I looked beautiful, and thus tried to push me down to make herself feel better." Mukadas's confidence grew. She recalled a proverb: "No one throws stones at a tree that does not bear fruit." She reasoned that the difficulties were a sign of her obedience; she must be bearing the fruit of her devotion.

Despite her desires for beauty, Mukadas chose to veil first and foremost in obedience to God and in an effort to ease familial tensions. Yet, she feared not being allowed back to work, she faced public admonishment, and she felt the weight of unheard community gossip. She also feared a change in her status as a modern woman. Not only had she confronted the stereotypes of her community, which equated wearing the hijab with extremism and the overturning of Soviet-era notions of gender equality, but she also dealt with an internal struggle of redefinition. In some ways, Mukadas, too, saw the hijab as antimodern—as a symbol of backwardness, of the uneducated, of a tradition given up long before the period of modernity in which she lived.

But her story also illustrates how modernity had become more complex since the fall of the Soviet Union. Thus, while Mukadas dealt with certain tensions inherent in veiling and being modern—tensions provoked by a century and a half of Western and Soviet/Russian interpretations of the veil—she simultaneously drew on new interpretations of the hijab and modernity in her community. Post-Soviet emphasis on consumption and the importance of exteriority, fashion, and youth had informed her desires to veil beautifully, but the emptiness of Western consumption and the perceived immorality of the post-Soviet period had forced her to reconcile these desires with the principles of ethical conduct she found in Islam. While Mukadas had not completely merged consumption with certain values in Islam, her attempts to veil fashionably nonetheless counteracted community notions that the headscarf was ugly or only for the old, redefining the veil in relation to at least one stereotype of modernity.

When Mukadas and other women like her seek to come "close to Islam"— whether through veiling or other techniques—and attempt to reconcile doing so with redefined notions of modernity, they confront, at least implicitly, one of the greatest tensions between Soviet and Western modernity. The Soviet version of modernity in Central Asia encompassed, however incompletely, individual as well as societal desires. It succeeded in providing institutional means to obtain these goals and provided a framework of morality to encompass the goals and the institutions. Despite imperfections, it was more inclusive and coherent than the fragmented, disembodied, desire-focused yet unattainable visions of Western modernity circulating in Kyrgyzstan after the fall of the Soviet Union. Mukadas's attempt to reinterpret modernity, to make herself obedient, modest, modern, educated, and "close to Islam"—in short, her creation of an Islamic modern—may be an antidote to these Western projects. Fashionable veiling intertwines with Western consumption while correcting its perceived immorality. If, as Saba Mahmood (2005, 195) rightly urges, the veil is about more than "women's (un)freedom," it can in the same measure be about more than just creating piety (see also Marsden 2005a, 251–52). Mukadas certainly understood her veiling as a pious act and one that transformed her inner dispositions, but her conception of what "the veil was performing," to borrow Mahmood's phrase, was not limited to this. The veil was also a means of realigning cultural landscapes and of creating herself as a modern individual through, within, and in reaction to "Western," "Soviet," and "Islamic" normative frameworks.

Mukadas's life, as well as her dilemma over the veil, illuminates the experiences, choices, commitments, and practices of those in Bazaar-Korgon who were interested in Islam and who had, to varying degrees, altered their lives as a response to it. It shows how they contemplated their decisions, how they lived the consequences, and how they read others in their town. Her story likewise sheds light on the struggles that many in Bazaar-Korgon had with locally new interpretations of Islam, of religion, as well as with those townsfolk who were interested in these new ideas. Islam was a contentious issue in a town whose population consisted almost entirely of Muslims and not just because there were debates about which practices or ideas were properly Islamic. Practices and material objects of Muslims were read and evaluated through specifically Soviet modernist discourses about Islamic extremism and acceptable religious behavior, both of which were created as a part of the Soviet project of secularism. At times these discourses melded easily with post-Soviet and global ideas; post-9/11 discourses of the "radical Muslim" and the fears about Wahhabis or extremists are a case in point. But at other moments they diverged, when, for example, they challenged local notions of Muslimness and proper public religion. This meant that in veiling, and in doing so in a way that was an attempt at being modern, Mukadas challenged certain ideas not only of modernity and secularity but also of religion. Her act was read by many in town, people like Nazgul, as, among other things, disputing the idea that religion was about belonging.

Contemporary Kyrgyzstan is not simply a place still in transition to modernity or in retreat from it. It is a place, like many the world over, where multiple modernities compete. But these various contemporary visions also compete with dreams from the past held by people who were already modern and who remained modern but who had to cope with the decay of their society. The tension that Mukadas felt arose not only from the variance between Western and Soviet notions of the modern but also from the disjuncture in how the two were enacted. Mukadas understood Soviet dreams to have been at least partially attainable. Western images, on the other hand, were incongruously mapped onto the realities she experienced in post-Soviet life, realities that in fact were the dark side of the West's development. The tensions provoked a sense of nostalgia for Soviet life, as well as a criticism of the present. They also fueled an alternative imagination of the future (see Rofel 1999, 128–31). In Mukadas's case, her simultaneous turn to Islam sparked the form that this reimagination took. But that turn—which was at odds with both Soviet and contemporary Western notions of gender equality and proper, moderate, religious behavior—necessitated yet another rethinking of the contentious notion of "modernity." Mukadas's was a complicated, multilevel dilemma; it was an attempt to realign and reinterpret the competing frameworks and material circumstances so that she could be a modern, veiling Muslim woman.

Mukadas's struggle with the veil and modernity presents an awkward map of modernity's "others." In visions of the modern, tradition is usually located in the past, more closely and distantly understood. In articulations of alternative modernities, the "other" is most often a spatial other. But how does Mukadas's experience fit with this? When thinking of herself as modern, to what is she comparing herself? While she certainly has a notion of tradition, it is one of a past long removed, one that occurred before the Soviet era. Similarly, she must position herself with reference to the dominant capitalist political economy and its incumbent culture. But where would the Soviet era—Mukadas's most immediate referent and source of contrast with the dominant vision of modernity—fit in such a schema?

In her study of Kemalist nostalgia in Turkey, Esra Özyürek (2006, 18–19) has uncovered a similar disjuncture in temporal experiences of modernity. She contends that Turkish citizens' "nostalgic take on modernity" is both a sentimental position and a political ideology, both of which attempt to make sense and make use of a history marked by multiple modernizing regimes and their variegated visions of modernity. Turkish citizens deal with contemporary neoliberal politics through the lens of past state-led modernization projects, she argues, leading her to conclude that anthropological literature needs to consider not only the spatial variation of modernity but its temporal one as well (2006, 18).

Similarly, I suggest that we still too strongly reflect a forward-looking thinking in our analyses of the modern. We end up with tradition behind us, modernity ahead, and the modern as the present. But is this the complete story? When James Ferguson (1999) charted the social experience of decline in the Zambian Copperbelt, he not only described the decline but offered means of interpreting the nonlinear, nonteleological trajectories he studied. In this way he critiqued the notion of progress and development found not only in modernization theory but also in much of the ethnography of developing countries. My argument parallels his attempt to "follow a range of reactions and strategies that shift over time in ways that do not sustain a simple linear narration" (1999, 20). However, I argue that in Kyrgyzstan it is not a matter of a modernity that was almost achieved but of one that was realized. Diverging from Ferguson, I see the contemporary situation in Kyrgyzstan not merely as one of decline. While there is this sense, especially regarding reduced living standards and the loss of societal modernity, the fact that Mukadas nonetheless sees herself as still modern despite the changed circumstances and attempts to create a new type of modernity—which incorporates Soviet, Western, and Islamic elements—signals that the experience of modernity is not just a matter of moving toward or away from something. The experience can be simultaneously one of loss, one of fulfillment, and one of desire—modernity as past, present, and future.

CHAPTER 5

THE PROPRIETY OF MOSQUES

In the telephone office an operator sits behind a switchboard plugging and un-plugging color-coded wires. Discarded theater seats lining the walls of the dark room, not bolted to the floor of their new location, creak and rock with the weight of a new occupant. The operator shouts a number. A man jumps up, runs to a cubicle, and picks up a phone. "HELLO! HELLO!" he cries, straining to hear a muffled voice through the cracks and pops of an old line. Others in the office wait for a numerical code scrawled on the back of old Soviet paperwork. In possession of the code, the bearer walks home, ten, twenty, even forty minutes away. She dials the operator and recites the number to prove she has paid to call outside of town. After the single call is exhausted, the procedure begins again. To avoid the time-consuming process, those who have the resources pay a higher subscription rate and get a "line out of town." However, even after the "open line" has been bought, there is no guarantee that the telephone service will be in operation; the whole system regularly goes out.[1]

In Bazaar-Korgon, the surest way to spread information was by word of mouth; word traveled amazingly fast. Despite the seemingly large number of inhabitants, the town functioned in many ways like a small village. Perhaps it is better to see Bazaar-Korgon as a series of small neighborhood-based communities linked to-

FIGURE 5.1. An old neighborhood of Bazaar-Korgon. Photograph by the author, 2015.

gether through a dense web of social relationships. These ties were important for social stability, support, and control. They also functioned as a communication center that spread information quickly and efficiently across town, from the oldest areas on the hill to the newest area, called Sai. Even though they said they got all the gossip, residents of Sai complained that their neighborhoods didn't have the solidarity of those in the old town. One young woman of twenty-six, born and raised in Sai, married into a family from an old neighborhood an hour's walk from her natal home. We had lunch together one afternoon at her parents' home, and she discussed the differences between her two neighborhoods. She said that neighbors in the old section of town helped one another. She described how they gave, lent, and traded produce from their gardens with one another to avoid the long trip to the bazaar. It was a contrast with her own neighborhood, she said, where she hardly talked to more than a handful of neighbors and people rarely helped each other in that way. She encouraged me to visit her in her new home, to see the differences for myself.

The woman was perhaps overstating her case, trying to create an air of desirability about her new marital home. Her frequent visits to her parents' home and the stories her younger sister told me revealed her unhappiness in her new situation. Nevertheless, her basic point coincided with similar, if more tempered stories indicating that the solidarity of residents living in Sai was not as strong as it was in other areas of town. Despite this seeming lack of cooperation, in the early 2000s a group of residents from the apartment buildings in Sai decided that a neighborhood mosque should be constructed in their area, and they organized themselves to achieve this end. With the help of Islamic and secular authorities in local, regional, national, and international arenas in the summer of 2004, construction began on their mosque, the twenty-eighth to be built in town.

In the early post-Soviet period, mosque construction grew steadily throughout the former Soviet Union, both in regions where Muslims were a majority as well as where they were a minority. This rise in construction garnered the attention of foreign observers, who saw it as among the most visible indicators of religious transformation facilitated by perestroika and, later, by the large-scale alteration of the political, legal, and economic environment brought on with the collapse of the Soviet Union. Mosque construction was understood and analyzed primarily in reference to missionary endeavors and/or as an aspect of religious foreign aid and charitable giving (e.g., Rashid 2002; Ghodsee 2010).

An analysis in this vein would make sense, at first glance, for the construction of the twenty-eighth mosque in Bazaar-Korgan. Foreign sponsors funded it, and a manager working for an anonymous foreign donor facilitated its construction. But, other than ensuring the construction of the building, the international actors had little to no influence on the residents of the neighborhood where it was built or the men who later came to pray there. This is quite remarkable, given many Bazaar-Korgonians' evaluations of extremist, foreign Muslims and their potentially detrimental influence on local communities and local Islamic practices.[2] Moreover, discourses regarding the supposedly nefarious nature of foreign Muslims and their interpretations of Islam were regularly deployed in the town as a means of invalidating "deviations" from widespread, communally held notions and practices of Islam and Muslimness. Yet, the mosque was positively evaluated and well received in the neighborhood and wider community. This was in sharp contrast to other displays of piety, like veiling, which were often viewed with suspicion and in which possible connections with foreign Muslims were regularly discussed. The mosque was an exception.

This chapter explores the exceptionality of the mosque—for those who built it and for those who interpret it. It asks two questions. First, what did the construction of the mosque do—for the neighborhood and for those involved in its construction? As the mosque construction neared completion, it became apparent that residents had built more than a religious structure. The project had brought people together for collective action, fostering solidarity in a neighborhood characterized by townsfolk for its lack of it. Moreover, because the mosque construction was tied to larger visions of modernization and progress, including efforts to transform Bazaar-Korgon from a village into a town, it initiated a new vision of social action and development. However, in contrast to previous efforts for the development of the town in the Soviet era, there was now space for Islam. The mosque not only restarted the development and rebuilding of the neighborhood, it was also woven into grander schemes for the town's growth and improvement.

Second, this chapter asks why the mosque project succeeded when other instances of Islam in public space, like veiling or missionary endeavors, were more negatively or suspiciously evaluated. It argues that its accomplishment was partly due to its perceived regulation by secular authorities. To residents, this regulation signaled the propriety of the actors and the project in which they were engaged. It also pushed capitalist development forward. Finally, the religious function of the mosque did not hinder its acceptance in the community; it was unproblematic, as it represented townspeople's reconnection with their perceived "lost" Muslim past, in a way that was not considered "extreme" religious behavior. In a multivocal landscape, the mosque was able to include competing, sometimes mutually exclusive, visions of Muslimness and successfully hold together visions of the past and dreams for the future that were likewise sometimes contradictory.

Development, Decay, and Postsocialist Religion

Ruslan, a mason in his fifties, remembers the 1970s in Bazaar-Korgon as an exciting time. He and many others of his age cohort had just finished their training in masonry, wiring, building design, and general construction. They had been charged with the task of creating a new Soviet town. As many remember it, the mid-1970s was when Bazaar-Korgon started to come into its own. At that time, it had been decided that Leninskii *rayon* would be split in two. The eastern

FIGURE 5.2. Bazaar-Korgon's main square, with the culture house (*dom kul'tury*) in the background. Photograph by the author, 2004.

half took the name of the town that became its administrative center: Bazaar-Korgon. Government offices, a house of culture (*dom kul'tury*), and a series of other edifices were erected to house the various administrative departments needed to run the district. The Sai River, which formed the northern limit of the town, was channeled, creating a new strip of usable land. In this area, apartment blocks were constructed for the workers brought into the district to run the rayon. The approximately three hundred apartments were the most prestigious places to live in the 1980s. They had indoor plumbing, electricity, and good heating; they were given to the administrators, doctors, teachers, and officials of the district government.

Ruslan was not among the new arrivals. His paternal family had a long history of living in Bazaar-Korgon. But, as he recounted, he was nonetheless excited to be involved in the construction of the new socialist town. He said he felt as if they were really working toward something. Although the focus was on the development of the new areas of town, the older parts were also included in the modernization projects. As the 1970s ended and the 1980s began, water mains were laid throughout the town and spigots were installed at the end of every street, bringing potable water reasonably close to nearly every home. New roads were built and others were paved. A second statue of Lenin was erected in the new town square on the new main street. Many residents remember the period as the moment when Bazaar-Korgon began to develop. Of course they had seen the development of other, larger urban areas—Jalal-Abad, the provincial capital, was only thirty minutes away by bus, and neither Andijan (in the Uzbek SSR) nor Osh was more than two to three hours away. These places had seen the fruits of Soviet infrastructure much earlier. Bazaar-Korgon had to wait a bit, but it too had its moment of glory.

Whatever level of development residents of Bazaar-Korgon may have felt they had achieved by the early 1980s—in the structural improvement of their town or in the increased literacy rates—they noted that the "progress" began to erode all too quickly. Just a bit more than a decade after the infrastructural improvements in town took place, the Soviet Union dissolved. The plans for the Sai neighborhood were never completed, and at least one apartment block remained unfinished, its husk a reminder of unfinished dreams. The infrastructure began to erode. By 2003, the prestigious apartments had become the least desirable accommodations in town. The water regularly failed to flow for long periods of time. People had to carry buckets of water from spigots a ten-minute walk away. Communal public outhouses had been built near the apartments to deal with the frequent water outages. Some residents on the ground floor had annexed the open land behind their homes. They kept animals and built private outhouses. Anyone living in the apartments who could afford to move out, and was still able to find land at a reasonable distance from the center of town, did so. Apartments faired less well when the services and infrastructure of the Soviet period failed and began to decay; they were the most highly dependent on those services and the least suited to return to a status in which there was a lack of stable, reliable public utilities. Water, electricity, and heat shortages could be managed better from homes with indoor fireplaces, external bathrooms, external kitchens, and nearby streams, for example.[3]

The demographics of the Sai neighborhood had also begun to change around the same time. A significant number of the highly educated Kyrgyz who were employed in government offices, hospitals, and schools moved out. Those moving in were Uzbeks from town who were often in difficult economic circumstances or separated from their social networks, as well as Kyrgyz who had relocated from the villages of the rayon after the collapse of the Soviet Union. They had come, by and large, to find work in the bazaar. It was at this same time, around the turn of the millennium, that Bazaar-Korgon had started to become known throughout Kyrgyzstan as a place where Islam was more publicly present. For residents of the town, as has already been noted, indicators of this public presence were the increasing numbers of men and boys attending the mosques, the rising numbers of women wearing headscarves that more fully covered the head, neck, and upper body than those worn by the majority of women, the popularity of home-based

Figure 5.3. Waiting in line for water. Photograph by the author, 2003.

study groups, and the public appearance of men inviting residents to come closer to Islam. Whereas outsiders generally cited the number of mosques as proof of increased public religiosity, in local residents' accounts the construction of mosques seemed uncontroversial and was never highlighted in discussions about the changing role of religion in public life. This change of physical landscape somehow fell outside of their evaluation.

After the Soviet Union collapsed, there were two periods of mosque building in town: the boom of the early 1990s and the smattering of construction of
the early 2000s. The earlier date is easy to interpret. While some mosques were
built at the end of the Soviet period when rules on religion were relaxed, the fear
that policy would again change precluded a construction boom. In the town of
Bazaar-Korgon, five new mosques were opened between 1987 and 1990.[4] Fourteen of Bazaar-Korgon's twenty-eight mosques, however, were built from 1991 to
1995. This period of construction coincides with many residents' feelings about
a sharp increase in formerly curbed practices just after the collapse of the Soviet
Union. While many Central Asians may not have welcomed the end of the Soviet
state, they did embrace certain opportunities this dissolution brought. One of
those was the opportunity to "reconnect" with a perceived lost Muslim past. As
described earlier, Central Asians' understanding of Muslimness may have been
profoundly changed over the Soviet period, but the notion that they were Muslims and that they had been prevented from practicing Islam or being the kind
of Muslims they were prior to the Soviet era persisted. In the early post-Soviet
era there was a strong desire to connect to this pre-Soviet past and to throw off
perceived unsavory elements of Soviet political control, such as the limitations on
religious expression. One of the most immediate and widespread ways these desires were manifested in Bazaar-Korgon (and among other Muslim populations
of the former Soviet Union) was in mosque construction.

One factor contributing to the massive growth in the number of mosques
surely was the relative ease at gaining funds for these kinds of projects. International Muslim NGOs, private Muslim donors from outside the former Soviet
Union, and even governments from Muslim-majority societies saw mosque construction—along with the distribution of religious materials such as Qurans—as
one of the main avenues for assisting "post-Soviet Muslims" in reconnecting to
Islam. Another facilitating factor was that for Bazaar-Korgonians, the buildings
served as an expression of Muslim attachment while their construction did not
necessitate any long-term personal commitment or religious transformation.
Moreover, their construction was a way of turning back the clock, so to speak—
an imagined undoing of what those involved in early antireligious campaigns
of the Soviet period had done—without challenging certain trumpeted values
of the late Soviet era. While mosques had been closed during the antireligious
campaigns, there was not a concomitant negative stereotyping of the buildings
as such. In fact, the Spiritual Directorate of Muslims of Central Asia and Kazakhstan, or SADUM, promoted mosques as the center of legitimate Islamic
life (Saroyan 1997, 70–71; Ro'i 2000, 181–286). While Soviet buildings such as
the houses of culture had been created as new loci for social life, they were never
presented as direct replacements for the closed mosques.[5] Veiled women in the

post-Soviet era, in contrast, could not have been viewed as a benign return to the past. The assertions made by Nazgul in chapter 4 are worth repeating here. While she was vehemently against more covered forms of veiling and linked those wearing the new style to Wahhabis, she evaluated mosque construction as acceptable. Over the course of the Soviet period, the veil had become a symbol not only of backwardness but also of religious extremism. Moreover, the promotion of gender equality and the advancement of women were presented as cures to the ills that the veil represented. A veil could not be worn in the post-Soviet years without confronting these notions.

A closer look at the periods of mosque construction in Bazaar-Korgon reveals interesting patterns. While there were fourteen mosques opened from 1991 to 1995, there were no mosques opened from 1995 to 1999. This early boom period is linked to a changed political and legal environment, and the end of the boom is likewise certainly linked to economic issues. By 1998, the post-Soviet economic collapse had reached its nadir. However, there is an interesting parallel with the performance of other religious practices not so dependent on financial resources. The period in which mosque construction declined was also one that residents recall showed a marked decrease in Islamic practice, such as regular prayer, which had temporarily surged just after the collapse of the Soviet Union. A second, more gradual rise in the numbers of those participating in these types of practices took longer to make its appearance. It was not until the early years of the 2000s that these religious transformations became apparent.

For example, a survey of fifty households I conducted showed that of those who began praying in 1990 or later, the majority had started after 1998. This observation coincided with the second phase of mosque construction, after the period from 1995 to 1999, when no mosques were opened. From 1999 until 2004, two mosques were opened, and at least one other was proposed; funding had yet to be found. A madrasa was scheduled to open in autumn 2004.[6] Importantly, the madrasa already had students waiting to attend, and the mosques were still well attended by 2004, something that could not be said for the majority of mosques built elsewhere in Kyrgyzstan since the collapse of the Soviet Union.[7]

It seems that the sort of practices that accompany long-term religious change in individuals and small social groups—teaching, study, working through social tensions, bodily disciplining, and institutional construction, to name a few—take time to grow and spread before their impact is felt. In other words, while the early boom of mosque construction and participation in certain rituals may have been a fad, as some residents argued, the signs of religiosity that residents of Bazaar-Korgon recognized by the early 2000s indicated slower but more permanent alterations in discourse and practice. Dramatic changes in governance, like the collapse of the Soviet Union, allowed for the expression of religious rituals, affiliation, or other religiously motivated acts, such as mosque construction, outside the home, in view of all—in short, "public," in one reading of the word. But these religious transformations became public in another way as well, because some of them, like the construction of the twenty-eighth mosque, were not only expressions of religious affiliation or acts of devotion and obedience but new forms of collective social action as well.

Making Connections, Building Mosques, Constructing Solidarity

In 2004, the only mosque within a reasonable walking distance of the Sai apartments was the Friday mosque of the entire rayon—the largest mosque in the area. Residents of the apartments recounted that in the early 1990s one unit had been used as a mosque, but it closed after a couple of years. The demographics of the area may give some clues as to why such a populated area lacked the kind of neighborhood mosque used by men for daily prayers. In the Soviet and initial post-Soviet period, the inhabitants of the apartment buildings were the most integrated in the Soviet system, the most removed from familial networks, and the most supportive of official party lines. In short, they were the least inclined to practice certain Islamic rituals. However, following independence, the demographics changed. Although some of the original inhabitants remained, new residents moved in, creating a more diversified population and one with a wider range of attitudes toward Islam.

In the early 2000s, a sizable number of residents had become interested in constructing a mosque in the area. Throughout Bazaar-Korgon, neighborhoods often had small neighborhood committees to deal with community issues and to mediate between the neighborhood and civic authorities. In this case, the neighborhood asked its *mahalla komitet* (neighborhood committee) leader to discuss the issue of a new mosque with the rayon head imam, Toktosun, an Uzbek. He approved of the idea, and together he and the mahalla komitet began to pursue the project. The mahalla komitet first approached the town government to get permission to use vacant land among the apartment complexes and behind the largest Kyrgyz school in the town.[8] The town government agreed, granting the deed to the community without payment, on the condition that a few years later they would begin to pay for the property. Toktosun's job was to help the community find a sponsor for the project. The mosque was one of three projects for which he was seeking financial assistance at the same time. Another community was also interested in building a mosque, and Toktosun, along with the imams of the rayon, were renovating the old mosque complex built in the early twentieth century. They planned to open the madrasa on its premises.

When the Sai community petitioned Toktosun to help them build a mosque, he sought the opinion and assistance of Tekebaev, Bazaar-Korgon's representative in parliament.[9] Tekebaev was not able to provide any financial assistance, but he did connect Toktosun with Isabek, a former Bazaar-Korgonian. Isabek Aldozob, a Kyrgyz man in his fifties, was originally from a small village in Bazaar-Korgon rayon. He had been the director of Bazaar-Korgon's house of culture in the late Soviet period and lived in the Sai apartments until 1996, when he moved to the capital of Kyrgyzstan. He had found work in Bishkek through his childhood friend, Tekebaev. After hearing of the proposed mosque, Isabek agreed to become the local foreman of the project. He headed up the project, hired the workers, made construction-related decisions, purchased materials and tools, and oversaw the building on a day-to-day basis.

Toktosun, however, still had to find the funding. He said that he searched for a long time and tried many sources before he finally located a willing sponsor—the World Assembly of Muslim Youth (WAMY). According to its website, WAMY is "an independent international organization and an Islamic forum that supports the work of Muslim organizations and needy communities the world over." The website further explains that mosque construction is one of the group's seven main humanitarian projects for Muslim communities.[10] Although the organization is behind the project, there is also an individual sponsor. In the banner displayed at the construction site, both WAMY and an "anonymous benefactor" are named. Furthermore, Toktosun and Isabek both refer to an "Arab man" in Bishkek as the source of the funds.[11] The man, however, was never present during the construction process.

Construction began in early 2004. The budget and timeline of construction were set by the Bishkek sponsor. He worked with the local community (i.e., Isabek and Toktosun) through his secretary, Marat, a Kyrgyz man from Bishkek. Marat visited the sites, checked the financial records, and handled all communication between the parties involved. On the Bazaar-Korgon side, Isabek was the contact person regarding construction, but the money was wired to a Jalal-Abad bank account in Toktosun's name. The funds were disbursed in stages. Marat checked both the actual construction of the project and the financial records before money for the next stage of the project was transferred.

In addition to conceiving the construction project, the neighborhood of Sai also participated in other aspects of it. Toktosun emphasized that the donor was very careful with his money and expected an account of every expenditure, as outlined in the budget. Thus, there was money for a mosque but no money to fund the trips Toktosun took to Bishkek to finalize legal and financial matters. The Sai neighborhood largely sponsored these trips. Furthermore, they took responsibility for regularly providing lunch to the construction workers employed

FIGURE 5.4. Project foreman Isabek Aldozob (*in front*) and the workers hold a sponsorship banner in front of the twenty-eighth mosque to be built in Bazaar-Korgon. Photograph by the author, 2004.

on the project. They also made donations to pay for the interior items of the mosque (carpets, lights, etc.). Finally, the future imam of the mosque, a close associate of Toktosun's, came from the neighborhood. As noted in the introduction to this chapter, Bazaar-Korgonians evaluated the neighborhoods as having varying degrees of cohesion and solidarity. The apartments in Sai were often thought to be the least cohesive neighborhood of any local community in the town. The fact that collective action was not taken in order to resolve common grievances like the frequent failure of water and electricity services demonstrates the lack of cohesion there. But, interestingly, the community did come together to help construct the mosque.

The mosque construction project in Bazaar-Korgon was an endeavor that required cooperation and trust on a number of different levels: among neighborhood members who cooked for construction workers, between higher- and lower-level public officials who sought and granted access to land, between religious and secular authorities working together to find funding, and between friends and new acquaintances establishing relationships in a common endeavor. It revealed the complex ways interactions among various (sometimes competing) communities, the state, and individuals worked to form not only community cohesion but also venues for solidarity in a new political and social environment.

Part of the novelty of the project was that Islamic discourses and Islamically motivated actions were the impetus and unifying factors around which action for the collective good was taken. In this way the mosque construction signaled the creation of what Dale F. Eickelman and Armando Salvatore (2004) have termed Muslim publics. In the post-Soviet period, collective action presented in, and justified with reference to, Islamic discourses was self-consciously done and was perceived by others to have been done at least partly out of an individual or collective desire to be obedient Muslims, to be compliant with the will of God. Thus, because actions like the mosque construction—presented in Islamic discourse, indeed presented as Islamic acts—were understood as having different motivations and goals, they held different significance as public acts. They indicated the presence of and a new role for Islam in collective life. Moreover, they indicated an end to the idea that social action or even development projects were and should be devoid of Islam.

The mosque was an important development in town. As infrastructure, utilities, and even buildings decayed, mosques were one of the few things being built, and nowhere was this so true as in the part of Sai where the apartment buildings were located. Several new buildings had been under construction when the Soviet Union collapsed. More than a decade later, the half-built structures and foundations of those remained. The mosque was set squarely in what would have been the green courtyard of the new buildings had they ever been finished. Instead, it sat in a dusty, rocky, brick-strewn expanse. The mosque was *development* restarted, but this time with an Islamic texture. If the construction project shows this change implicitly, Isabek's perspective on and role in it are a more explicit example of new modes of social action. Toktosun and the community viewed the project as a joint endeavor of many parties, but Isabek took much more personal credit for the project. He saw the construction of the mosque as something he had initiated and enabled. Moreover, he saw it as the first stage in a larger development project he had in mind—the construction of a *mikro-rayon* (suburb of a town or town neighborhood).

In 2004, Bazaar-Korgon began the legal process of trying to upgrade its status from that of a village (*aiyl*) to that of a town (*shaar*) or at least a small town (*shaarcha*). In order to accomplish this, Bazaar-Korgon had to reach a series of benchmarks. For example, a small microbus route was opened to carry travelers from one side of the town to the other—inner-city transport being one of the hallmarks of a town. In conjunction with this larger project, Toktosun wanted to develop the apartment complex area into an official mikro-rayon of the new "town." He dreamed of officially naming the area Ene-Sai (Mother Sai), getting

FIGURE 5.5. Mosque construction among the ruins in the Sai neighborhood of Bazaar-Korgon. Note the never-completed apartment building in the background, one of many Soviet-era projects halted when the union collapsed. Photograph by the author, 2004.

the microbus route to run through the complex, and generally improving the physical conditions of the neighborhood. For Isabek, the mosque was an important religious building, but it was just one part of what he saw as a larger effort to develop his home area and ultimately the entire town.

While for most Soviet citizens religion had long been thought to be incompatible with progress or development, projects like the mosque show that, for Bazaar-Korgonians, new practices and notions of development were being generated (see Borbieva 2012). Structural progress that contributed to the economic development of a community, such as Isabek's vision of a mikro-rayon, could include religious structures in post-Soviet Bazaar-Korgon. And while there were many instances in which religion was being used only as a discourse to shore up support for national projects in an otherwise primarily secular endeavor, there were cases, like the mosque in Bazaar-Korgon, that were more thoughtful, reflexive approaches at creating a new kind of religious public space. Isabek's vision of the development of Sai indicates the public utility of religion—the capacity for religiously inspired projects to help create order and social cohesion—even among those not subscribing to the notions held by the organizers of the project. It also demonstrates the way conceptions and practices of development and modernization were being created in a community where socialist and liberal "secular" notions dominate the landscape.

An Act of Merit

Residents of Sai, together with Toktosun, Isabek, Marat, WAMY, and the anonymous donor, built the mosque; in doing so, they created a new kind of religiously textured public space, as well as a new vision for development. They built solidarity among themselves and, importantly, built a collective space for prayer, learning, and fellowship in a neighborhood that lacked one. The mosque likewise played a part in individual religious projects. Isabek's role in the project is particularly insightful here. When Toktosun sought the assistance of Tekebaev, who connected him to his old friend Isabek, it transpired that Isabek's interest in the project came not only from his desire to undertake development and his allegiance (or perhaps social debt) to his friend. He had other motivations as well. In 2002, Isabek had begun praying *namaz* and had quit drinking alcohol. He started to take Islam more seriously, he said. As argued, the majority of those who had become interested in Islam in Bazaar-Korgon were those who, during the Soviet era, were less formally tied to and thus monitored by, local Soviet structures like the schools, administrative offices, and executive leadership of the collective farms. They were by and large Uzbek peasants. However, this was not universally true, as Isabek's religious experiences demonstrate. Since his new commitment to Islam, Isabek said he'd also had a desire to do something for Bazaar-Korgon as an act of merit (*soop*).

For Isabek, the mosque was more than *symbolic* of the return of religion to public space in post-Soviet Kyrgyzstan, more than *emblematic* of the global nature (and all that that might bring) of post-Soviet Islam in Central Asia, and more than *indicative* of the means by which Islam was constructed and lived in a new political and economic environment. Isabek saw his participation as a means of living Islam and doing good. Similar to the Orthodox Christians in Russia, studied by Tobias Köllner (2013), who contribute labor or money for church construction as an act of penance, Isabek saw his role in the building project as a religious act. As Nadia Fadil and Mayanthi Fernando (2015, 64) remind us, there are all kinds of ways that Muslims work to be good Muslims and to form an ethical subjectivity that are "not immediately recognizable as 'religious.'" For many in the Sai neighborhood, the construction of the mosque was an aspect of working on themselves as religious practitioners. The building, in Oskar Verkaaik's (2012, 2013) terms, played an active role in their religious experience. What is interesting is that it did this for and to people with differing, sometimes contradictory, notions of Muslimness.

The Propriety of Religion

Why was it acceptable to build a mosque in Bazaar-Korgon but not to participate in a study group or to veil? As discussed, elements of Muslim life in Central Asia, such as veiling, had been vilified over the course of the twentieth century and had become central themes in representations of Islam as backward and threatening. International networks among Muslims and the subversive potential of such connections likewise constituted a primary trope employed in negative depictions of Islam, beginning in British colonial writings on Central Asia, running through Russian imperial-era portrayals, and continuing in later Soviet discourse on the region. The discourse changed over the years but remained largely consistent into the twenty-first century, when fears about underground terrorist cells in the region and their connection to larger international networks formed a dominant framework for interpreting the religious landscape of Central Asia. These fears as articulated in Central Asia and their convergence with similar fears on a more global scale demonstrate not only the power and salience of political myth in the contemporary period but also the intertwined history of the modernizing regimes of Central Asia and the West.[12]

Thus, despite the fact that both veiling and international Muslim connections had been negatively stereotyped and given central importance in discourses about the "evils" of Islam, reactions to actual instances of veiling and international Muslim connections differed. If elements of each self-reflexively Islamic act could have been evaluated by Bazaar-Korgonians as potentially threatening and subversive, why was one negatively viewed while the other was not? After all, the mosque project was in fact paid for with foreign money, and it came from an organization with roots in Saudi Arabia. What determined the propriety of one act and the impropriety of the other? Why did the mosque project succeed?

One part of the explanation lies in the role of WAMY in the community. The fact that the international donor was given little attention in the above account of the mosque construction project is not without purpose. While the WAMY website mentions that the organization is a "member of the United Nations NGOs" and is recognized worldwide for its humanitarian efforts, a lawsuit was launched against it by some relatives of the victims of the 9/11 attacks (Benthall and Bellion-Jourdan 2003).[13] WAMY has denied allegations of involvement in those attacks. Despite this notoriety, WAMY does not prominently figure in this ethnography because it has operated only in the background. The organization had no direct lasting impact in Bazaar-Korgon, as its cooperation with the community ended with the completion of the mosque. It did not even distribute religious publications. Its role in and impact on the religious landscape in Bazaar-Korgon was important, facilitating not only the construction of a place of prayer but also

FIGURE 5.6. Construction of the twenty-eighth mosque in Bazaar-Korgon. Photograph by the author, 2004.

community cohesion and religious social action. While the mosque project was unthinkable without WAMY, the group was largely invisible to the community.[14]

Another mitigating factor in the mosque construction project's success was not only that it was regulated by secular and religious authorities but that it was perceived to be under the supervision of these leaders. As was demonstrated, regulation of religious activities by the official religious leadership ensured, for those residents not partaking in these activities, that the activities were not deviant or extreme. The supervision and involvement of secular authorities added weight to this regulating function. Wearing a *hijab*, by contrast, was not perceived to be under this secular supervision. Moreover, it was associated with "foreign forms" of Islam. The propriety of the religious beliefs of hijab-wearing women was unknown and difficult to control.

The mosque project should also be understood in terms of the town's history of modernization. Building the mosque was a step toward reconstructing the infrastructure that had broken down following the collapse of the Soviet Union. The explicitly Islamic tone of the project did signal new modes of social action and visions of a religious modernity that would be objectionable to some residents committed to the idea of secular public actions and having different definitions of (acceptable) religion. However, the project occurred in a form—the mosque—that had been, since the early 1990s, a standard mode of "reconnecting" with a past and a communal sense of ethnoreligious identity that was understood as having been lost or suppressed during the Soviet era. Participation in, or validation of, the mosque construction project did not necessitate the kind of altered conceptions, discourses, and actions understood to accompany other behavior, such as wearing a headscarf. The new mosque did not counteract the widespread notions of Muslimness present in the community—those that understood it to be part of ethnonational belonging—but instead strengthened it.[15] At the same time, it was a project supported by those who had "come close to Islam" because it provided a place for the collective performance of rituals and may have been seen as the re-Islamization of social space.

John Peel (2009) has argued that people convert either because the truth-value or the identity-value of the new religion becomes stronger than that of the former normative order. For Peel, truth-value indicates the way a religion's message "expresses the reality of things" for potential converts, while identity-value is the compatibility of a new religion with what a convert "feel[s] or want[s] themselves to be" (2009). The conflict between those who had "gone to Islam" and others in the community can in many ways be seen as revolving around this divide. For the former, the way others in the community value Islam as a source of ethnonational belonging is at odds with their conception of it as a truth-system, one that requires participation in proscribed rituals, observances, and bodily fashioning and one that sees "Muslim" as primarily a faith-oriented identity. What is interesting about this distinction in terms of the mosque construction project is that while many acts and discourses that locally are understood as differentiating those who had "gone to Islam" from others—like veiling—necessitate valuing Islam for its truth-value and criticizing its role as an ethnonational identity marker, the mosque project allowed both conceptions of Islam to coexist, without necessitating the rejection of the other.

This is one of the moments in which the different notions of Muslimness, bound up with varying definitions of religion, coalesce, and do so without necessitating the explicit interrogation or negation of the other. The mosque construction was an inclusive, multivocal project in which Muslims with heterogeneous interpretations of both the meaning and the work of this specific mosque, as well as differing notions of Islam and religion more generally, could hang together. The mosque construction project was successful, but not because its participants were of one mind in what the construction and the mosque did or represented. There was a plurality of experience and vision. But in contrast to other public Islamic expressions, the mosque remained more open to a variety of uses and interpretations, allowing it to work.

It was a project, variously interpreted but universally seen as connected to Islam and Muslimness, that brought Muslims of the town together despite their differing views, and it produced something that was nearly unanimously seen as productive for the community. The mosque spoke to residents because of its value in identity projects, truth projects, and development projects. Like the construction of the rayon Friday mosque that had opened five years earlier, it signaled successful participation in new economic orders in which international donors and grants were one of the surest routes to economic achievement. And while aesthetically it may not have dramatically altered the landscape of the Sai neighborhood complex, it at least indicated that the community was trying to change the state of its decaying environment.

Why did this project succeed when other interventions of religion into public space, like veiling or missionary endeavors, were more negatively or suspiciously evaluated? Part of that success could be attributed to the project's perceived regulation by secular authorities. This regulation, for residents, signaled the propriety of the actors and project in which they were engaged. But the fact that it was a building—construction—also played a role in the positive evaluation of the mosque. Much like the Friday mosque built a decade earlier, this newer building activity and the physical presence of the mosque in one of the most dilapidated parts of town was a counterweight to the postsocialist decay that had been dogging the town for more than a decade. It not only represented development but was progress itself, in terms of both the alteration of the physical environment and the new economic setting in which accessing funds through donors had become a primary means of acquiring capital and a highly sought-after skill. Importantly, the religious function of the mosque did not hinder its acceptance in the community; it was unproblematic, as it represented and enabled townspeople's reconnection with their perceived "lost" Muslim past, in a way that was not considered "extreme." Finally, the mosque, as a project, could be read as being safely outside the bounds of religious extremism because it was able to include competing visions of Muslimness and successfully hold together visions of the past and dreams for the future that, in the Soviet period, were contradictory. Nonetheless, it did so in a way that sanctioned Soviet- and post-Soviet-era secularism, namely the regulation of Islam, and it built on a history of development and construction. It was an Islamic project that was spacious enough for the heterogeneity of Muslim life in Bazaar-Korgon.

This was a significant change, given the specific conception of and limitations on public religion in the Soviet period. Interestingly, precisely because the mosque construction was a religious act in a new political, economic, and legal environment—the postsocialist situation—it also did something not only to and for the religious practitioners. To move Verkaaik's argument forward, the material force of the mosque extended beyond the bounds of the Islamic community directly involved—and not in the antagonistic forms of identity politics so often discussed in the Muslim minority context of western Europe. Religion played a public role in urban renewal and social cohesion beyond simply the direct involvement of religious practitioners. It included others with differing views of Islam, Muslimness, and religion. In the case of the mosque construction project, heterogeneous notions of Islam, Muslimness, and development, along with varied types of solidarity, piety, and urban renewal, mingle, and to some degree coalesce, in the project (see Hammond 2014).

While these developments could be charted without reference to the Soviet period, an exclusively contemporary view of the project—the way it created community cohesion and constructed public space for the articulation of religiously inspired social and infrastructural development projects—might read these developments as a criticism of or reaction to the Western visions of modernity and associated development projects that have bombarded the country since 2000 (Boehm 1999; Anderson 2003). But the significance of the mosque construction project lay equally in its dialogue with Soviet notions and projects of modernization—the way it upheld some Soviet notions (e.g., the equation of construction with progress), questioned others (e.g., the value of religion in societal progress), and rested on a balance between late Soviet-era ideas of (the propriety of) religion and post-Soviet ones. The success of the project was partly rooted in the way it addressed the various normative orders competing for dominance in the contemporary landscape, including the legacies of Soviet notions. And although these legacies are dying out, they still manage to shape the contemporary debates over religion in Bazaar-Korgon to some degree.

CHAPTER 6

WATCHING *CLONE*

Farida, Saodat, and Dilafruz were gathered around the television talking while commercials played. Suddenly, one sister hushed the others and drew their attention to the images on the screen. The pictures were of beautifully dressed Muslim women, swirling strands of DNA, and images from Brazil and Morocco. It was a promotional trailer for the new Brazilian soap opera, *Clone*.[1] The sisters and I, seated together in their small home in Bazaar-Korgon, Kyrgyzstan, watched, enraptured for the short clip. When I asked the girls what the new serial was about, they replied that they weren't sure but mentioned that it had something to do with Brazilians and Muslims. While the images of the Moroccan Muslims had grabbed their attention, the girls said nothing about the rather unique central topic of the soap opera: human cloning.

The sisters were not the only ones silent on that aspect of the show. For many viewers around the world, it was the lavishly presented, and highly romanticized, Moroccan "other" that made the soap opera so popular. One observer noted that Armenia had gone "Arabic over [the] wildly popular soap opera" (Grigoryan 2004). Another reported that "'El Clon' is leaving Latin America wide-eyed and drop-jawed for all things Arab" (Eisele 2002). But much commentary on the program criticized its inaccurate portrayals. Sheik Abdelmalek Cherkaoui Ghazouani, the Moroccan ambassador to Brazil, noted in a public statement that "the novela turned out to be a gross farce, portraying mediocre images, and a sham of the Arab-Muslim culture and reality" (quoted in Barbosa 2005, 48). In contrasting the "two worlds" of Brazil and Morocco, *Clone*'s creators objectified the featured places, lifestyles, and communities, presenting them as fundamentally different from one another. Moreover, through text and visual imagery, they rendered a highly orientalized portrayal of Muslims and Muslim life, especially regarding issues of gender.

Partly due to the romanticism central to its depictions, *Clone* achieved tremendous popularity in Bazaar-Korgon. Residents said the soap opera was so fascinating because it was the first serial they had seen with (non–Central Asian) Muslims as leading characters. In short, they explained, watching the soap was a chance for them to see how Muslims "really" lived. As they collectively viewed the program, chatted about the serial at cafés and the market, or analyzed episodes with friends and acquaintances, *Clone* became a part of the daily discussion in the community over the nature of Islam and Muslimness. *Clone*'s broadcast not only signaled a political shift in Kyrgyzstan that included a relatively free religious environment; it also helped create that shift by producing a discursive space where viewers could interrogate norms (see Das 1995, 180).

In its portrayal of the lives of Moroccans, *Clone* flatteringly depicted practices that in Bazaar-Korgon were seen as excessive religious behavior or indicators of extremism—like veiling. Orientalization, in Gerd Baumann's (2004) formulation, is a complex process of representation that creates romanticized notions of the other as much as it produces negative stereotypes. The orientalized view in *Clone* may have been patronizing, but it was romantic and beautiful, creating an air of desirability and normalcy around practices like veiling that, in Bazaar-Korgon, would otherwise have been interpreted as threatening. By recasting these practices, the depictions of Muslim life in *Clone* served as a positive resource for residents reevaluating their understandings of Islam, Muslim behavior, and public religious life.

Apart from political changes, the end of socialism also meant an alteration in economic order and the adoption of capitalism, with its incumbent property relations, structural adjustment programs, goods—including media—and desires. *Clone* appeared at a moment when the number and kind of goods, along with their proliferation in even the remotest of regions, had really taken off. A part of this influx of goods, *Clone*'s international credentials—a Brazilian-made serial about Moroccans broadcast by a Russian network in Kyrgyzstan—signaled just as they created the reach and complexities of the new material regime. *Clone* also indicated that the new forms of goods possible in the post-Soviet environment—soap operas, market stalls, and scarves completely covering the hair and neck—were being used in religious projects.

Yet, in the case of *Clone*, the material gathered and utilized to construct religious subjectivities, to aid individuals' desire for obedience to God and pious living, and to mark out boundaries of proper religious thought and practice was not by anyone's definition religious in itself. While it has been noted that the construction of the secular and religious are intimately and inherently linked (Asad 2003) and that proper religious behavior is often built by demarcating its negative "other" (e.g., Armbrust 2006), more ambiguously classifiable material—material that is not strictly religious but not exactly "secular," "forbidden," "sinful," or any of religion's other opposites—can likewise be employed to "do religion." In this chapter I show that the particular history of Islam in Soviet and post-Soviet spaces created an environment in which ambiguously classifiable material like *Clone*, with its stereotypical, orientalist portrayals of Muslim life, could be used to expand the imagination and practice of Islam in ways that were experienced by Bazaar-Korgonians as novel and emancipating. Although used in religious projects, *Clone* was not transformed by residents into something religious; its ambiguous status remained.

The Materiality of Islam in Bazaar-Korgon

Ways of being Muslim at the end of the Soviet period included more than just ideas—Muslimness was crafted materially and inscribed on the body. These material forms had changed dramatically over the course of the Soviet period, partly in response to the antireligious campaigns. By the late Soviet period, for example, unmarried girls never veiled, and while most married women donned a headscarf while at home, it did not cover the hair completely. It was usually tied at the nape of the neck, and women often removed their scarves in public and especially in the workplace. By the end of the Soviet period, men and women drank vodka and ate pork products regularly. Few Islamic texts were available. Moreover, access to information about other Muslims, other ways of understanding Islam and thinking about religion, and access to materials such as texts, cassettes, or television programs that could have been used to cultivate other ideas, bodily dispositions, and ritual practices were virtually impossible to obtain.

As discussed earlier, despite the Soviet Union's collapse, the material conditions through which people understood and acted out their Muslimness, as well as the notions about Muslimness themselves, remained fairly stable throughout the 1990s, the early 1990s religious burgeoning notwithstanding. By the turn of the millennium, however, things began to shift as the number of those "interested in Islam" increased. But those who had "turned and gone to Islam" (*dinge burulup getkin adamdar*) were derided and gossiped about in town and their al-

Figure 6.1. Material ways of being Muslim from the early Soviet era, like this *paranji*, were largely eliminated while new modes, like the headscarf shown right, replaced them. Photograph by the author, 2003.

ternative visions of Muslimness were contested. One of the newer practices introduced in Bazaar-Korgon and promoted as central to proper Muslim behavior was the donning of headscarves that completely covered the hair. The headscarf became not only a way of being an obedient Muslim and of cultivating piety but also, unwittingly, a public pronouncement of adherence to locally "new" interpretations of Islam. Headscarves became, in short, a way in which those who had "turned and gone to Islam" could be identified.

In the 1990s very few objects—foreign or domestic—that would have been locally associated with the "new" interpretations of Islam were available in the marketplaces of Bazaar-Korgon, though tracts on proper prayer and the five pillars of Islam were exceptions. But commodities from outside the region in general were also absent. By then only the biggest names in global capitalism were available in the local market—for example, Coca-Cola or Snickers. Kyrgyzstan's post-Soviet economic decline reached its nadir at the end of the 1990s, so by 2004 economic prospects had slightly improved and the diversity of goods available had reached a level stunning to those accustomed to socialism. Russia, Turkey, and China had become the main sources of imported goods.

The influx of goods associated with Islam and the "new" interpretations seemed to rise in tandem, both with the increase of commodities generally and with the number people who had become "interested in Islam."[2] It also mirrored a similar commodification of Islam seen in other Muslim-majority societies (Jones 2010; D'Alisera 2001; Starrett 1995). By 2004 there were many Islamic objects on the scene—plastic prayer beads, skull caps, posters of the Ka'ba, cassette recordings of religious messages, and many, many types of written texts featuring ideas about Islam and proper Muslim behavior. These types of items were usually sold together and often in front of mosques, as well as at special bazaar stalls. Importantly, they were almost never grouped and sold alongside objects like bracelets bearing the protective eye, herbs and wood burned like incense for the cleansing of spaces and bodies, or headscarves (see Soares 2005, 80–81). These items were found at most any market stall—the protective eye bracelets near the car parts and the twine sellers in one bazaar or by the makeup and toiletries in another; herbs and wood might be in the housewares area, near the grains, or by the brooms.

Headscarves, so important in a woman's daily life and in gift exchanges, could be and were bought everywhere. However, these kinds of headscarves were of a size and pattern that would not trigger public commentary, so common and ubiquitous were they. They were also the kinds of scarves that had been worn in the same way for at least thirty years (i.e., since the late Soviet period in the 1970s and 1980s) and perhaps a bit longer. Ironically, although a local increase in women's veiling that more fully covered the body—the style now internationally known as the *hijab*—was one of the indicators to many residents that something was happening with Islam in Bazaar-Korgon, there was no place in town to buy clothing to suit these women's needs and desires in 2004. Even in the much larger nearby urban center of Jalal-Abad dedicated searches had to be made to cobble together enough items to make a suitable outfit.[3] The only headscarves around were the small, normal, "nonthreatening" ones.

Despite this lack of available clothing for headscarf-wearing women, the number and variety of materials dealing with Islam or Muslims entering Kyrgyzstan from abroad was impressive compared with the situation five or ten years earlier. These objects—religious objects or objects about religion—and residents' evaluation of them were included in the discussions that had arisen in the community about what Muslimness should be precisely because they introduced and fostered the development of new ideas about and novel approaches to living Islam into the community. Absent among all these things until *Clone*'s appearance was any fictional media depicting or discussing non–Central Asian Muslims in which central Islamic practices like veiling or prayer were portrayed and discussed.

The Soap Opera and Its Imagery

Clone was produced by the Brazilian media giant TV Globo and aired in Brazil in 2001. Subsequently the program was syndicated and shown around the world, including throughout the former Soviet Union. As previously noted, the seemingly unique element of this soap opera was that it had a cloned human being as one of its central characters. The main storyline revolved around the love affair of a Brazilian man, Lucas, and a Brazilian-born woman of Moroccan decent, Jade (ZHA-dee). The couple, who met in Morocco after Jade moved there to live with the family of her mother, began their love affair in the 1980s. The affair was ill fated. Jade was married by her family to Said, and Lucas, too, married. The soap opera followed their lives—and attempts to be together—as well as the various friends, relatives, and colleagues who surrounded them.

Where did the clone come in? Lucas was a twin whose brother had been killed as a teen. One of Lucas's father's closest friends was a geneticist, Dr. Albieri. The scientist, saddened that his friend had lost his son, secretly took a cell sample from Lucas, successfully cloned the cell, and implanted the embryo into a woman, Deusa, who had come to his clinic for in vitro fertilization.[4] No one knew of the doctor's deeds. Once the clone was born, he "disappeared" for nearly two decades, returning only when Lucas and Jade had reached their forties. In the meantime, Jade had become disenchanted with Lucas, who, she felt, had lost his physical appeal, his sense of romance, and the ambitions of his youth. When the clone appeared, Jade fell in love with him, creating what the serial's creator Glória Perez called an uncommon love triangle: Lucas became his own rival. In the end, Dr. Albieri and the clone—the former unable to come to terms with what he had done and the latter, with what he was—wandered off together into the desert and so the soap opera ended (Massarani and Moreira 2002).

FIGURE 6.2. A screen shot of the *Clone* character Jade dancing.

But what of the Muslims? A soap opera about a love triangle that includes a clone could easily have been set entirely in Brazil; the main dilemma of the program does not require Muslims to make it tenable. Nonetheless, the writer decided to add a "Muslim twist" to this tale. Perez's serials are known for engaging with social issues like alcohol or drug abuse. And while she addressed some of these themes in *Clone*, she said she chose to include Muslims to make the program more multicultural.[5] While Bazaar-Korgonians credited the role of Muslims in the soap as the key to its success, I assert that its popularity was dependent on the highly romantic fashion in which the Muslims were portrayed, especially when compared to the Brazilians. The romance of Muslims in the soap began with the visual imagery used to depict Muslims and their spaces. The Moroccans in *Clone* were depicted as wealthy, except for their servants. They were lavishly dressed, wore vibrant colors, and were adorned with jewels. They lived in large, attractive homes. The physical environment and backdrop of the scenes in Morocco were simply breathtaking—rolling sand dunes bathed in golden light, narrow alleyways lined with fabrics and other fantastical treasures. Nearly every event portrayed in the lives of the Moroccans called for an accompanying dance. In these scenes groups of women—or sometimes individuals—were shown erotically performing for the pleasure of a few male guests.

FIGURE 6.3. A Moroccan home interior, as featured in *Clone*.

FIGURE 6.4. A Brazilian home interior as featured in *Clone*.

When the action of the soap opera shifted from one country to the other, "typical scenes" of the new location were shown to indicate where the action would take place. The Brazilian shots include beaches, palm trees, and large highways. Those of Morocco showed sand dunes, camel trains, men praying, and stereotypical images of "Eastern" bazaars. The images painted a very beautiful picture of Morocco. The rich fabrics, unique jewelry, beautiful women, and lavish "harems" were some of the most popular parts of the show. Nevertheless, the visual portrayal of Moroccan life was highly exotic and the contrast between Brazil and Morocco was plain. Moroccan streets were devoid of cars. The servants of wealthy Moroccans characters cooked over open fires. Other than a telephone—a rotary dial with a cord—there were no other electronic devices present in the homes of Moroccans. The stereotyping of the home was so strong that the interior of Moroccan-owned houses appeared the same regardless of whether they were in Morocco or Brazil. They all resembled typical orientalized images of "Arab interiors" as can be found in other clichéd portrayals, like Disney's *Aladdin*. All in all, the visual picture presented was one of an atemporal existence of beauty and sensuality—one that was fundamentally different from Brazil.

The orientalization of the Moroccans that was accomplished through the depiction of their physical environment also occurred within the storylines. The episodes that dealt primarily with the Moroccans touched precisely on the subjects where the variance with Brazilian life was perceived to be the greatest. Many of these storylines revolved around issues related to gender: seclusion of women, patriarchal society, polygamy, or dress. Characters in *Clone* moved quite easily and frequently between Brazil and Morocco, except for the heroine, Jade. According to the portrayal of Moroccan life in the show, Jade had to obtain the signature of a male relative in order to leave the country. Her many attempts to reach Brazil—to visit Lucas or see her daughter, for example—were plots for a number of episodes. What was always highlighted was Jade's inability to control her own movement and, by extension, her life.

If the depiction of Jade's struggles to travel displayed the "evils" of patriarchal society, other episodes that dealt with gender relations and female subordination tried to present at least one positive counterpoint to every negative instance. For example, a main theme running through the whole serial was Jade's arranged marriage and the ensuing troubles she had in her relationship with her spouse. But her cousin's marriage—also arranged—was portrayed as having a "happy ending." Similarly, when two young girls faced the prospect of veiling, one was shown to be excited—trying out headscarves and talking happily about the event with her mother—while the other tried to avoid it and was forced to deceive her parents. Other episodes addressed the issue of women's power in the home, or the maneuvering ability women have in a male-dominated society.

These point/counterpoint portrayals in *Clone* utilize the binary logic of orientalized dichotomies. However, they nonetheless offer a positive valuation of these practices, especially on aesthetic grounds. As Gerd Baumann (2004, 20) notes, orientalization is not just, or even necessarily, the demonizing of another. It involves a positive reversal as well as a negative mirroring of the other (20). This reversal, based on a longing for certain elements "we" have lost but that the other still has, resulted in the flattering portrayals that helped make *Clone* so popular. Although Muslims were depicted as "lacking" in terms of technology and certain "modern" values, they were nonetheless beautiful depictions that valorized aspects of (perceived) Moroccan culture.

Other mechanisms of representation in *Clone* likewise contributed to its success and to the creation of material that could be used to nuance and diversify conceptualizations about Muslims. The use, display, or "practice" of objects always co-constitutes the context for their reading (Morgan 2008, 228). Certain objects owned or used by the Moroccans portrayed in *Clone*—telephones, wood-burning stoves, and headscarves—were commonly interpreted as signs of tradition. But their use and presentation by women who themselves "embodied" modernity through their comportment or bodily adornments, for example, created new readings of these items (see Moors 2000, 873). So when Jade and Latifa wore covered forms of dress, the women's bodies created a context for interpreting these material expressions of tradition rather than the other way around. As beloved, beautiful, modern heroines, they therefore constructed a notion of modernity that celebrated and was compatible with valued elements of tradition, such as veiling (Moors 2000). This was a novel reading in Bazaar-Korgon.

Watching *Clone*

While there were many venues through which "those interested in Islam" could explore and debate Islam in Bazaar-Korgon, *Clone* and its portrayal of Muslims provided a space where norms concerning the propriety of particular observances were interrogated by a wider spectrum of the community (see Das 1995, 180). This process is perhaps most evident in reference to ideas about bodily fashioning. Some of the most popular and most discussed aspects of *Clone* were the beautiful female Moroccan characters and their clothes. Importantly, all the Moroccan women wore variations on the hijab when depicted in spaces outside the home. The headscarves in *Clone* were perceived by residents of Bazaar-Korgon as glamorous. Importantly, as noted, they were worn by the most popular characters, characters whom residents rated as modern, beautiful, and enviable women.

The garments of the female Moroccan characters were stunning in color and design, so much so that they were as much an item of discussion as the actual

FIGURE 6.5. The Moroccan character Jade in *Clone*.

storyline. Just a few months into the show's year-and-a-half run, a certain style of jewelry worn by the Moroccan characters in the show could already be found at every market stall in Bazaar-Korgon. New stores took on the names of beloved characters, and there were even dresses that were called "Jade." *Clone* offered an alternative view concerning the aesthetics and meaning of the veil. Young women in Bazaar-Korgon who were considering veiling often talked about their dreams of having a collection of scarves and clothes as wonderful as Jade's or Latifah's. Through these characters, young women in Bazaar-Korgon saw that Islam and veiling were not at war with fashion. Interestingly, even some women who had not considered veiling said that they experimented with the veil because of the influence of *Clone*.

Gulmira, a twenty-year-old college student at home in Bazaar-Korgon for the weekend, had commented on her interpretation of the hijab extensively when she and I met in fall 2003. She had interpreted her neighbor's changes in bodily fashioning as an indicator of Wahhabi tendencies (McBrien 2006). When we met again in spring 2004, it was evident that Gulmira had been reconsidering her thoughts on Islam and Muslimness. We were discussing the Islamically in-formed ideas and practices of mutual friends and acquaintances when, compar-ing herself to them, Gulmira said that although she called herself a Muslim, she was no longer entirely sure what she meant when she said that. She explained that she'd come to question what she understood Muslimness to mean. When

Figure 6.6. The Moroccan characters Jade and Latifah in *Clone*.

she looked at the practices of some of her friends and acquaintances who prayed daily and fasted at Ramadan, she commented, "I am not doing anything with my religion."

Gulmira was also an avid *Clone* watcher. She reported that, after viewing *Clone* and seeing the fabulous clothes and veils, she went home and tried on her mother's headscarves. What Gulmira didn't do was tie them like her mother wore them, at the nape of the neck.[6] Rather, she experimented with the various ways Jade and Latifah tied theirs, all of which fully covered their hair and neck. Gulmira said, "I did it because I wanted to know how it would feel and whether, if I someday wanted to wear my scarf like this, it would suit the shape of my face." Gulmira said she'd never seriously considered becoming a more devout Muslim, and in light of her friends' practices and her respect for them, she sometimes wondered whether she should even identify herself as one.

Clone did not directly help her with her questions, but she remarked that it did influence the way she thought about the veil. She said that she no longer believed that the veil was always ugly or that it was only for the old or for "extremists." It could be a very beautiful and fashionable form of dress, she explained, but one that was worn by Muslims more involved with Islam than herself. When looking at the divergence in the opinions Gulmira expressed in the fall and the spring, it's impossible to say whether she'd made a long-term alteration, temporally changed her view, or was unaware of the differences in her two evaluations.

However, her varying opinions show powerfully the kind of alternative notions of Muslimness that *Clone* was helping foster.

Lisa Rofel's (1994, 701) work on soap operas in China has pointed to the way that popular culture can serve "as a site for the constitution of national subjects." Similarly, Purnima Mankekar's (1993, 544) study of soap operas in India traced the "connections between responses to television and the continuous constitution of national and gendered subjectivities." What is intriguing about the broadcast, viewing, and discussions of *Clone* in Bazaar-Korgon is that it too was debated because of the way it commented on the construction of national identity. However, unlike those analyzed by Mankekar (1993), Rofel (1994), or Lila Abu-Lughod (1993, 1995, 2004), *Clone* was not viewed by individuals who identified with the national subjectivities portrayed in it. It was not designed to teach, model, shape, or project images for or about Kyrgyz or Uzbeks.

Yet, it did present images and storylines about Muslims, a religious subjectivity with which the Kyrgyz and Uzbeks who viewed the program could identify. Because widespread, local conceptions of Muslimness in Bazaar-Korgon were intertwined with ethnonational belonging, as outlined in the introduction, the soap opera widened the discursive space for interrogating these notions. Interestingly, it therefore simultaneously contributed not only to national and gendered subjectivities but to religious ones as well.

This interrogative process had already been under way in town for several years, as those who had "gone to Islam" had been challenging the premise that "Muslimness" was necessarily intertwined and bound up with ethnonational belonging and asserting instead that it was inherently, if not exclusively, a matter of belief. In this reading, religion and ethnonational belonging were not and could not be mutually constitutive. Residents associated the practices and bodily fashioning depicted in *Clone* with the interpretations of Islam and the practices of those who had "gone to Islam." But they did not perceive the characters in the show to be threatening, backward, or overly religious in the way that those who had "gone to Islam" were often understood to be. The characters—even the apparent antagonist, Said—were well loved in Bazaar-Korgon. Like most soap opera characters, they were beautiful and enviable. This explains why seeing their participation in certain religious practices may have caused residents to rethink, if only partially, their views.

Moreover, unlike other forms of media that conveyed scripture-oriented messages about Islam—such as recorded sermons or booklets—*Clone* was a form of media consumed by more viewers than just those who were "interested in Islam." *Clone*'s public was wider and more diverse, a trend found in publics of popular religious entertainment throughout the world (Meyer 2006; McAllister 2003).

What makes *Clone* unique in this respect was that it was not produced by the Muslim community it portrayed but by a secular media giant.

Those in Bazaar-Korgon who had "gone to Islam" watched and loved the soap as much as those who—like Gulmira—had not. But for them, the material they gathered while viewing *Clone* was not only about breaking down norms and stereotypes; it was also about gaining support in their attempts at obedience and piety. Just after her marriage in 2000, Mukadas, a resident of Bazaar-Korgon, said she and her husband came "close to Islam" (*dinge jakyn*). A few years later, at age twenty-six, Mukadas slowly began to transform her mode of dress and veiling, covering more and more of her body. Mukadas was an avid fan of *Clone*, as were nearly all members of her immediate and extended families. Mukadas said that she learned something new from *Clone* every time she watched it, because, as she explained, the characters in the program dealt with the same kinds of problems she faced. She was sometimes stared at when walking in public, and often she would overhear harsh comments on her mode of dress. When she watched *Clone*, Mukadas said, she could relate to the feeling of difference that the veiled Moroccans in Brazil encountered. Beyond that, she said she found validation for her form of dress through them. For Mukadas, seeing beautiful young women veiling in very fashionable ways confirmed her idea that veiling did not indicate that Islam was an antiquated religion, as the critics in her town intimated.

Critical Views

In Bazaar-Korgon there is a sense that during the seventy years of socialism, Muslims in Central Asia lost the knowledge (and practice) of true Islam and proper Muslim behavior.[7] As a result, many residents of the town perceived themselves as less knowledgeable about "real" Islam, or at least they characterized themselves that way when discussing *Clone*.[8] One of the most oft-repeated phrases I heard when viewing or discussing the program with others was the epiphanic statement, "Oh, so that's how Muslims really do it." Many residents thus attributed educational value to the soap opera and commented on how much they were learning from it. This is certainly due to the special status of its content—the first fictional program about non–Central Asian Muslims, with debates about proper Muslim behavior at the heart of many of its themes. But it is likewise related to the general popularity of soap operas in town, as well as to the "aura" of importance and factuality given by the form of its disseminations—television being an "authorizing medium par excellence" (van de Port 2006, 457).

Despite this, residents, while lauding what they learned through the program, simultaneously commented critically on certain aspects of it. *Clone* is therefore best understood not only as a course on "Islam for Beginners," as residents made it out to be, but also as a program that widened their exposure to alternative ways of living and interpreting Islam. In addition, it became a resource they drew from when constructing their own views about Islam.

Ziyod, the twenty-six-year-old bazaar merchant who was married to Mukadas, had also come "closer to Islam." For two years he had been studying in a small, home-based group led by one of the most popular religious leaders in the community. There he learned to recite the Quran and received instruction from his teacher about proper Muslim behavior. Ziyod was slowly becoming known in his neighborhood as a person knowledgeable about Islam; neighbors were beginning to come to him—or his wife—for advice. Ziyod frequently watched *Clone* but said that he did not always agree with it. He explained that some episodes showed the Moroccans doing things that Muslims should not be doing, like dancing or publicly kissing at wedding ceremonies. He explained that both practices were un-Islamic. Despite this caveat, he said, he still enjoyed the program.

Maksat, a local schoolteacher in his late fifties, was wary of the recent changes he had seen in Bazaar-Korgon. He adamantly defended his belief in God but often expressed concerns about the interpretations of Islam that were becoming more widespread in town, chafing at the calls of those who said he must pray or go to the mosque. On more than one occasion, men had knocked on his door, given him written materials on Islam, and invited him to attend meetings being held at his neighborhood mosque. When recounting incidents like this, his description took on disparaging tones. He employed phrases like "sneaking off," "hiding," and "doing something bad" and accused them of coercing others—like him—into adopting their understanding of being a Muslim.

Maksat was a fan of *Clone* and watched it nightly. Like Ziyod, however, Maksat was sometimes critical of the program. He found fault with some of the actions of the Moroccan characters. On one occasion, Maksat contrasted various customs shown in the program with those kept in Kyrgyzstan—such as practices that establish a girl's virginity at marriage—concluding that they were unnecessary components of proper Muslim behavior. The important thing in a Muslim's life, he said, was that one had faith and behaved decently to others. The performance of rituals was not the proper measure.

The practices Maksat criticized in this instance were, interestingly, more similar to the kinds of life-cycle events and rituals understood to be part of Muslimness by most townsfolk, himself included, than they were to the rituals, such as prayer, being advocated by those "close to Islam." Nevertheless, his criticism of the practices shown in *Clone* was similar to what he had said about those "close to Islam" in his community—that there was not a definite core of rituals to which all Muslims must adhere. He used *Clone* to argue for a broader view of acceptable Muslim behavior, implicitly engaging with those in his community who sought to define it more narrowly. Ziyod, however, employed the material he gathered from *Clone* to make the opposite argument—for more strictly defined notions of propriety, using the soap opera to do the very thing Maksat so opposed.

Ziyod's and Maksat's critical approaches to the serial ended differently—one drew on *Clone* to narrow appropriate Muslim behavior while the other employed the soap to widen it—but both were nonetheless utilizing the soap as a resource in renegotiating, and then asserting, their interpretations of Muslimness. Muka-das, however, had a different reaction. She chose not to make normative claims about the actions of the Moroccan Muslims. She said, "In *Clone* they do some Muslim things differently. I don't know if they are wrong or if the Muslims there are just a different type of Muslim. Before, I thought there were only Muslims and Christians. Now I am learning that there are many types of Muslims." All three comments on the portrayals seen in *Clone* revealed a certain kind of reflexivity. The material gathered while viewing *Clone* facilitated an individual contemplation of one's own practices and ideas about Islam vis-à-vis communal norms.

The Materiality of *Clone*

Opinions cultivated through the viewing (and discussing) of *Clone* were used in debates about being Muslim and about being Kyrgyz or Uzbek, as well as in personal religious projects. *Clone* thus served to widen perspectives on Muslim life, providing encouragement and expanding views in some instances. But what kind of material was *Clone*? Reflecting on the way the soap opera was viewed and used, observing that its storylines were debated and discussed as frequently as the lives of real-life neighbors, or looking at the manner in which *Clone* became materially present in town through notebooks with Jade's picture on the cover, cafés bearing her name, and women "dressing up" as that character, we might then ask what can be said about *Clone*'s material form. We might also ask what this form says about contemporary constructions and enactments of religion in post-Soviet Kyrgyzstan.

Clone was definitely a unique commodity in the marketplace, and it was distinct in at least three important ways from other religious objects or objects about religion circulating in the region at that moment. First, *Clone* was not associated with the kinds of foreign interpretations of Islam understood to be nefarious or threatening. Hijabs and certain styles of male dress (long white tunics with coordinating white trousers) were tagged as imported, foreign Islam and associated with extremist interpretations and enactments of the religion. On the contrary, through the beauty of its imagery—and perhaps because of Bazaar-Korgonians' lack of preconceptions about Morocco and its Muslim inhabi-tants—*Clone*'s portrayal of Muslims was far removed from any threatening

Корпорация "КиноХит" представляет

O CLONE

Бразильский сериал-бестселлер

КЛОН

1 - 30 серии

FIGURE 6.7. *Clone* DVDs were still available in 2010. Photograph by the author, 2012.

interpretations that Bazaar-Korgonians imagined, creating a far less negatively biased interaction with the material it provided. Moreover, it was one of the few material sources about Muslims and religious practices like prayer and veiling that those who did not have a particular interest in Islam were nevertheless exposed to, creating a rather unique, unthreatening venue for interrogating notions concerning the propriety of religious observance and the constitution of national and religious subjectivities. These practices were not only beautifully and lavishly portrayed, and not only performed by enviable, modern characters, as previously noted, but they also were depicted as occurring in a context utterly removed from Bazaar-Korgon. In this way, *Clone* offered a more distant vantage point from which to consider Muslimness. *Clone* as popular culture served not only as a means through which national and gendered subjectivities were constituted, but it presented material and created space for the interrogation and fashioning of religious ones as well.[9]

Second, *Clone* was, obviously, a form of media, a visual and aural representation of Muslim lives. But it was one created for entertainment purposes. It was not meant to mediate spirituality, instruct about Islam, or aid anyone's interaction with God. In this way it differed significantly from all the other forms of religious commodities available in town in that it was not purported by residents to "do" or to assist them in "doing" anything religious—such as enlighten the mind, ward off evil spirits, cultivate piety, or even entertain in a "pure" way. In this way it likewise differs significantly from the majority of media, commodities, and objects about religion explored by anthropologists (e.g., Starrett 1995; Hirschkind 2001; van de Port 2006; Schulz 2006; Kendall et al. 2010). Their attention has largely been focused on religious things, with religious purposes, made by or for practitioners of the religion.

Clone was, however, created to entertain and—as its writer, Glória Perez, suggests—to expose viewers to other ways of life. Bazaar-Korgonians were certainly not the viewers of Perez's imagination—non-Muslim Brazilians and perhaps, the broader non-Muslim, Spanish-speaking, North and South American world. Her aim was nonetheless fulfilled in the Central Asian town. The majority of townspeople used material from the serial to expand their understandings of other Muslims and to widen the acceptable array of legitimate understandings and enactments of religious and national subjectivities.

Perez's inclusion of Muslims in a fictional television program made by and for Brazilians signals and continues to constitute the religious textures of our contemporary, interconnected, mediated world (see Meyer and Moors 2006; Csordas 2009). It also indicates, as Gregory Starrett (2010, 214) has argued, that "Islam and Muslims are objects of imagination, and this imagination has implications for politics and for experiences of the modern by non-Muslims." Starrett's examination of the controversy surrounding simulation of Islamic ritual as a part of the US elementary school curriculum demonstrates how these ritual performances can be read as commitment to and creation of a set of culturally salient ideas for non-Muslim Americans—"the values of tolerance, cosmopolitanism, and diversity" (2010, 227). Similarly, for many of those non-Muslims involved in developing *Clone*—like Perez and those who worked to script, design, and perform the lives of Muslims—the implication of these performances had less to do with "teaching Islam" than with inculcating "multiculturalism."

It was this commitment to tolerance that, in part, contributed to a flattering portrayal of Islam, which allowed many Muslim viewers of *Clone* to use material gathered from it in a way never imagined by Perez—to assist them in their religious lives. This leads to the third point regarding *Clone*'s uniqueness as a "thing." The most obvious yet important observation is that it was not a religious object. While *Clone* was about Muslims—and included performances of their religious lives—it would not have been considered religious or sacred in any way by anyone in town, nor would any external observer have classified it as such. It was rather, on one level at least, a metadevice providing the ground upon and language through which many could think about religion. Ideas developed in these interrogations were used to help form boundaries around proper religion, improper religion, and the secular. In this way *Clone* was used to "do" religion, even if only at times through an "othering" process in which, by defining oneself as not religious, the religious was delineated (Armbrust 2006, 208–9).

Yet, *Clone* was also used to deal with doubt and persecution for those who had started veiling and to stir reflection on understandings of what it means to be a Muslim, which for some included a turn toward piety. In these instances *Clone* was used by some in their attempts at religious obedience. It was material being drawn upon to help fulfill what they understood to be God's will, to create a religious subjectivity, and in some cases to act as a witness of proper Muslim behavior to others. These aspects go beyond "othering" and show that in the case of *Clone* in Bazaar-Korgon nonreligious materials are important in "doing" religion, pushing us to look more broadly when attempting to understand and map "how religion happens materially" (Meyer et al. 2010, 209). "Obviously religious objects" are used to build religious worlds; profane things, bodies, places, or projects are consecrated; religions articulate attitudes toward things (2010, 210), and "new media technologies affect the contents and forms of religious debate" (Schulz 2006, 211). But "nonreligious objects"—including the material gathered from media—play a role in the construction of religious worlds as well—and not just as a counterpoint or a larger contextual whole.

The anthropological literature on media has focused on power relations between producers and viewers, arguing that viewers can "simultaneously 'submit' to and 'resist' the texts" of the programs they view (Mankekar 1993, 544) or, neither opposing nor acquiescing to a "message," can create alternative meanings and construct new subjectivities from media (Kulick and Wilson 2002). The various ways of viewing and using *Clone* among Bazaar-Korgonians show how complex the relationship between produced text and viewed text can be and how novel are the ways people can use texts (see Abu-Lughod 1995).

Drawing on the orientalized view of Moroccans imagined and created by Brazilians, Bazaar-Korgonians interpreted *Clone* in light of Soviet-era notions of proper Muslim behavior and the dangers of religious extremism, as well as the post-Soviet situation of a market economy, religious plurality, and discourses of a supposed Islamic "threat." Understanding the social role(s) the media can play, the various meanings that can be created using material gathered through it, or the importance placed upon it is dependent on the various social contexts of the producer or the viewer, including the spatiotemporal node in which either lives (Abu-Lughod 2004). While in other situations the orientalized texts and images of *Clone* have been interpreted as reinforcing negative stereotypes of Muslims and contributing to rifts between "Muslims" and "the West," residents of Bazaar-Korgon utilized the material to expand their understanding of the variety of Muslim experiences. Moreover, they employed the soap opera to debate interpretations of proper Muslim behavior and to assist them in their attempts at obedience and piety. In short, rather than being used to reinforce clichéd, narrow views of Muslims, or as a means to counteract and reverse these interpretations, the material gathered from *Clone* and the way it was used in discussions about and enactments of proper Muslim behavior show an interpretation of the material that fell outside the dialectic.

The production of *Clone* and the uses it was put to point to another change in the landscape that can be seen as simultaneously emancipating and constraining. The ability of Central Asian viewers to see the program was possible because the collapse of the Soviet Union had ushered in a new economic system of consumer capitalism. The availability of products—consumer goods of all kinds, including religious commodities—provided access to ideas about Islam from outside the community and to materials that suggested new ways of imaging and enacting Islam. It also meant that Islam was being enacted in a new way—through objects bought and sold at a market stall, a development unprecedented in the socialist or presocialist history of the region. But *Clone* was unique among the other religious commodities in several ways, first and foremost because it was not a religious commodity at all. It nonetheless served as a powerful material for constructing religious subjectivities and creating religious worlds.

CONCLUSION

The five mosques that were built in Bazaar-Korgon during the late 1980s would be difficult for most outsiders to find today. It is not that they are falling apart or are in disrepair. They are simply small neighborhood mosques, lacking much decoration, unremarkable in size and location. They are set between houses on unmarked streets. They are known to those who use them and to those who live nearby. They were constructed during the period of "openness" (glasnost), one of several moments over the long Soviet period when restrictions on religion were eased. The Bazaar-Korgon district Friday mosque, on the other hand, sits atop a hill overlooking the town's main square; it is large and looming, and everyone who drives into town sees it. Construction on it began only three years after the five neighborhood mosques were built. And yet, despite this continuity, something had changed. It was not just another mosque; the process for authorizing, funding, and carrying out its construction followed new routes and encountered new roadblocks. And once it was built, it signaled something new for residents. What had happened in those three years was the end of the Soviet Union.

Mosques, headscarves, prayer, shrine visitation, and knowledge of Islamic law, not to mention amulets, circumcision, and ways of preparing food, had long been features of life in Bazaar-Korgon. However, the political and economic transformation of the early 1990s, often summed up with terms like "collapse" or "transition," meant a different kind of social and political location for religion, a different space for interpreting and living Islam, a different mode of power and set of logics exercised by the state. This is precisely what I was interested in when I went to Bazaar-Korgon to conduct fieldwork in 2003. I therefore asked one simple question when I arrived in Kyrgyzstan: what were the contours of religious life approximately ten years after the end of state pursued atheism? I wanted to understand, for example, what kinds of rituals people were participating in, what sorts of ideas about Islam they were articulating, and how these things related to the way they constructed their lives and their town in the early post-Soviet period. I was also keenly interested in what the Soviet atheist past had been like and how it had formed the early post-Soviet condition.

What I found, and what this book has shown, is that this new public religious life was hallmarked by vibrancy, diversity, and debate, but it was also characterized by a sense of unease and discomfort. Bazaar-Korgonians were teaching, learning, and encountering Islam in a variety of ways. They were reading books, listening to cassette tapes, and seeing things on the street. Some women and even some men changed their mode of dress. Others attended study groups or aided in the construction of a mosque. And as townsfolk experimented with, committed to, modified, or rejected a variety of ideas and practices of Islam, they created the post-Soviet religious landscape. There was not merely a singular interpretation of Islam circulating in town, and there certainly was not a hegemonic way of living Islam. Townsfolk discussed and interrogated these matters whether they used material from television, from local religious leaders, or from statements made by a wedding speaker. They evaluated the clothes they saw women wearing. They talked about the buildings being constructed and the regulation (or lack thereof) of Islamic teachers and education. In short, they experimented with, contested, modified, and adopted a variety of practices of and ideas about Islam.

This atmosphere of debate and public religiosity was in contrast to the situation in the Soviet period but also to the state of affairs in contemporary Uzbekistan, the two most immediate referents of comparison for people in town. Compared to these two denotata, the religious world that was emerging in Bazaar-Korgon in the early 2000s was public, multivocal, and variegated. Debate, however, does signal difference—of opinion, practice, and power. So, just as debate was a primary characteristic of religious life in Bazaar-Korgon around the turn of the millennium, so was the experience of difference. In some cases this situation led to enrichment and expansion, as in the case of *Clone*, for example. In other instances, the experience of difference was confrontational, creating a sense of unease and uncertainty. This was true when it came to an alternative definition of Muslimness being articulated in town. This alternative conceptualization came, in part, from outside the region but was likewise created and articulated by those in town who had "turned and gone to Islam." It asserted that Muslimness was primarily and essentially a category of belief. This was counter to the most widespread understanding, cultivated over the long Soviet period and still dominant in the early 2000s, which prioritized belonging as the primary characteristic.

This idea of Muslimness as principally a category of religious-ethnonational belonging unintentionally resulted from the intertwining of Soviet-era antireligious campaigns, the promotion of scientific atheism, and the policies and programs created to cultivate and promote the nations of the Soviet Union during the Soviet period. The Soviet antireligious campaigns were perhaps the harshest and most thorough form of state-led secularizing attempts; they eventually led to the eradication, limitation, and demonization of many aspects of Muslim life in Central Asia. However, there were aspects of Muslim life that persisted over the course of the Soviet period, though certainly altered in form, meaning, and consequence. These included rituals related to the home, shrine visitation, and the network of (un)official scholars, for example. Through these and other ways, Muslims continued to live and interpret Islam and to cultivate a particular notion of being Muslim during the Soviet period and, importantly, as a part of their lives more broadly as Kyrgyz, Uzbeks, and Soviets.

Concurrent with the antireligious struggles, particular romantic, folklorized ideas of national belonging were cultivated in Central Asia over the course of the Soviet period; these became tied up with notions of Muslimness. By the end of the Soviet period, to be Kyrgyz or Uzbek was to be Muslim. This particular variety of inchoate religious-ethnonational belonging was the unintended consequence of policies intended to rule and develop Central Asia, but it was also tied with programs—like the nationalities policies (*korenizatsiya*)—aimed at equality and opportunity for the union's peoples. In this way, Muslimness, as an important characteristic of ethnonational belonging, became tied up with particular routes to power and resources that relied on its strategic deployment. It arose as one element of a series of compromises made to achieve a grander vision of societal evolution, momentarily accepted as in-the-meantime states on the way to a postnational, postreligious, communist utopia. The public articulation of Muslimness in this form was not only necessary but, due to the particularities of Soviet secularism, also the only sanctioned public expression and enactment possible. The antireligious campaigns and the campaigns for scientific atheism had foreclosed, eliminated, and/or demonized other practices and articulations of Muslimness. Finally, and importantly, Muslimness understood in this manner could co-constitute a field in which overlapping and mutually supporting ideas about being (a good) Muslim, Kyrgyz or Uzbek, and Soviet could be formulated and articulated.

This concept of Muslimness, as primarily about belonging, was still present in the early post-Soviet period, especially among those in Bazaar-Korgon, for example, who had come to maturity during the Soviet era. The collapse of the Soviet Union had, of course, profound effects on the region, allowing, among other things, new access to ideas, peoples, institutions, and objects from around the world, including notions, practices, and representations of Muslims and Islam. These frequently emphasized that being Muslim was primarily about belief. This view was disturbing to the majority of residents in town because it upset understandings and practices of Muslimness that focused on belonging; it likewise invalidated their everyday mode of religious and ethical life. Importantly, this understanding of Muslimness as a category of belief was also unsettling because it was not simply an alternative; it negated the idea of Muslimness as belonging. The two were, in the new formulation, incompatible. This was upsetting to many people.

This new idea of Muslimness centered on belief not only came from outside the region but was advocated by many of those "interested in Islam" (*dinge kyzyktuu bölüp kaluu*) in town as well. The discourses and actions of those close to Islam were perceived of by many others in town as linked with the kinds of ideas and practices attributed to religious extremists in regional discourses about Wahhabis, making their presence, their practices, and their ideas, including those about Muslimness, more complex and troubling. Regional discourse about Wahhabis, circulating since the 1970s, built on older tropes of religious extremism. The geopolitical environment of the 2000s—with the U.S.-led "global war on terror"—and the pressure Russia, Europe, the United States, and China put on Kyrgyzstan to do its part in this "war," fortified negative discourses about Wahhabis and heightened the perceived need to monitor and control certain Islamic behaviors and teachings. These discourses were a palpable part of how religion was understood and evaluated in town and not just by those who might be skeptical of the interpretations and practices of Islam gaining ground. Those "interested in Islam" too were worried about the so-called "terrorists." Thus, just as debate characterized the post-Soviet religious landscape of Bazaar-Korgon and just as unease with and contestation of alternative ideas about Muslimness likewise depicted the post-Soviet religious landscape, so too did wrestling with the idea of extremism.

In the early 2000s the specter of Muslim extremism and the supposed radicalization of Central Asian Islam were all-pervasive in the literature on religion in the region. And yet these depictions of the region as a hotbed for religious extremism seemed very disconnected from what I saw in Bazaar-Korgon. The post-Soviet religious world was, of course, open to and more influenced by a wider array of ideas, people, and things. These likely included Salafi-oriented interpretations of Islam and Muslims with particular notions of "the state," as feared by foreign political observers. However, things like *Clone* were equally present, as were ideas like those taught by Tajideen and the wedding speaker, for example; these were, I would argue, more influential in the construction of religious life. The religious landscape of Bazaar-Korgon at the turn of the millennium was vibrant and diverse, dispelling the notion that a monolithic, nefarious Islam had somehow swept through and gathered up the unsuspecting Muslims of the region or that the flourishing of religion automatically led to uniformity or conservatism. Certainly this lively religious landscape was not always positively experienced or evaluated by townsfolk, but it was one in which residents actively interrogated, contested, experimented with, and shaped various interpretations of Islam and Muslimness. These were the primary hallmarks of religious life in Bazaar-Korgon at the very beginning of its post-Soviet flourishing.

Soviet Religion and Theories of Secularism

The statue of Lenin, long the focal point of the main square in Bazaar-Korgon, remained after the Soviet Union collapsed. Concerted move or tired oversight, the socialist icon had not been removed despite the political shifts, economic alterations, and decades that had passed. The socialist experience persisted. Lenin remained. But Lenin now shared the square with the mosque; the statue's outstretched hand pointed right to it. It made a difficult landscape to interpret, but it reflected, as it created, the contradictory, unexpected, and unsettling experience the residents had had with the political projects that had shaped the region over the previous hundred years, including varied ideas about religion articulated by the two unique but related projects of secularism.

Throughout this book I have argued that many Bazaar-Korgonians' ambiguous and unsettled reactions to the interpretations of Islam circulating in town had to do with the way they challenged their notions and practice of Muslimness. But I have also argued that this unease was sparked by challenges of another kind, namely, challenges to concepts of "religion" and "culture." It was a disquiet that lay not with how a specific religion was imagined or enacted but with how religion as a category per se was interpreted and experienced. What many of my interlocutors were struggling with, then, was an articulation of religion that premised the idea of individual, internal belief rather than a definition in which belonging was the most essential characteristic.

This empirical observation can, I assert, be used to reevaluate theoretical notions in the study of religion and secularism. Following Talal Asad, I argue that the authority and power of the modern state are derived, in part, from its control over the definition of religion; secularism, a political project, monitors this articulation and practice of religion to keep it within its proper borders. Therefore, that standard definition of religion as individual, internal belief, rather than being universal—as in a Geertzian articulation—is merely a modern secular formation. However, moving the argument forward, I suggest that this articulation must be even more thoroughly situated. Religion as individual, internal belief is merely a liberal secular articulation and one that suits the logics of liberal secular power. The notion of religion that forged and was forged by Soviet secularism, on the contrary, was one more premised on ideas about intersubjectivity, for example. A different secularism built around different logics and a different history created a different notion of religion—religion as belonging.

This particular articulation of religion was co-constituted in a milieu in which collectivity was emphasized and valorized, as in republican notions of citizenship or economics organized around redistribution, rather than the individual rights-bearing, independent economic agent of more liberal visions. Romantic, folklorized ideas of ethnicity and the nation were prominent, and religious traditions such as Islam and Orthodox Christianity provided particular scripts about religion, the community and person, and generative action, for example. All of these contributed to the particular idea of religion as it developed over the course of the Soviet period and within the Soviet secular project—an idea of religion not premised on individualized, internal belief but based primarily on the notion of collective belonging.

It is not, I argue, that other ideas about religion were not present in the Soviet Union. Certainly the idea of belief as part of religion was present in the Kyrgyz SSR during the Soviet period. However, under the conditions of Soviet secularism there was only one definition of religion that could be publicly articulated that did not essentially contradict or challenge the power of the state; that definition was wrapped up, however inadvertently, with the conditions for the state's existence. There was only one definition that, when publicly deployed as a part of ethnonational-religious identity, was important for gaining access to certain rights, goods, and privileges and that was, in some cases, necessary to obtain those benefits. There was likewise only one articulation that co-created a field in which one could imagine oneself as a good Muslim, Kyrgyz or Uzbek, and Soviet. This was religion as belonging, an understanding that had been (inadvertently and temporarily) cultivated by, and in conversation with, Soviet secularism.

An Afterword on Violence, Fear, and Research in Bazaar-Korgon

I embarked on a study of Islam in Bazaar-Korgon at what was, in hindsight, an exceptional moment in the growth and spread of Islam in Kyrgyzstan. When I arrived in Kyrgyzstan in 2003 and began talking to people in Bishkek, in Osh, and in Bazaar-Korgon itself, everyone commented that Bazaar-Korgon was the right spot for research on Islam. Something was happening there, they said. They turned out to be right. Missionary groups were coming to the town, from which other such groups were departing for other places. New-style weddings were being organized. A soap opera that everyone loved featured Muslims. I was led into a network of home-based religious schools and the various meetings they organized. Books, pamphlets, and other printed materials were becoming increasingly available, and cassette tapes with recordings of well-known Islamic speakers were circulating. In addition, everyone was discussing these things—and not only in interviews with me. I overheard conversations at public and semipublic events; I listened to and participated in discussions at local cafés, parties, and all sorts of meetings or gatherings. I was fortunate to be in the right place at the right time.

I was not new to Bazaar-Korgon when I began my fieldwork, and it was not by chance that I chose the town as my research site. I had lived and worked there for two years as a Peace Corps volunteer from 1998 to 2000. This prior residency in the town facilitated my anthropological research. I knew and was known by many and was familiar with daily life and the "workings" of the town. I had connections, I knew the languages, and I could feel at home. I was also aware of public discussions, local gossip, and political issues in town. In short, the town had become my home. When I returned three years later with my children, I returned to a network of acquaintances, former students, friends, and adopted family. I could easily and happily settle in and start my work. Everyone was more than willing to help and support me. It made for an easy, engaging, and wonderful research period, professionally and personally. I was lucky.

What is interesting to note, when thinking about how pleasant my fieldwork experience was, is that the region had long been characterized in academic, policy-oriented, media-generated, or NGO-produced writings as ripe for violence. Reading about the region could make one fear to venture there. In the 1990s the fear was about ethnic violence, likely to "flare up," the literature predicted, because of the region's variegated ethnic composition, its densely populated land, and its water-related issues. Later, it was violence in the name of Islam that occupied the imaginations of observers. The Fergana Valley was seen as a particularly dangerous place in the wider region of Central Asia—also broadly characterized as a "hotbed" of Islamic radicalism. I found these fears to be terribly unfounded and rooted in concerns far from Central Asia itself.

When I conducted my fieldwork, academic and popular writings about Islam in Central Asia had two general foci—the threat of radical Islam and/or the celebration of religion "released" or "revived" from seventy years of Soviet atheism. These foci, not coincidentally, lined up with the two main perceived "threats" or "enemies" of American politics over the last century—the communist atheist

FIGURE C.1. By 2015, a new entrance to the mosque complex had been built. Photograph by the author, 2015.

and the radical Muslim. In the American imagination both enemies suppress "freedom" and pose unique religious threats. The communist atheist is seen as suppressing religion at best and aiming to destroy it at worst. The radical Muslim supposedly distorts and radicalizes religion, or at least the wrong religion, and his victory, much like that of the atheist, would signal the end of the "American way of life," including freedom of religion. Given the spread of the "global war on terror" and Russia's own fixation with Islamic extremism, a similar preoccupation with so-called Islamic extremism exists in the literature on religion in Central Asia produced by many scholars from the former Soviet Union, including Russians and Central Asians.

The fear of these enemies, given form as analytical lenses and research agendas with which to examine the region, profoundly shaped investigations of religion in the region. But once I started my research it became clear very quickly that the way religion in Central Asia was being interpreted in the literature did not square with the actual lived experiences of my interlocutors or with the way I understood power, religion, or personal agency to work. What made things more complex for me, however, was that suspicions of religious extremism in the town itself were very high and figured prominently in understandings and practices of religion—even if there was little to no evidence of the suspected interpretations of Islam and its proponents in town. And while both frames—the communist atheist and the radical Muslim—were problematic from empirical and theoretical standpoints, the notion of religious radicalism, at the time I conducted my research, was a dangerous and very political one as well.

I had vigorously avoided discourses of religious extremism when I initially set out to do my research. But as I watched and listened to the flourishing of religious life, and the concomitant construction of a secular one, I could not ignore the role that the suspicion of religious extremism played in the production of both. I included the social lives of these tropes and rumors in my work, even as I disavowed the fixation with "religious extremists" found in the literature.

My fieldwork on religion in Bazaar-Korgon constituted my second extended stay in Kyrgyzstan. I would make two additional research trips between then and the publication of this book. However, I never returned there to research religion following the fieldwork conducted for this book in 2003 and 2004. There is no real update as to what happened, though I have made a few observations, of course. In 2009, for example, Ziyod had serious questions about his commitment to Islam and it no longer occupied the place it once had for him. Traces of *Clone* could still be found in the market but were nearly gone. There were a few places in nearby Jalal-Abad where you could buy the kind of clothes Mukadas had desired in 2003. Gulmira was not "doing much" more with Islam, to use her words, than she was five years earlier.

By 2015, Mukadas had changed her style of veiling again, covering her nose and mouth when she left the home. Two of her three younger sisters had begun wearing a *hijab*, as had her eldest daughter. Both of her daughters studied at a summer madrasa for girls that had recently opened. Construction on the Friday

FIGURE C.2. Bazaar-Korgon rayon Friday mosque. Photograph by the author, 2015.

FIGURE C.3. Entrance to the Friday mosque complex (*center*) with additional prayer room (*left*). Photograph by the author, 2015.

FIGURE C.4. Gilded Lenin, 2015. Photograph by the author, 2015.

mosque had continued, and a new, external prayer room on an adjacent lot had been built, as had a new gate to mark the entrance to the complex. A separate women's section that had been planned never materialized. When I observed attendance during Ramadan in 2015, not only were the mosque complex, the porch of the teahouse, and the prayer room full, but all the outdoor space surrounding these was as well. The hijab appeared more widespread, and there were stalls at the Bazaar-Korgon bazaar where you could purchase a wider variety of clothes suitable to women wishing to cover more of their bodies. The bazaar itself had dramatically expanded, ballooning across the adjacent road and on to the other side, and now it was constructed out of cheap shipping containers. More neighborhood mosques had been constructed. Both Lenin statues remained, though in 2015 they had both been painted gold, like all Lenin statues across Kyrgyzstan.

Although these things were visible to me, the social landscape of the town had radically changed in the intervening years, making follow-up research impossible. Two revolutions had profoundly marked the political and economic terrain of the country, but, more importantly, the 2010 ethnic violence in southern Kyrgyzstan had left deep, profound changes and very painful scars. Any new research in town would have to take those events into account, and I was not prepared to do so. Unfortunately, the worries from the 1990s literature on the region

FIGURE C.5. One of two cafés operated by two businesswomen, and frequented by the author during 1998–2000 and 2003–4, burned during the violence in 2010. The charred building remained in 2015. Photograph by the author, 2015.

about ethnic violence had proven to be true, but not for the reasons often speculated about then. Much of the writing produced at that time and again in 2010 relied on reified notions of ethnic identity and supposed "ancient" or "inherent" difference and tension, which led, in these explanations, inexorably to violence, ignoring the messy multidimensionality of identity work and the way specifically located political crisis and violence become ethnicized (Reeves 2010b).

Bazaar-Korgon was a site of major violence in 2010. During three horrible days, I received a number of terrified phone calls and several emails describing horrendous events. I have never asked, but given the variety and number of people I know, I very likely know perpetrators of crimes as well as victims. I wrote two articles on the violence—at the behest of my friends there—and decided shortly thereafter not to do so again. I simply could not and did not want to deal, in an academic way, with the horrors of that moment. I knew that no matter what topic I might research, that moment of violence and what it did would come up. I decided to close the book on my research in town not long after the violence occurred.

My suspicions proved to be true. When I visited Bazaar-Korgon in 2015, five years after the violence, I never asked about it, but everyone brought it up. "War" (*sogush*) was the word my friends used to speak about it. It took some getting used to the vocabulary, as I'd always reflected on the events with the English word *violence* in mind. I was jarred when friends would say, "Oh, you know, the war. . . ." At first I got lost in the conversation, trying to think about which war they meant. It took several conversations to realize that that was the way the ethnic violence came to be spoken of in town. As I began to hear stories and as I saw pictures of the events, I realized why. In addition to the violence perpetrated by civilians, there had been all manner of military vehicles and weaponry in town. For residents, it must have felt like a war. I could see and hear the trauma in my friends' words, eyes, dispositions, and stories.

No research could simply "follow up" and see how things had developed without considering the enormity of what had changed and without facing the trauma that had marked the town. It was a task I was unwilling undertake. My research ended when I left, and what is here is the situated knowledge of religious life in a small Kyrgyz-Uzbek town produced from that period of fieldwork in 2003 and 2004. It was a unique moment in which religious life was flourishing, the economic crisis was easing, and residents of Bazaar-Korgon were negotiating, creating, and contesting what it meant to be a Muslim in the early post-Soviet period.

APPENDIX

NOTES ON FIELDWORK

This book is based on fourteen months of anthropological fieldwork conducted in Kyrgyzstan in 2003 and 2004. Eleven months were spent in the town of Bazaar-Korgon and three months in the capital, Bishkek. This period of formal fieldwork was supported by two years of prior residence in Bazaar-Korgon (1998–2000), during which I worked as a Peace Corps volunteer teaching English in a local secondary school. During that time I not only learned Kyrgyz and made a start at Uzbek, but I also began to understand daily life in the small town, including how to live in a place gripped by economic and infrastructural decay. I also made friends, developed relationships with colleagues, students, and their families, and built extensive social networks in town and throughout the *rayon*. When I returned in 2003 to conduct fieldwork, my interlocutors initially came from these networks. These networks then branched out further and deepened; I also reached out to meet people outside my usual circles. Some of these were of course people who had "become interested in Islam" and who were teaching or learning Islam. But it was simultaneously important to me to develop relationships with those who were not among the individuals considered to have drawn "close to Islam." My interlocutors were male and female, Kyrgyz and Uzbek, young and old, and primarily poor or middle class.

During the eleven months I conducted research in town, I employed four methods of investigation: participant observation, in-depth interviewing, collecting of life histories, and conducting surveys. During my fieldwork, I attended religious meetings, witnessed rituals, took part in religious education courses, followed the construction of another new mosque, and even "observed" friends undergoing personal religious transformation. Importantly, I also watched and participated in the lives of those who did not take part in any religious events. In addition to the use of participant observation, I also conducted in-depth interviews with people in town. These fell into several categories: interviews aimed at eliciting specific information about practices, rituals, social life, and organizational matters; topical interviews into various themes relevant to my main research topic; interviews that sought to cross-check information I had gained through other means or through other interviews; and interviews conducted to elicit opinions. Most of these interviews were recorded, always with the permission of the interviewee.

I complemented these interviews with the collection of life histories. After six months of research, I chose eight individuals from whom I would collect life histories. These were people with whom I was already well acquainted. I chose the life-history approach specifically because I wanted to see if and how certain opinions, choices, and actions regarding various interpretations of Islam were related to elements in a person's biography. Having already noted that age, gender, ethnicity, and socioeconomic status affected the type and degree of an individual's religious participation, I chose people who came from various constellations of these demographic features. I also considered their religious beliefs (or lack thereof) and the individual's observance of religious prescriptions. I conducted between five and ten interviews of at least two hours each with each of these individuals. In addition, I spent significant time with them on an "informal" basis and interviewed their family and friends or other community members who had relevant opinions about them. Two of these situated life histories—Tajideen's and Mukadas's—are presented at length in this book.

Finally, I undertook two surveys during my fieldwork. The aim of these surveys was to provide additional insight concerning the relationship between biographical features—age, gender, education, socioeconomic status, ethnicity—and participation in certain religious observances. I had developed some impressions early on in my fieldwork and used the surveys to get a broader view. I conducted one series of surveys among ninth-grade students in three schools, two of which used Uzbek as a language of instruction while one used Kyrgyz. The second survey was a household survey also focusing on participation in religious observances. I conducted this survey in four different neighborhoods—two with exclusively Uzbek residents, one of mixed Uzbek-Kyrgyz households,

and one predominantly Kyrgyz neighborhood. I chose the neighborhoods because their ethnic composition reflected the main demographic patterns of the
town. I chose two all-Uzbek neighborhoods simply because the majority of the
population (80 percent) is Uzbek. In each case I chose a neighborhood where I
had a few personal contacts. I selected one street of approximately ten to fifteen
houses in each location and surveyed every household on the street. In the instances where I did not know a member of a particular household, I took along
a friend or acquaintance who lived on the same street to introduce me. In the
case of the predominantly Kyrgyz neighborhood, I conducted the survey in an
apartment building. I used the survey as a structured interview, verbally asking
and explaining each question and writing the answers myself. The total number
of household surveys completed was fifty-one.

NOTES

Introduction

1. On the persistence of Lenin statues in Kyrgyzstan, see the book by Liu (2012, 69–73).

2. See, e.g., works by Brenner (1996), Deeb (2006), Hefner (2005), Hirschkind (2006), Mahmood (2005), Saktanber (2002), Smith-Hefner (2007), Werbner (2007), and White (2002).

3. On these disappointments see, e.g., works by Boehm (1999) and Pelkmans (2005).

4. Those in town who were "interested in Islam" were a primary source for encounters with these ideas, though, importantly, there were other sources for the notion that religion was primarily, if not exclusively, about inner faith. These included television serials, printed materials, and Kyrgyzstani citizens who had traveled abroad for a variety of reasons, as well as Muslim and Christian missionaries, NGO workers, and a whole host of materials about democracy, the rule of law, and capitalism that came as a part of Kyrgyzstan's so-called transition from socialism to democracy.

5. For notable exceptions, see works by Smolkin-Rothrock (2010), Luehrmann (2011), and Wanner (2012, 1–26).

6. The literature on religion and/or collective belonging in (post) socialist spaces is replete with examples of, and references to, the inseparability of religion and national belonging. See, e.g., works by Bringa (1995), Ro'i (2000), Privratsky (2001), Pelkmans

(2006), Khalid (2007), Louw (2007), Wanner (2007), Hilgers (2009), Ghodsee (2009), Rogers (2009), İğmen (2012), and Wanner (2012).

7. A similar conclusion can be read in Gregor McLennan's (2010, 5) discussion of the postsecular turn, in which he notes "commentators like José Casanova (2006, 20) and William Connolly (2006, 75) perceive Asad as systematically challenging not only 'the established unconscious of European culture,' but also 'the secular self-understanding of modernity that is constitutive of the social sciences.'"

8. For example, see works by van der Veer (1994), van der Veer and Lehmann (1999), Navaro-Yashin (2002), Mahmood (2005), Hirschkind (2006), Bowen (2007, 2010), Engelke (2009), Cannell (2010), Verkaaik and Spronk (2011), Bubandt and van Beek (2012), Bracke and Fadil (2008), Fadil (2013), and Agrama (2012).

9. The important works reviewed were by Warner, VanAntwerpen, and Calhoun (2010), Calhoun, Juergensmeyer, and VanAntwerpen (2011), and Mendieta and VanAntwerpen (2011).

10. For examples, see the works of Hann and Goltz (2010), Wanner (2012), Mahieu and Naumescu (2008), Naumescu (2007), Köllner (2013); Benovska-Sabkova et al. (2010), Makrides (2012), and Fokas (2012).

11. Russians' evaluation of Orthodox Christianity during the development of a modern sense of nation is a case that shows the ambiguous normative evaluation of religions but no ambiguity about the idea of religion as being about belonging. In his discussion of colonial Tashkent, Jeff Sahadeo (2007, 72), for example, sketches the way that Russian officials perceived of themselves vis-à-vis Europe, their "civilizing mission" in Turkestan, and their role as Russians in a colonial city. Sahadeo argues that in 1866 the military analyst Lev Kostenko saw the link between Orthodoxy and the Russian state as a sign of backwardness compared to states in Europe; Tashkent was, for him and others, to be a place of religious freedom, and they saw themselves as on a civilizing mission, not a religious one. At the same time, Orthodox Christianity in Tashkent "appeared during selected ceremonies as a primary, if not only, marker of Russian nationhood" (72). Moreover, despite the stated areligious nature of their civilizing mission, both Governor-General Konstantin von Kaufman and General M. A. Ternet'ev linked their mission in Turkestan to a "greater Christian mission" or "Christian cosmopolitanism" (72). Thus, religion was negatively evaluated as backward while being consolidated as a primary marker for collective (national) belonging. Also apparent was the desire to create a political and social space (a Russian imperial Tashkent) free from religion in order to allow freedom for all religions while at the same time framing the supposedly areligious "mission" that brought the Russians to the area in terms of a Christian, civilizing one. The landscape of religion and politics was complex and contradictory, but written all over it was religion bound up with collective belonging and processes of identification.

12. As Wanner (2007, 4) describes for Ukraine in the eighteenth century, for example, the arrival of Protestantism introduced another notion of religion in which

personal conviction, rather than "ascriptive attribute of identity bestowed at birth" was its primary feature.

13. For example, Catherine the Great's policies and notions were cultivated in line with European Enlightenment ideals (Crews 2006, 2). As previously mentioned, German intellectuals and travelers directly contributed to ideas of "nation" and the means of classifying and understanding them that were prominent during the time of Peter the Great, but these ideas were influenced by romanticism and orientalism. The Jadids, Muslim intellectuals and reformers in Central Asia, understood their work as a campaign to modernize Islam (Khalid 1998) and can be linked to similar reformist movements in the Crimea, Turkey, and Iran (Geraci 1997). It is also known that a prominent Tatar reformer studied at the Sorbonne and attended lectures by Émile Durkheim (Geraci 1997), whose own ideas about religion emphasized solidarity, collective effervescence, and cohesion. Similarly, in territories that are part of contemporary Ukraine, eighteenth-century Protestant missionaries who had liberal ideas of religion not only taught about particular religious notions but "introduced the possibility that religious practice did not have to be an ascriptive attribute of identity bestowed at birth, as was historically the cultural and legal norm throughout the Russian Empire. Protestant proselytizers proposed that religious identity was a personal choice, a conscious decision based on conviction developed after a spiritual encounter" (Wanner 2007, 4). This was threatening, explains Catherine Wanner, "because it represented the decoupling of nationality and religion as an organic entity" (4).

14. Adrienne Lynn Edgar (2004, 17–40) indicates, for example, that the Turkmen elite were able to conceive of a Turkmen nation, in the modern sense of the word, and thus engage with and sometimes support the nation-building efforts, because there was already a sense of wider belonging among the various tribes based on lineage.

15. The paranji was a large, shirtlike covering worn by some female inhabitants of the Fergana Valley at the end of the tsarist era and beginning of the Soviet period. The garment was draped over the head and hung loosely over the body. It was open in the front and was either pulled closed by the woman wearing it or was worn with a *chachvan*, a rough horsehair veil that extended from the top of the paranji over the face and down the length of the body.

16. Hujum is the name given to the campaign aimed at liberating Central Asian women. Its iconic feature was the unveiling of women.

17. This is not unlike other parts of the Muslim world where Western colonial powers sought control. The issue of Islam's supposed oppression of women, as symbolized through her "imprisonment" in the veil, became central to debates about deficiencies in Islam and Muslim societies (Ahmed 1992, 164; Moors 1998, 210). Instead of taking issue with the colonial focus on women and with the veil as the appropriate symbol of Islam, Muslims' counterarguments implicitly accepted the veil's new symbolic role, and they launched their retaliation by extolling its virtues. Thus, it was as much the colonized as

the colonizers who made gender and gender seclusion central to the debates over Islam. For an important discussion of the role of gender in the socialist secularizing projects of Yugoslavia and Bulgaria, see the article by Ballinger and Ghodsee (2011).

18. See, e.g., works by Ro'i (1984), Carrère d'Encausse (1979), and Kowalewski (1980).

19. See the piece by Verdery (2006) for similar arguments about socialist Europe.

20. See the article by Khalid (2003) for an excellent description of this process.

21. Regarding citizenship, Dov Yaroshevski (1997) argues that ideas from the late Russian imperial era, from which as least some socialist practices and ideas arose, were rooted in a republican as opposed to a liberal interpretation. They prioritized "value-oriented activity in joint endeavors of citizens striving for the good of each one and contributing to the good of others, and through this participation aiming at the well-being of the whole. It emphasizes a community of values shared by associations of citizens. One of the basic principles of this sort of citizenship is that private ends should be subjected to the public good" (1997, 60).

22. Artemy Kalinovsky's (forthcoming, 154–55) work on post–World War II development projects in Tajikistan illustrates this articulation of the interpersonal logics. He demonstrates how efforts to "develop" this part of the Soviet Central Asian periphery were rooted in a material alteration of the environment, as in the construction of the Nurek Dam and the projects associated with it. Those who were involved imagined and enacted transformation at the level of, and based on, the collective efforts of the nation or the family, for example. Roads and sanitation projects, he argues, get bound up with nationality politics, and raising living standards was to be accomplished by transforming the village. United efforts made change, and the change was imagined as happening to the collective, even if this meant reinforcing and inadvertently creating a sense of belonging (to a community, whether Tajik, Muslim, or nuclear family) that would someday be superseded.

23. In Asad's example, the Greek Orthodox Church alleged that a change in information on identity cards in connection with Greece's entering the European Union "curtail[ed] the right of citizens to express their religious affiliation publicly if they so desire." Removing their religious affiliation from the IDs was a breach of their rights, the Church argued. The state did not agree, insisting that the alteration was not a threat to the Orthodox faith. In doing so, the government "claim[ed] to identify the essence of that faith" (Asad 2003, 139), moving the discussion from what Orthodox Church members "regard as vital to their religious being" to "what does and what does not affect their freedom of religious belief" (140). Mahmood's work deals with Muslims' appeal to hate speech laws in reaction to the Danish cartoons depicting the prophet Mohammad in 2005 and 2008. The redress they sought on these grounds was considered invalid by legal critics who argued that the hate speech laws were designed with race in mind—an identity based on (biological) belonging, not belief. Muslims' articulations of their Muslimness

were invalid, the critics argued, because Muslimness had to do with religion—essentially defined as a matter of choice dealing with belief—and not the type of belonging the law had in mind.

24. For some interesting inquiries and comparisons of Western secularisms and the variant understandings and regulation of religion, see the literature on secularisms previously mentioned, as well as investigations on religion by, for example, Hann (2006, 153–76) and Werbner (2007).

25. The attempt to eliminate religion occurred in different modes, however, some of which allowed for toleration of religion "in the meantime" (Tasar 2010).

1. On Being Muslim in Bazaar-Korgon

1. In the same location during the late Soviet period there had been a small market where inhabitants bought and sold fruit, vegetables, and meat produced on their domestic plots. The new bazaar is much larger than the old market and the range of products available much greater.

2. Sergei Abashin (2006, 278–79) observed a similar event during his research in "village O," Tajikistan, in the late 1980s. Villagers of "O" similarly classified the visitors as "Wahhabis."

3. This is quite similar to the way Magnus Marsden (2005a, 8–23) describes religious experience among Muslims in northwestern Pakistan.

4. See the work of Ibañez-Tirado (2015) for an interesting challenge to the idea of "post-Soviet."

5. Despite its classification as a village (*aiyl*) I call Bazaar-Korgon a town because of its physical size, the size of its population, and its function as a center of economic and bureaucratic activity. Moreover, in 2003 procedures were set in motion to have it administratively reclassified as a small town (*shaarcha*) or town (*shaar*).

6. On the violence, see the work of Reeves (2010a, 2010b).

7. One sotik is one-hundredth of a hectare.

8. Cotton was the most common crop, but sunflowers, onions, and potatoes were also prominent.

9. On labor migration and remittances, see works by Isabaeva (2011), Reeves (2012), and Rubinov (2014).

10. It is difficult to judge these statistics because the documents gave no information regarding how poverty was defined for the study or how the statistics were gathered.

11. The students and development workers were discussing bride kidnapping (*ala kachuu*).

12. Judith Beyer (2016, chap. 3) argues similarly for Talas, Kyrgyzstan, noting that "international organizations are today regarded as the main providers and caretakers," especially as "the state is increasingly perceived as unreliable even in the presence of its officials."

13. For a wide-ranging overview, see especially the articles collected in *ISIM Review* (vol. 20, Fall 2007, http://openaccess.leidenuniv.nl/handle/1887/4949).

14. Alisher Khamidov (2013, 148–49) comes to a similar conclusion and provides an excellent analysis of local politics and their role in whether or not religion becomes a mobilized category in acts of protest and violence.

15. All names are pseudonyms except for those of public figures whose identity would be impossible to conceal.

16. *Davatchi* means one who gives *davat* (an invitation to participate in Islam); for a full discussion of davat, see chapter 3.

17. For more detailed discussions of the "great" and "little" tradition in Islam in reference to Central Asia, see the work of Rasanayagam (2006a). For a more recent inquiry into the problems and benefits of this kind of conceptualization in anthropological studies of religion, see the edited volume by Schielke and Debevec (2012).

18. I have no evidence for this claim about drug trafficking save for gossip and observation. The wealth of two or three families in town—even when compared with that of the owners of the most profitable cotton business—is too great not to be of suspicious origins.

19. For examples of this kind of logic in the media, see the editorial in the *Bishkek Observer*, 29 July 2003, or an interview with then–Kyrgyz president Askar Akaev, 24 June 1997, at www.eisenhowerinstitute.org.

20. According to statistics gathered by the town government, by 2001, 25 percent of the town's population was Kyrgyz.

21. Examples of these regulated practices include veiling, fasting at Ramadan, *zakat* (alms), pilgrimage, and Islamic education outside of the two approved madrasas in Bukhara and Tashkent. A number of practices were technically permitted, but oral histories indicate that attendance was monitored and highly discouraged for those who were not party members; party members could not attend.

22. This is not an explanation that can be applied, through inference, to the whole country, however.

23. One particular Soviet reading of Marx—as exemplified by Poljakov's (1992) work—would argue that those who were "religious" in the post-Soviet period were the people never completely "reached" by the Soviet economic, political, and antireligious campaigns and thus were those still attached to "traditional" ways of life, including religious commitment.

2. Listening to the Wedding Speaker

1. The acronym ZAGS refers to the office for the registration of civil status.

2. A moldo is a religiously knowledgeable man.

3. Nikoh (Uzbek), or nike (Kyrgyz), was the part of a marriage ceremony officiated by a religious specialist. It is usually done at home and is, for most residents, the minimal requirement for a marriage.

4. Sunnat (Uzbek) refers to practices in Islam derived from the Prophet's teachings and habits. Ibodat (Uzbek) means worship. Unlike the weddings studied by Sophie Roche and Sophie Hohmann (2011, 122), however, this attempt to create an Islamic wedding did not explicitly link the practice of proper Islam to an imagined pre-Soviet Central Asia.

5. However, there is another reason why I find economic interpretations less than satisfactory in explaining these changes. Although ascribing changes in the wedding rituals to religion might sometimes be a means of presenting a change made for socially unacceptable (i.e., financial) reasons in a more morally satisfactory manner (i.e., by recourse to religion), the religious explanations, as well as the interpretations of Islam to which they are attached, are not well received in Bazaar-Korgon. In fact, I would wager that similar changes justified in explicitly economic terms would be more acceptable in the town than those explained through Islamic discourses.

6. Namaz or *salat* is the name for the prayers to be performed five times daily.

7. Noruz is a holiday locally thought of as the Muslim New Year. It is celebrated on 21 March.

8. The hayits are the religious holidays commemorating Ibrahim's willingness to sacrifice his son (Kurban Hayit) and the end of Ramadan (Roza Hayit).

9. Such a discussion would reveal an interesting facet of the weddings and the debate over orthodoxy (Asad 1986, 15–16). I have argued in this chapter that the wedding is part of the debate over orthodoxy between those who understand religion to be primarily about belief and those who do not (in essence, those for whom it is more a category of belonging). However, the wedding is also a public space where debates over orthodoxy occur among Muslims who, by and large, all adhere to scripturally oriented interpretations of Islam and share a common idea about the nature of religion. This discussion would further reveal the complexity of religious ideas in the community.

10. The texts referred to in the wedding speaker's message were the Quran, hadiths, and writings from the Hanafi legal school.

11. Zaochno is a Russian word and describes a program of "distance learning." A student is officially registered at a university but is allowed to study at home. Students are required to appear in person at the university at the end of each term to take their exams. Studying zaochno is much less costly than a regular course of study.

12. I use the term hijab here to refer to the style of veiling in which a headscarf fully covers the hair and ears. It is fastened below the chin, fully covering the neck. The remainder of the scarf is draped over the shoulders. Residents themselves, however, rarely use the term. If it is, it is used to describe the overcoatlike covering worn by many Muslim women worldwide, rather than the style of veil.

13. Spaces and activities are often gendered in Bazaar-Korgon, with men at a party eating in one room and women in another. However, the wedding ceremony was different because of the curtain that prohibited the sexes from even seeing one another. In this way the practice of separation was heightened and the idea behind the practice somehow

altered. Whereas in other contexts the separation can be read as "men should eat/be with men" and "women with women," here the implicit meaning was "men and women should not be together nor see one another."

14. There are interesting parallels between the role of the new weddings in religious exploration and the role of the peer groups in the lives of youth in Bazaar-Korgon and the place of religious lessons among the youth in Dushanbe, studied by Manja Stephan (2010).

15. On varying articulations of Muslimness, see works by Hilgers (2006) and Rasanayagam (2006c). Christian groups' creation and use of rituals further heightened the post-Soviet politicization of culture. On this point see Pelkmans's (2007) article.

3. Living and Learning Islam

1. Limited coverage of the episode was provided by the Keston News Service, 16 August 2001, http://www.starlight.co.uk/keston/kns/2001/010816KY-02.htm, last accessed 2008.

2. I have used Tajideen's real name because it would be impossible to hide his identity even if a pseudonym was used. I also have used the real names of all his teachers. Names of all other Bazaar-Korgon residents are pseudonyms.

3. The attendance numbers vary on a weekly and especially on a seasonal basis. Numbers are higher in the winter, when agricultural work is at a minimum. The numbers cited here are based on my own observations. I collected my data in two ways. First, I regularly went to the mosques on Fridays, and although I was not allowed inside, I was able to count the shoes that were left outside the building. Second, I waited outside on the grounds until prayers concluded and was thus able to perform a rough count as the men left the building and socialized on the grounds. In his 2004 report to the qazi, the imam of the rayon reported average attendance as between one thousand and twelve hundred. Attendance peaked at the end of Ramadan (November 2003), when approximately thirty-five hundred men attended Friday prayers. A large portion of them prayed outside the building. I gathered my data then through similar methods, but in this case I was also able to obtain a copy of a video recording that had been made inside the building during the Ramadan prayers. I was thus able to more easily count the number of men inside. Since I was outside the building that morning, I was also able to count the number of men outside the mosque.

4. This figure was documented by the rayon head imam in his 2004 report to the qazi on the mosques and imams under his supervision.

5. Attendance for Friday prayers in this smaller Friday mosque is two hundred to three hundred men.

6. Judith Beyer (2016) describes a similar process in Talas, Kyrgyzstan.

7. See Johan Rasanayagam's (2006a) piece for a thorough discussion of the Soviet-era scholarship. See the article by Peshkova (2014) for a discussion of how this dichotomy was likewise gendered.

8. See, e.g., works by Kemper, Motika, and Reichmuth (2010), Kemper (2014), Sartori (2010), all of the articles in the special edition (vol. 50, no. 3–4) of *Die Welt des Islams* published in 2010, Epkenhaus (2011), and Dudoignon and Noack (2013).

9. For a related argument concerning Old Believers in rural Russia, see the monograph by Rogers (2009, 185–89).

10. See also Tasar's (2010) dissertation on the issue of being Soviet and Muslim.

11. Luehrmann's (2011) work on Soviet secularism in the Volga region of Russia details a similar pattern in which didactic skills utilized in the Soviet period for antireligious campaigns are deployed in the post-Soviet context for religious education.

12. The historical account that follows is a synthesis of works on the Central Asian ulama by Babadjanov (2004), Babadjanov and Kamilov (2001), Babadzhanov (1999), Saroyan (1997), and Shahrani (2005).

13. According to Babadjanov and Kamilov (2001, 201), "many Hanafite theologians in the Ferghana consider [Hakimjon] to be (perhaps with justification) the father of all 'neo-Wahhabist' groups in the Valley."

14. I have chosen the designation "reformers," though with certain reservations because of the likely heterogeneity of the group. It most likely involved ulama with Salafi orientations—those typically labeled as reformers in much of the anthropological literature on Islam, as well as Hanafi ulama involved in criticizing the so-called popular forms of Islam. Of course, those potential Salafis and critical Hanafis differed in their opinions, but the existing literature does not reveal whom the Soviet authorities allowed more liberties.

15. See the work of Sergei Abashin (2006) for a similar argument about labels. He states that "moderation and aggressiveness, tolerance and dogmatism, local and foreign are terms that are ascribed to this dichotomous model. However, in my opinion they do not characterize *hajis*, *mashrums*, or any group such as the descendants of saints. They are tools and perceptions which these groups manipulate in the complex game they play out in the religious field, which in turn mediates access to positions of status and influences in the community" (2006, 283). See also Hilgers's (2009) monograph.

16. The terms "terrorist" and "extremist" are also used in Bazaar-Korgon. Even when Kyrgyz or Uzbek are being spoken, however, the Russian words for these terms—which themselves are English cognates—are used.

17. Babadjanov and Kamilov (2001) continue to use this term in an otherwise excellent article.

18. Tablighi Jamaat is a global Islamic devotional movement primarily concerned with teaching good Muslim faith and practice.

19. The texts Amina said she used were the Quran, hadiths, and Chagatai texts that she said were by "our own religious scholars." She named Imam Bukhori, Attermiziy, and Ibn Kassir.

20. On this point see also works by Ro'i (2000, 144), Dudoignon (2011), and Peshkova (2014), but for a contrasting view about the Islamic revival in Kazakhstan see the article by Schwab (2012).

21. This is not to say that everyone who attends a study group necessarily takes a pious turn, attends the groups regularly, or retains a sustained interest in learning about Islam. However, the number does at least give an indication of the widespread interest in learning more about Islam in Bazaar-Korgon.

22. See the article by Dudoignon (2011, 72) for a similar argument about Tajikistan, as well as works by Kemper, Motika, and Reichmuth (2010) and Kemper (2014) for arguments about other Muslim regions of the former Soviet Union.

23. It is intriguing to compare the debates and movements in Soviet Central Asia to what Barbara Metcalf (2002) has called the "traditional" reformist groups of the Tablighi and the Deobandi. There are congruencies between the Deobandis and Tablighis and the Central Asian reformists. And while there is a solid basis for believing that there have been recent and long-term connections, there are no firm data (however, see the work of Dudoignon [2011]). Beyond the practice of davat, one of the other most striking similarities between the ulama in Bazaar-Korgon and the Deobandi is the articulation of a reformist, yet apolitical agenda (with variation in the degree and severity of reform) and an emphasis on proselytizing. Metcalf (2002, 16) notes that "the historical pattern launched by the Deobandi *ulama* for the most part treated political life on a primarily secular basis." However, without firm evidence of historical connection between the groups to explain the similarity, one could also argue that the congruence was a result of the shared framework of secularism, nation-states, and modern conceptions of religion and politics. The matter awaits further investigation. By the late 2000s, the Tablighi Jamaat was publicly present in Kyrgyzstan, and Kyrgyzstani Tablighi were open about their membership. On the Tablighi in Kyrgyzstan, see the work of Balci (2012, 2015). However, in 2003–4, no one I knew in Bazaar-Korgon made reference to them, claimed to be a member, or even seemed to know what or who they were. Although groups like Hizb ut-Tahrir were present in town and spoken of, I never once encountered the term "Tablighi" in Bazaar-Korgon—even in a negative sense—and no one seemed to know what it was.

24. By 2016 this situation had changed and lessons were being offered in the summer to elementary and high school girls at madrasa. This is also in contrast to urban centers like Almaty, in Kazakhstan, where other forms of Islamic education are open to women (see Schwab 2012).

25. See also Liu's (2012, 117–20) comments on *ziyofat*s in Osh.

26. For a similar discussion on transnational discourses about Muslim women, modernity, and civilization, see the essay by McBrien (2006), and see also the article by Deeb (2009).

27. Tolombai claims that he opposed Tajideen because Tajideen was a Wahhabi and got his money from Osama bin Laden. He describes the architecture of the mosque as fitting for a fortress, not a place of prayer. He says it does suit Tajideen and all his "terrorist" followers who need a place to hide. Tolombai remains in his teahouse day and night so as to "protect it" from "terrorists" who he believes want to burn it down.

28. By that time, Tajideen's own connection in the rayon government was no longer around.

29. Others who had talked to Tajideen directly or who had heard accounts of Tajideen's side of the story similarly remarked on his unwillingness to blame or make accusations against his opponents. They cited his ability to refrain from defaming those who had launched such an attack against him as evidence of his pure character.

30. No major work was done on the grounds of the mosque while I was researching the topic. In the summer of 2004, prior to the awaited visit of the president of Kyrgyzstan to Bazaar-Korgon, some ground was cleared and new decorative fencing was placed around the grounds. Toktosun informed me that no other major work was planned, as there were no further funds available.

31. On Jadids, see Khalid's (1998) book.

4. Mukadas's Struggle

1. See the work of Abu-Lughod (2002) and Moors (2007).

2. On Suleiman's Mountain, see the work of Liu (2012, 36–38).

3. Eisenstadt (2000a) deals only with the communist and socialist revolutions. For a fuller discussion of the Soviet Union as modern, see works by Arnason (1993, 2000). For theories of multiple modernities, see various works by Eisenstadt (1992, 2000a, 2000b, 2003). For an argument against multiple modernities based on post-Soviet fieldwork, see the book by Mostowlansky (2017).

4. For a similar assessment in Uzbekistan, see works by Hilgers (2006, 2009) and Rasanayagam (2006c, 2011).

5. For a similar situation in Bulgaria, see the Ghodsee's (2005) article.

6. For a comparison in the context of Turkey, see the book by Özyürek (2006).

7. Literally translated, the word *eskicha* means "old language." It is a common way of referring to the Arabic language. People who are learning to recite the Quran or who attend Islamic study groups in Kyrgyzstan are said to be studying eskicha. It is assumed that these people are "close to Islam."

5. The Propriety of Mosques

1. In September 2003, the then-dominant Kyrgyz mobile phone company—Mobi-Card—built a cell tower near Bazaar-Korgon. However, with so few able to afford a cell phone and the cost of calls, its effects on communication in the community were imperceptible.

2. Similar worries have been articulated by observers of the region, leading some to speak of the radicalization of Central Asian Islam, for example, Ahmed Rashid (2002).

3. On similar situations in Russia, see the book by Collier (2011).

4. Statistics about mosques and their construction come from documents provided by the imam of the Bazaar-Korgon rayon.

5. Victoria Smolkin-Rothrock (2010) has argued, however, that in the Khrushchev era there was a more general attempt by those involved in pro-atheism and antireligious campaigns to replace religion in the Soviet Union with a "Soviet spirituality." This campaign envisioned the culture houses as places where the leisure activity of the modern Soviet citizen would occur (2010, 67).

6. The madrasa would be open to men who had already completed secondary school and wished to pursue religious education. The rayon head imam, who oversaw the project, indicated that other subjects, such as computers and English, would be taught as well.

7. In the northern area of the country, many of the newly opened mosques remained largely empty, although in Bishkek this was not the case.

8. There are only two schools in town that use Kyrgyz as the language of instruction. The one that lies near the new mosque is the largest. It was built in the late 1970s as a part of the larger development projects going on in town. The other is a small boarding school located on a hill in an older area.

9. In 2000, Tekebaev was a candidate for president, but his candidacy was nullified by the courts. The charges were largely believed to be false and spurred protests in Bazaar-Korgon in 2000. Tekebaev was an opposition leader in the March 2005 revolutions and served as leader of the new parliament.

10. "WAMY's headquarters are based in Riyadh, Saudi Arabia. WAMY has regional as well various branches in and outside Saudi Arabia. Established in 1972, it has presence in 55 countries and an associate membership of over 500 youth organizations around the world. WAMY is a member of the United Nations NGOs (Non-Governmental Organizations), and recognized for its vast scope of humanitarian and relief work that encompasses about 60% of the Muslim World." World Assembly of Muslim Youth, United Kingdom, http://www.wamy.co.uk/index.htm, last accessed 2008.

11. Information regarding the funding of the mosque was a slightly sensitive topic, largely because the benefactor wished to remain anonymous. For this reason, it was difficult to obtain more detailed information.

12. On political myth, see the article by Bottici and Challand (2006).

13. For a concise view of the "overreaction" to Muslim charities, see the article by Benthall (2007).

14. WAMY's relative absence from the local community stands in contrast to other areas of the former socialist world where, for example, mosques funded by foreign donors have remained much more connected to those donors, international Muslim NGOs, and other actors (see, e.g., Ghodsee 2010, 130–58). Sustained connections may also be more prominent in larger urban centers such as Bishkek.

15. For a link between mosques and ethno-national-religious identity in the Soviet era, see the commentary by Ro'i (2000, 698).

6. Watching *Clone*

1. The original Portuguese title was *O Clone*, and the Spanish title was *El Clon*. I have rendered the title *Clone*. I chose to eliminate the definite article for my English translation of the title partly because it was referred to without the article in Kyrgyzstan.

2. For an excellent study of material religion and the way objects are used to cultivate piety in Kazakhstan, see works by Schwab (2012, 2014).

3. By 2009 this situation had changed. There were special stores in Jalal-Abad catering to these women, mostly at prices that the average inhabitant of Bazaar-Korgon could not afford.

4. *Deusa* is the Portuguese word for goddess.

5. Glória Perez, "*The Clone*: Plot Summary," IMDb.com, accessed 16 November 2004, http://www.imdb.com/title/tt0289800/plotsummary.

6. Gulmira's mother wore headscarves only at home.

7. Morten Axel Pedersen (2011, 9) describes what, in my opinion, is an analogous situation in northern Mongolia, where the Darhad people experienced a loss of shamanic knowledge and expertise needed to deal with the spiritual situation of the chaotic postsocialist environment. He sums up by saying that in the postsocialist period there was "plenty of shamanism but hardly any shamans."

8. While it is true that many residents acknowledge widespread ignorance about even the most basic tenets of Islam, they nonetheless take pride in themselves as some of the most "modern" or "advanced" Muslims. Residents thus have ambiguous feelings when they compare themselves to Muslims outside the region.

9. Interestingly, however, the makers of *Clone* employ an equation of religion and national identity similar to the Soviet-era idea. In *Clone*, Moroccans are, by definition, Muslims, while Brazilians are more variously portrayed as nonreligious, or Catholic, or involved with Candomblé, and so forth.

REFERENCES

Abashin, Sergei. 2006. "The Logic of Islamic Practice: A Religious Conflict in Central Asia." *Central Asian Survey* 25 (3): 267–86.

Abashin, Sergei. 2014. "A Prayer for Rain: Practicing Being Soviet and Muslim." *Journal of Islamic Studies* 25 (2): 178–200.

Abu-Lughod, Lila. 1993. "Islam and Public Culture: The Politics of Egyptian Television Serials." *Middle East Report* 180:25–30.

Abu-Lughod, Lila. 1995. "The Objects of Soap Opera: Egyptian Television and the Cultural Politics of Modernity." In *Worlds Apart: Modernity through the Prism of the Local*, edited by Daniel Miller, 190–210. London: Routledge.

Abu-Lughod, Lila. 2002. "Do Muslim Women Really Need Saving? Anthropological Reflections on Cultural Relativism and Its Others." *American Anthropologist* 104 (3): 783–90.

Abu-Lughod, Lila. 2004. *Dramas of Nationhood: The Politics of Television in Egypt*. Chicago: University of Chicago Press.

Agadjanian, Alexander, and Kathy Rousselet. 2010. "Individual and Collective Identities in Russian Orthodoxy." In *Eastern Christians in Anthropological Perspective*, edited by Chris Hann and Hermann Goltz, 311–28. Berkeley: University of California Press.

Agrama, Hussein Ali. 2010. "Secularism, Sovereignty, Indeterminacy: Is Egypt a Secular or a Religious State?" *Comparative Studies in Society and History* 52 (3): 495–523.

Agrama, Hussein Ali. 2012. "Reflections on Secularism, Democracy, and Politics in Egypt." *American Ethnologist* 39 (1): 26–31.

Ahmed, Leila. 1992. *Women and Gender in Islam: Historical Roots of a Modern Debate.* New Haven: Yale University Press.

Akiner, Shirin. 1993. *Political and Economic Trends in Central Asia.* London: British Academic Press.

Anderson, John. 2003. "Coping with Otherness: Dealing with Religious Minorities in Kyrgyzstan and Turkmenistan." Paper presented at the fourth annual Central Eurasian Studies Society conference, Harvard University, Cambridge, MA, 2–5 October.

Armbrust, Walter. 2006. "Synchronizing Watches: The State, the Consumer, and Sacred Time in Ramadan Television." In *Religion, Media, and the Public Sphere*, edited by Birgit Meyer and Annelies Moors, 207–26. Bloomington: Indiana University Press.

Arnason, Johann P. 1993. *The Future That Failed: The Collapse of Communism in Eastern Europe.* London: Routledge.

Arnason, Johann P. 2000. "Communism and Modernity." *Daedalus* 129 (1): 61–90.

Arnason, Johann P. 2001. "Comment on Joel Kahn: 'Anthropology and Modernity.'" *Current Anthropology* 42 (5): 664–65.

Asad, Talal. 1986. *The Idea of an Anthropology of Islam.* Washington, DC: Center for Contemporary Arab Studies, Georgetown University.

Asad, Talal. 1993. *Genealogies of Religion.* Baltimore: Johns Hopkins University Press.

Asad, Talal. 2003. *Formations of the Secular: Christianity, Islam, Modernity.* Stanford: Stanford University Press.

Asad, Talal. 2011. "Thinking about the Secular Body, Pain, and Liberal Politics." *Cultural Anthropology* 26 (4): 657–75.

Asad, Talal, Wendy Brown, Judith Butler, and Saba Mahmood. 2009. *Is Critique Secular? Blasphemy, Injury, and Free Speech.* Berkeley: Townsend Center for Humanities, University of California, Berkeley.

Babadjanov, Bakhtiyar. 2004. "From Colonization to Bolshevization: Some Political and Legislative Aspects of Molding a 'Soviet Islam' in Central Asia." In *Central Asian Law: An Historical Overview; A Festschrift for the Ninetieth Birthday of Herbert Franke*, edited by W. Johnson and I. F. Popova, 153–72. Topeka: Society for Asian Legal History, University of Kansas.

Babadjanov, Bakhtiyar, and Muzaffar Kamilov. 2001. "Muhammadjan Hindustani (1892–1989) and the Beginning of the 'Great Schism' among the Muslims of Uzbekistan." In *Islam in Politics in Russia and Central Asia: Early Eighteenth to Late Twentieth Centuries*, edited by Stéphane A. Dudoignon and Komatsu Hisao, 195–219. London: Kegan Paul.

Babadzhanov, Bakhityar. 1999. "The Ferghana Valley: Source or Victim of Islamic Fundamentalism?" In *Political Islam and Conflict in Russia and Central Asia*, edited by L. Jonson and M. Esenov, 112–23. Stockholm: AB Publishing House.

Balci, Bayram. 2012. "The Rise of the Jama'at al Tabligh in Kyrgyzstan: The Revival of Islamic Ties between the Indian Subcontinent and Central Asia?" *Central Asian Survey* 31 (1): 61–76.

Balci, Bayram. 2015. "Reviving Central Asia's Religious Ties with the Indian Subcontinent? The Jamaat al Tabligh." *Religion, State and Society* 43 (1): 20–34.

Ballinger, Pamela, and Kristen Ghodsee. 2011. "Socialist Secularism: Religion, Modernity, and Muslim Women's Emancipation in Bulgaria and Yugoslavia, 1945–1991." *Aspasia* 5 (1): 6–27.

Baran, Zeyno, S. Frederick Starr, and Svante E. Cornell. 2006. "Islamic Radicalism in Central Asia and the Caucasus: Implications for the EU." In *Silk Road Papers*. Washington, DC: Central Asia–Caucasus Institute and Silk Road Studies Program.

Barbosa, Elizabeth. 2005. "The Brazilian Telenovela 'El Clon': An Analysis of Viewers' Online Vicarious and Virtual Learning Experiences." PhD diss., Lynn University.

Baumann, Gerd. 2004. "Grammars of Identity/Alterity: A Structural Approach." In *Grammars of Identity/Alterity: A Structural Approach*, edited by Gerd Baumann and Andre Gingrich, 18–50. New York: Berghahn Books.

Bennigsen, A., and Chantal Lemercier-Quelquejay. 1979. "Official Islam in the Soviet Union." *Religion in Communist Lands* 7 (3): 148–59.

Bennigsen, A., and S. E. Wimbush. 1985. *Mystics and Commissars: Sufism in the Soviet Union*. London: Hurst.

Benovska-Sabkova, Milena, Tobias Köllner, Tünde Komáromi, Agata Ładykowska, Detelina Tocheva, and Jarrett Zigon. 2010. "'Spreading Grace' in Post-Soviet Russia." *Anthropology Today* 26 (1): 16–21.

Benthall, Jonathan. 2007. "The Overreaction against Islamic Charities." *ISIM Review* 20:6–7.

Benthall, Jonathan, and Jérôme Bellion-Jourdan. 2003. *The Charitable Crescent: Politics of Aid in the Muslim World*. London: I. B. Tauris.

Berger, Peter. 1999. "The Desecularization of the World: A Global Overview." In *The Desecularization of the World: Resurgent Religion and World Politics*, edited by Peter Berger, 1–18. Grand Rapids: Eerdmans.

Berger, Peter. 2006. "An Interview with Peter Berger," by Charles T. Mathews. *Hedgehog Review* 8 (1–2): 152–61.

Beyer, Judith. 2016. *The Force of Custom: Law and the Ordering of Everyday Life in Kyrgyzstan*. Pittsburgh: University of Pittsburgh Press.

Bielo, James S. 2015. "Secular Studies Come of Age." *Thesis Eleven* 129 (1): 119–30.

Boehm, Christian. 1999. "Democracy as a Project: Perceptions of Democracy within the World of Projects in Former Soviet Kyrgyzstan." *Anthropology of East Europe Review* 17 (1): 49–58.

Borbieva, Noor O'Neill. 2012. "Empowering Muslim Women: Independent Religious Fellowships in the Kyrgyz Republic." *Slavic Review* 71 (2): 288–307.

Bottici, Chiara, and Benoît Challand. 2006. "Rethinking Political Myth: The Clash of Civilizations as a Self-Fulfilling Prophecy." *European Journal of Social Theory* 9 (3): 315–36.

Bowen, John R. 2007. *Why the French Don't Like Headscarves: Islam, the State, and Public Space.* Princeton: Princeton University Press.

Bowen, John R. 2010. *Can Islam Be French? Pluralism and Pragmatism in a Secularist State.* Princeton: Princeton University Press.

Bracke, Sarah, and Nadia Fadil. 2008. "Islam and Secular Modernity under Western Eyes: A Genealogy of a Constitutive Relationship." *EUI Working Paper RSCAS 05.* Florence: Mediterranean Programme, Robert Schuman Centre for Advanced Studies, European University Institute.

Bräker, Hans. 1994. "Soviet Policy toward Islam." In *Muslim Communities Reemerge: Historical Perspectives on Nationality, Politics, and Opposition in the Former Soviet Union and Yugoslavia,* edited by Andreas Kappeler, 157–82. Durham: Duke University Press.

Brenner, Suzanne. 1996. "Reconstructing Self and Society: Javanese Muslim Women and 'the Veil.'" *American Ethnologist* 23 (4): 673–97.

Bringa, Tone. 1995. *Being Muslim the Bosnian Way: Identity and Community in a Central Bosnian Village.* Princeton: Princeton University Press.

Brower, Daniel R. 1997. "Islam and Ethnicity: Russian Colonial Policy in Turkestan." In *Russia's Orient: Imperial Borderlands and Peoples, 1700–1917,* edited by Daniel R. Brower and Edward J. Lazzerini, 115–37. Bloomington: Indiana University Press.

Brower, Daniel R. 2003. *Turkestan and the Fate of the Russian Empire.* London: RoutledgeCurzon.

Brower, Daniel R., and Edward J. Lazzerini, eds. 1997. *Russia's Orient: Imperial Borderlands and Peoples, 1700–1917.* Bloomington: Indiana University Press.

Bubandt, N. O., and M. van Beek, eds. 2012. *Varieties of Secularism in Asia: Anthropological Explorations of Religion, Politics and the Spiritual.* London: Routledge.

Burbank, Jane. 2006. "An Imperial Rights Regime: Law and Citizenship in the Russian Empire." *Kritika,* n.s., 7 (3): 397–431.

Calhoun, Craig, Mark Juergensmeyer, and Jonathan VanAntwerpen, eds. 2011. *Rethinking Secularism.* Oxford: Oxford University Press.

Cannell, Fenella. 2010. "The Anthropology of Secularism." *Annual Review of Anthropology* 39:85–100.

Carrère d'Encausse, Hélène. 1979. *Decline of an Empire: The Soviet Socialist Republics in Revolt.* New York: Newsweek Books.

Casanova, José. 1994. *Public Religions in the Modern World.* Chicago: University of Chicago Press.

Collier, Stephen J. 2011. *Post-Soviet Social: Neoliberalism, Social Modernity, Biopolitics.* Princeton: Princeton University Press.

Creed, Gerald. 2002. "Economic Crisis and Ritual Decline in Eastern Europe." In *Postsocialism: Ideals, Ideologies, and Practices in Eurasia*, edited by Chris Hann, 57–73. London: Routledge.

Creed, G., and J. Wedel. 1997. "Second Thoughts from the Second World: Interpreting Aid in Post-Communist Eastern Europe." *Human Organization* 56 (3).

Crews, Robert D. 2006. *For Prophet and Tsar: Islam and Empire in Russia and Central Asia*. Cambridge: Harvard University Press.

Csordas, Thomas. 2009. "Introduction: Modalities of Transnational Transcendence." In *Transnational Transcendence: Essays on Religion and Globalization*, edited by Thomas Csordas, 1–29. Berkeley: University of California Press.

D'Alisera, JoAnn. 2001. "I ♥ Islam: Popular Religious Commodities, Sites of Inscription, and Transnational Sierra Leonean Identity." *Journal of Material Culture* 6 (1): 91–110.

Das, Veena. 1995. "On Soap Opera: What Kind of Anthropological Object Is It?" In *Worlds Apart: Modernity through the Prism of the Local*, edited by Daniel Miller, 169–89. London: Routledge.

Davie, Grace. 1990. "Believing without Belonging: Is This the Future of Religion in Britain?" *Social Compass* 37 (4): 455–69.

Davie, Grace. 1994. *Religion in Britain since 1945: Believing without Belonging*. Hoboken: Wiley-Blackwell.

Davie, Grace. 2015. *Religion in Britain: A Persistent Paradox*. 2nd ed. Hoboken: Wiley-Blackwell.

Deeb, Lara. 2006. *An Enchanted Modern: Gender and Public Piety in Shi'i Lebanon*. Princeton: Princeton University Press.

Deeb, Lara. 2009. "Piety Politics and the Role of a Transnational Feminist Analysis." *Journal of the Royal Anthropological Institute* 15 (s1): S112–26.

Dragadze, Tamara. 1993. "The Domestication of Religion under Soviet Communism." In *Socialism: Ideals, Ideologies, and Local Practice*, edited by Chris Hann, 141–51. London: Routledge.

Dudoignon, Stéphane A. 2011. "From Revival to Mutation: The Religious Personnel of Islam in Tajikistan, from De-Stalinization to Independence (1955–91)." *Central Asian Survey* 30 (1): 53–80.

Dudoignon, Stéphane, and Christian Noack, eds. 2014. *Allah's Kolkhozes: Migration, De-Stalinisation, Privatisation, and the New Muslim Congregations in the Soviet Realm (1950s–2000s)*. Berlin: Klaus-Schwarz Verlag.

Economist. 2013. "Remittance Man: Russia Attempts to Draw Tajikistan and Kyrgyzstan Back into Its Orbit." 7 September. http://www.economist.com/news/asia/21584999-russia-attempts-draw-tajikistan-and-kyrgyzstan-back-its-orbit-remittance-man.

Edgar, Adrienne Lynn. 2004. *Tribal Nation: The Making of Soviet Turkmenistan*. Princeton: Princeton University Press.

Edgar, Adrienne Lynn. 2006. "Bolshevism, Patriarchy, and the Nation: The Soviet 'Emancipation' of Muslim Women in Pan-Islamic Perspective." *Slavic Review* 6 (2): 252–72.

Eickelman, Dale F., and James Piscatori. 1996. *Muslim Politics*. Princeton: Princeton University Press.

Eickelman, Dale F., and Armando Salvatore. 2004. "Muslim Publics." In *Public Islam and the Common Good*, edited by Armando Salvatore and Dale F. Eickelman, 3–28. Leiden: Brill.

Eisele, Kimi. 2002. "Arab Affinities: Sci-Fi Soap Opera 'Clone' Sweeps Latin America." *Pacific News Service*, 27 November. http://www.laprensa-sandiego.org/archive/november27-02/scifi.htm.

Eisenstadt, Shmuel Noah. 1992. "A Reappraisal of Theories of Social Change and Modernization." In *Social Change and Modernity*, edited by Hans Haferkamp and Neil J. Smelser. Berkeley: University of California Press.

Eisenstadt, Shmuel Noah. 2000a. "Multiple Modernities." *Daedalus* 129:1–29.

Eisenstadt, Shmuel Noah. 2000b. "The Reconstruction of Religious Arenas in the Framework of 'Multiple Modernities.'" *Journal of International Studies* 29 (3): 591–611.

Eisenstadt, Shmuel Noah. 2003. *Comparative Civilizations and Multiple Modernities*. Vol. 1. Leiden: Brill.

Engelke, Matthew. 2009. "Strategic Secularism: Bible Advocacy in England." *Social Analysis* 53 (1): 39–51.

Epkenhaus, Tim. 2011. "Defining Normative Islam: Some Remarks on Contemporary Islamic Thought in Tajikistan; Hoji Akbar Turajonzoda's Sharia and Society." *Central Asian Survey* 30 (1): 81–96.

Fadil, Nadia. 2013. "Performing the Salat [Islamic prayers] at Work: Secular and Pious Muslims Negotiating the Contours of the Public in Belgium." *Ethnicities* 13 (6): 729–50.

Fadil, Nadia, and Mayanthi Fernando. 2015. "Rediscovering the 'Everyday' Muslim: Notes on an Anthropological Divide." *HAU: Journal of Ethnographic Theory* 5 (2): 59–88.

Ferguson, James. 1999. *Expectations of Modernity: Myths and Meanings of Urban Life on the Zambian Copperbelt*. Berkeley: University of California Press.

Finke, Peter. 2014. *Variations on Uzbek Identity: Strategic Choices, Cognitive Schemas and Political Constraints in Identification Processes*. New York: Berghahn Books.

Fitzpatrick, Sheila. 1999. *Everyday Stalinism: Ordinary Life in Extraordinary Times*. Oxford: Oxford University Press.

Fitzpatrick, Sheila, ed. 2000. *Stalinism: New Directions*. London: Routledge.

Fokas, Effie. 2012. "'Eastern' Orthodoxy and 'Western' Secularisation in Contemporary Europe (with Special Reference to the Case of Greece)." *Religion, State and Society* 40 (3–4): 395–414.

Frank, Allen. 2012. *Bukhara and the Muslims of Russia: Sufism, Education, and the Paradox of Islamic Prestige.* Leiden: Brill.

Fumagalli, Matteo. 2006. "State Violence and Popular Resistance in Uzbekistan." *ISIM Review* 18:28–29.

Fumagalli, Matteo. 2010. "Islamic Radicalism and the Insecurity Dilemma in Central Asia." In *Russia and Islam: State, Society and Radicalism*, edited by Roland Dannreuther and Luke March, 191–208. London: Routledge.

Geertz, Clifford. 1973. *The Interpretation of Cultures.* New York: Basic Books.

Geiss, Paul Georg. 2003. *Pre-Tsarist and Tsarist Central Asia: Communal Commitment and Political Order in Change.* London: Routledge.

Gellner, Ernest. 1981. *Muslim Society.* Cambridge: Cambridge University Press.

Geraci, R. 1997. "Russian Orientalism at an Impasse: Tsarist Education Policy and the 1910 Conference on Islam." In *Russia's Orient: Imperial Borderlands and Peoples, 1700–1917*, edited by David R. Brower and Edward J. Lazzerini, 138–62. Bloomington: Indiana University Press.

Ghodsee, Kristen. 2005. "Examining 'Eastern' Aid: Muslim Minorities and Islamic Foundations in Bulgaria." *Anthropology of East Europe Review* 23 (2): 63–71.

Ghodsee, Kristen. 2009. "Symphonic Secularism: Eastern Orthodoxy, Ethnic Identity and Religious Freedoms in Contemporary Bulgaria." *Anthropology of East Europe Review* 27 (2): 227–52.

Ghodsee, Kristen. 2010. *Muslim Lives in Eastern Europe: Gender, Ethnicity, and the Transformation of Islam in Postsocialist Bulgaria.* Princeton: Princeton University Press.

Göle, Nilüfer. 1996. *The Forbidden Modern: Civilization and Veiling.* Ann Arbor: University of Michigan Press.

Grant, Bruce. 1995. *In the Soviet House of Culture: A Century of Perestroikas.* Princeton: Princeton University Press.

Grant, Bruce. 2005. "The Traffic in Brides." *American Anthropologist* 107 (4): 687–89.

Grant, Bruce. 2011. "Shrines and Sovereigns: Life, Death, and Religion in Rural Azerbaijan." *Comparative Studies in Society and History* 53 (3): 654–81.

Grigoryan, Marianna. 2004. "Armenia Goes Arabic over Wildly Popular Soap Opera." Armenianow.com, 10 November. http://www.armeniandiaspora.com/archive/6280.html.

Hammond, Timur. 2014. "Matters of the Mosque: Changing Configurations of Buildings and Belief in an Istanbul District." *City* 18 (6): 679–90.

Hanganu, Gabriel. 2010. "Eastern Christians and Religious Objects: Personal and Material Biographies Entangled." In *Eastern Christians in Anthropological Perspective*, edited by Chris Hann and Hermann Goltz, 33–55. Berkeley: University of California Press.

Haniffa, F. 2008. "Piety as Politics amongst Muslim Women in Contemporary Sri Lanka." *Modern Asia Studies* 42 (2–3): 347–75.

Hann, Chris. 1996. Introduction to *Civil Society: Challenging Western Models*, edited by Chris Hann and Elizabeth Dunn, 1–26. London: Routledge.

Hann, Chris. 2006. *"Not the Horse We Wanted": Postsocialism, Neoliberalism, and Eurasia.* Münster: LIT Verlag.

Hann, Chris. 2012. "Personhood, Christianity, Modernity." *Anthropology of This Century*, no. 3 (January). http://aotcpress.com/articles/personhood-christianity-modernity.

Hann, Chris, and Hermann Goltz, eds. 2010. *Eastern Christians in Anthropological Perspective.* Berkeley: University of California Press.

Hann, Chris, Caroline Humphrey, and Katherine Verdery. 2002. "Introduction: Postsocialism as a Topic of Anthropological Investigation." In *Postsocialism: Ideals, Ideologies and Practices in Eurasia*, edited by Chris Hann, 1–28. London: Routledge.

Hann, Chris, and Mathijs Pelkmans. 2009. "Realigning Religion and Power in Central Asia: Islam, Nation-State and (Post) Socialism." *Europe-Asia Studies* 61 (9): 1517–41.

Harris, Steven E. 2013. *Communism on Tomorrow Street: Mass Housing and Everyday Life after Stalin.* Washington, DC: Woodrow Wilson Center Press; Baltimore: Johns Hopkins University Press.

Hefner, Robert. 2005. Introduction to *Remaking Muslim Politics: Pluralism, Contestation, Democratization*, edited by Robert W. Hefner, 1–36. Princeton: Princeton University Press.

Hervieu-Léger, Danièle. 1990. "Religion and Modernity in the French Context: For a New Approach to Secularization." *Sociological Analysis* 51 (S): S15–25.

Hervieu-Léger, Danièle. 2000. *Religion as a Chain of Memory.* New Brunswick: Rutgers University Press.

Hervieu-Léger, Danièle. 2006. "In Search of Certainties: The Paradoxes of Religiosity in Societies of High Modernity." *Hedgehog Review* 8 (1–2): 59–68.

Hilgers, Irene. 2006. "The Regulation and Control of Religious Pluralism in Uzbekistan." In *The Postsocialist Religious Question: Faith and Power in Central Asia and East-Central Europe*, edited by Chris Hann et al., 75–98. Münster: LIT Verlag.

Hilgers, Irene. 2009. *Why Do Uzbeks Have to Be Muslims? Exploring Religiosity in the Ferghana Valley.* Berlin: LIT Verlag.

Hirsch, Francine. 2005. *Empire of Nations: Ethnographic Knowledge and the Making of the Soviet Union.* Ithaca: Cornell University Press.

Hirschkind, Charles. 2001. "The Ethics of Listening: Cassette-Sermon Audition in Contemporary Egypt." *American Ethnologist* 28 (3): 623–49.

Hirschkind, Charles. 2006. *The Ethical Soundscape: Cassette Sermons and Islamic Counterpublics.* New York: Columbia University Press.

Hirschkind, Charles. 2011. "Is There a Secular Body?" *Cultural Anthropology* 26 (4): 633–47.

Hirschon, Renée. 2010. "Indigenous Persons and Imported Individuals: Changing Paradigms of Personal Identity in Contemporary Greed." In *Eastern Christians in Anthro-*

pological Perspective, edited by Chris Hann and Hermann Goltz, 289–310. Berkeley: University of California Press.

Human Rights Watch. 2005. "'Bullets Were Falling Like Rain': The Andijan Massacre, May 13, 2005." *Human Rights Watch* 17 (5): D.

Human Rights Watch. 2010. "'Where Is the Justice?' Interethnic Violence in Southern Kyrgyzstan and Its Aftermath." *Human Rights Watch*, 16 August. https://www .hrw.org/report/2010/08/16/where-justice/interethnic-violence-southern-kyrgyzstan -and-its-aftermath#page.

Humphrey, Caroline. 2002. *The Unmaking of Soviet Life: Everyday Economies after Socialism*. Ithaca: Cornell University Press.

Huq, M. 2008. "Reading the Qur'an in Bangladesh: The Politics of 'Belief' among Islamist Women." *Modern Asia Studies* 42 (2–3): 457–88.

Ibañez-Tirado, Diana. 2015. "'How Can I Be Post-Soviet If I Was Never Soviet?' Rethinking Categories of Time and Social Change; A Perspective from Kulob, Southern Tajikistan." *Central Asian Survey* 34 (2): 190–203.

İğmen, Ali. 2012. *Speaking Soviet with an Accent: Culture and Power in Kyrgyzstan*. Pittsburgh: University of Pittsburgh Press.

Ilkhamov, Alisher. 2001. "Uzbek Islamism: Imported Ideology or Grassroots Movement?" *Middle East Report* 221:40–46.

International Crisis Group. 2003. "Radical Islam in Central Asia: Responding to Hizb ut-Tahrir." *ICG Report* 58.

International Crisis Group. 2005. "Uzbekistan: The Andijon Uprising." *Asia Briefing*, no. 38, 25 May.

Isabaeva, Eliza. 2011. "Leaving to Enable Others to Remain: Remittances and New Moral Economies of Migration in Southern Kyrgyzstan." *Central Asian Survey* 30 (3–4): 541–54.

Ismailbekova, Aksana, and Emil Nasritdinov. 2012. "Transnational Religious Networks in Central Asia: Structure, Travel, and Culture of Kyrgyz Tablighi Jama'at." *Transnational Social Review* 2 (2): 177–95.

Jones, Carla. 2010. "Materializing Piety: Gendered Anxieties about Faithful Consumption in Contemporary Urban Indonesia." *American Ethnologist* 37 (4): 617–37.

Kalinovsky, Artemy. Forthcoming. *Laboratory of Socialist Development: Decolonization, Cold War Politics, and the Struggle for Welfare and Equality in Soviet Tajikistan*. Ithaca: Cornell University Press.

Kamp, Marianne. 2006. *The New Woman in Uzbekistan: Islam, Modernity and Unveiling under Communism*. Seattle: University of Washington Press.

Kandiyoti, Deniz. 1996. "Modernization without the Market." *Economy and Society* 25 (4): 529–42.

Kandiyoti, Deniz. 2002. "Post-Colonialism Compared: Potentials and Limitations in the Middle East and Central Asia." *International Journal of Middle East Studies* 34:279–97.

Kandiyoti, Deniz. 2009. "Islam, Modernity and the Politics of Gender." In *Islam and Modernity: Key Issues and Debates*, edited by Muhammad Khalid Masud, Armando Salvatore, and Martin van Bruinessen, 91–124. Edinburgh: Edinburgh University Press.

Kandiyoti, Deniz, and Nadira Azimova. 2004. "The Communal and the Sacred: Women's Worlds of Ritual in Uzbekistan." *Journal of the Royal Anthropological Institute*, n.s., 10:327–49.

Kappeler, Andreas. (2001) 2013. *The Russian Empire: A Multi-Ethnic History*. London: Routledge.

Kappeler, Andreas. (2001) 2014. eBook ed. *The Russian Empire: A Multi-Ethnic History*. London: Routledge.

Karagiannis, Emmanuel. 2006. "Political Islam in Uzbekistan: Hizb ut-Tahrir al-Islami." *Europe-Asia Studies* 58 (2): 261–80.

Keane, Webb. 2008. "The Evidence of the Senses and the Materiality of Religion." *Journal of the Royal Anthropological Institute* 14:110–27.

Kehl-Bodrogi, Krisztina. 2006. "Who Owns the Shrine? Competing Meanings and Authorities at a Pilgrimage Site in Khorezm." *Central Asia Survey* 25 (3): 235–50.

Kehl-Bodrogi, Krisztina. 2008. *Religion Is Not So Strong Here: Muslim Religious Life in Khorezm after Socialism*. Münster: LIT Verlag.

Keller, Shoshana. 1992. "Islam in Soviet Central Asia, 1917–1930: Soviet Policy and the Struggle for Control." *Central Asian Survey* 11 (1): 25–50.

Keller, Shoshana. 2001a. "Conversion to the New Faith: Marxism-Leninism and the Muslims in the Soviet Empire." In *Of Religion and Empire: Missions, Conversions, and Tolerance in Tsarist Russia*, edited by Robert P. Geraci and Michael Khodarkovsky, 311–34. Ithaca: Cornell University Press.

Keller, Shoshana. 2001b. *To Moscow, Not Mecca: The Soviet Campaign against Islam in Central Asia, 1917–1941*. Westport: Praeger.

Kemper, Michael. 2014. "*Ijtihad* into Philosophy: Islam as Cultural Heritage in Post-Stalinist Daghestan." *Central Asian Survey* 33 (3): 390–404.

Kemper, Michael, Raoul Motika, and Stefan Reichmuth, eds. 2010. *Islamic Education in the Soviet Union and Its Successor States*. London: Routledge.

Kendall, Laurel, Vũ Thị Thanh Tâm, and Nguyễn Thị Thu Hu'o'ng. 2010. "Beautiful and Efficacious Statues: Magic, Commodities, Agency and the Production of Sacred Objects in Popular Religion in Vietnam." *Material Religion* 6 (1): 60–85.

Khalid, Adeeb. 1998. *The Politics of Muslim Cultural Reform: Jadidism in Central Asia*. Berkeley: University of California Press.

Khalid, Adeeb. 2003. "A Secular Islam: Nation, State, and Religion in Uzbekistan." *International Journal for Eastern Studies* 35 (4): 573–98.

Khalid, Adeeb. 2006. "Backwardness and the Quest for Civilization: Early Soviet Central Asia in Comparative Perspective." *Slavic Review* 65 (2): 231–51.

Khalid, Adeeb. 2007. *Islam after Communism*. Berkeley: University of California Press.

Khamidov, Alisher. 2002. "Ethnic Uzbeks Stoke Unrest in Southern Kyrgyzstan." *Eurasianet*, 26 June. http://www.eurasianet.org/departments/civilsociety/articles/eav062 602.shtml.

Khamidov, Alisher. 2013. "The Lessons of the 'Nookat Events': Central Government, Local Officials and Religious Protests in Kyrgyzstan." *Central Asian Survey* 32 (2): 148–60.

Kharkhordin, Oleg. 1999. *The Collective and the Individual in Russia*. Berkeley: University of California Press.

Khodarkovsky, Michael. 1997. "Ignoble Savages and Unfaithful Subjects: Constructing Non-Christian Identities in Early Modern Russia." In *Russia's Orient: Imperial Borderlands and Peoples, 1700–1917*, edited by Daniel R. Brower and Edward J. Lazzerini, 9–26. Bloomington: Indiana University Press.

Kligman, Gail. 1988. *The Wedding of the Dead: Ritual, Poetics, and Popular Culture in Transylvania*. Berkeley: University of California Press.

Köllner, Tobias. 2013. "Works of Penance: New Churches in Post-Soviet Russia." In *Religious Architecture: Anthropological Perspectives*, edited by Oskar Verkaaik, 83–98. Amsterdam: Amsterdam University Press.

Kotkin, Stephan. 1995. *Magnetic Mountain: Stalinism as a Civilization*. Berkeley: University of California Press.

Kowalewski, David. 1980. "Religious Belief in the Brezhnev Era: Renaissance, Resistance and Realpolitik." *Journal for the Scientific Study of Religion* 19 (3): 280–92.

Kulick, Don, and Margaret Wilson. 2002. "Rambo's Wife Saves the Day: Subjugating the Gaze and Subverting the Narrative in a Papua New Guinean Swamp." In *The Anthropology of Media: A Reader*, edited by Kelly Michelle Askew and Richard R. Wilk, 270–85. Oxford: Blackwell.

Kyrgyzstan Inquiry Commission. 2011. *Report of the Independent International Commission of Inquiry into the Events in Southern Kyrgyzstan in June 2010*.

Lampland, Martha. 2002. "The Advantages of Being Collectivized: Cooperative Farm Managers in the Postsocialist Economy." In *Postsocialism: Ideals, Ideologies and Practices in Eurasia*, edited by Chris Hann, 31–56. London: Routledge.

Latour, Bruno. 1993. *We Have Never Been Modern*. Cambridge: Harvard University Press.

Ledeneva, Alena. 2006. *How Russia Really Works: The Informal Practices That Shaped Post-Soviet Politics and Business*. Ithaca: Cornell University Press.

Lehmann, David. 2013. "Religion as Heritage, Religion as Belief: Shifting Frontiers of Secularism in Europe, the USA and Brazil." *International Sociology* 28 (6): 645–62.

Lewis, David. 2008. *The Temptations of Tyranny in Central Asia*. New York: Columbia University Press.

Liu, Morgan. 2012. *Under Solomon's Throne: Uzbek Visions of Renewal in Osh*. Pittsburgh: University of Pittsburgh Press.

Lorenz, Richard. 1994. "Economic Base of the Basmachi Movement in the Farghana Valley." In *Muslim Communities Reemerge: Historical Perspectives on Nationality, Politics, and Opposition in the Former Soviet Union and Yugoslavia*, edited by Andreas Kappeler, 277–303. Durham: Duke University Press.

Louw, Maria. 2007. *Everyday Islam in Post-Soviet Central Asia*. London: RoutledgeCurzon.

Luehrmann, Sonja. 2010. "A Dual Struggle of Images on Russia's Middle Volga: Icon Veneration in the Face of Protestant and Pagan Critique." In *Eastern Christians in Anthropological Perspective*, edited by Chris Hann and Hermann Goltz, 56–78. Berkeley: University of California Press.

Luehrmann, Sonja. 2011. *Secularism Soviet Style: Teaching Atheism and Religion in a Volga Republic*. Bloomington: Indiana University Press.

Luehrmann, Sonja. 2012. "A Multireligious Region in an Atheist State: Unionwide Policies Meet Communal Distinctions in the Postwar Mari Republic." In *State Secularism and Lived Religion in Soviet Russia and Ukraine*, edited by Catherine Wanner, 272–301. Washington, DC: Woodrow Wilson Press; Oxford: Oxford University Press.

Mahieu, Stéphanie, and Vlad Naumescu, eds. 2008. *Churches in-Between: Greek Catholic Churches in Postsocialist Europe*. Berlin: LIT Verlag.

Mahmood, Saba. 2005. *Politics of Piety: The Islamic Revival and the Feminist Subject*. Princeton: Princeton University Press.

Mahmood, Saba. 2009. "Religious Reason and Secular Affect: An Incommensurable Divide?" In *Is Critique Secular? Blasphemy, Injury, and Free Speech*, edited by Talal Asad, Wendy Brown, Judith Butler, and Saba Mahmood, 64–100. Berkeley: Townsend Center for the Humanities, University of California.

Mahmood, Saba. 2011. New preface to *Politics of Piety: The Islamic Revival and the Feminist Subject*. 2nd ed. Princeton: Princeton University Press.

Makarov, Dmitrii, and Rafik Mukhametshin. 2003. "Official and Unofficial Islam." In *Islam in Post-Soviet Russia: Public and Private Faces*, edited by Hilary Pilkington and Galina Yemelianova, 117–63. London: RoutledgeCurzon.

Makrides, Vasilios N. 2012. "Orthodox Christianity, Modernity and Postmodernity: Overview, Analysis and Assessment." *Religion, State and Society* 40 (3–4): 248–85.

Mandaville, Peter. 2007. "Globalization and the Politics of Religious Knowledge: Pluralizing Authority in the Muslim World." *Theory, Culture & Society* 24 (2): 101–15.

Mandel, Ruth. 2002. "Seeding Civil Society." In *Postsocialism: Ideals, Ideologies and Practices in Eurasia*, edited by Chris Hann, 279–96. London: Routledge.

Mankekar, Purnima. 1993. "National Texts and Gendered lives: An Ethnography of Television Viewers in a Northern Indian City." *American Ethnologist* 20 (3): 543–63.

Marsden, Magnus. 2005a. *Living Islam: Muslim Religious Experience in Pakistan's North-West Frontier*. Cambridge: Cambridge University Press.

Marsden, Magnus. 2005b. "Muslim Village Intellectuals: The Life of the Mind in Northern Pakistan." *Anthropology Today* 21 (1): 10–15.

Martin, David. 2005. *On Secularization: Towards a Revised General Theory.* Aldershot: Ashgate Publishing.

Martin, David. 2007. "What I Really Said about Secularisation." *Dialog: A Journal of Theology* 46 (2): 139–52.

Martin, Terry Dean. 2001. *The Affirmative Action Empire: Nations and Nationalities in the Soviet Union, 1923–1939.* Ithaca: Cornell University Press.

Marx, Karl. (1844) 2002. "Critique of Hegel's Philosophy of Right." In *Marx on Religion*, edited by John Raines, 170–81. Philadelphia: Temple University Press.

Massarani, Luisa, and I. de Castro Moreira. 2002. "Human Cloning: A Soap Opera as a Science Communication Tool." Paper presented at the Seventh Conference on the Public Communication of Science and Technology, Cape Town, South Africa, December. https://www.researchgate.net/publication/237588844_Human_cloning_A _soap_opera_as_a_science_communication_tool.

Massell, Gregory. 1974. *The Surrogate Proletariat: Moslem Women and Revolutionary Strategies in Soviet Central Asia, 1919–1929.* Princeton: Princeton University Press.

McAlister, Melani. 2003. "Prophecy, Politics, and the Popular: The *Left Behind* Series and Christian Fundamentalism's New World Order." *South Atlantic Quarterly* 102 (4): 773–98.

McBrien, Julie. 2006. "Extreme Conversations: Secularism, Religious Pluralism, and the Rhetoric of Muslim Extremisms in Southern Kyrgyzstan." In *The Postsocialist Religious Question: Faith and Power in Central Asia and East-Central Europe*, edited by Chris Hann et al., 47–74. Münster: LIT Verlag.

McBrien, Julie. 2007. "Brazilian TV & Muslimness in Kyrgyzstan." *ISIM Review* 19 (Spring).

McBrien, Julie. 2009. "'Mukadas' Struggle: Veils and Modernity in Kyrgyzstan." *JRAI*, n.s., 15:S127–44.

McBrien, Julie. 2011. "Leaving for Work, Leaving in Fear." *Anthropology Today* 27 (4): 3–4.

McBrien, Julie. 2013. "Afterword: In the Aftermath of Doubt." *Ethnographies of Doubt: Faith and Uncertainty in Contemporary Societies*, edited by Mathijs Pelkmans, 251–68. London: I. B. Tauris.

McBrien, Julie, and Mathijs Pelkmans. 2008. "Turning Marx on His Head: Missionaries, 'Extremists,' and Archaic Secularists in Post-Soviet Kyrgyzstan." *Critique of Anthropology* 28 (1): 87–103.

McGlinchey, Eric. 2009. "Islamic Revivalism and State Failure in Kyrgyzstan." *Problems of Post-Communism* 56 (3): 16–28.

McLennan, Gregor. 2010. "The Postsecular Turn." *Theory, Culture & Society* 27 (4): 3–20.

McLeod, Arlene E. 1991. *Accommodating Protest: Working Women, the New Veiling, and Change in Cairo*. New York: Columbia University Press.

Megoran, N. 2002. "The Borders of Eternal Friendship? The Politics and Pain of Nationalism and Identity along the Uzbekistan-Kyrgyzstan Ferghana Valley Boundary, 1999–2000." PhD thesis, University of Cambridge.

Megoran, Nick. 2004. "The Critical Geopolitics of the Uzbekistan-Kyrgyzstan Fergana Valley Boundary Dispute, 1999–2000." *Political Geography* 23 (6): 731–64.

Megoran, Nick. 2006. "For Ethnography in Political Geography: Experiencing and Re-Imagining Fergana Valley Boundary Closures." *Political Geography* 25 (6): 622–40.

Mendieta, Eduardo, and Jonathan VanAntwerpen, eds. 2011. *The Power of Religion in the Public Sphere*, by Judith Butler, Jürgen Habermas, Charles Taylor, and Cornel West. New York: Columbia University Press.

Metcalf, Barbara. 2002. *"Traditionalist" Islamic Activism: Deobands, Tablighis, and Talibs*. ISIM Paper Series. Leiden: ISIM.

Meyer, Birgit. 2006. "Impossible Representations: Pentecostalism, Vision, and Video Technology in Ghana." In *Religion, Media, and the Public Sphere*, edited by Birgit Meyer and Annelies Moors, 290–312. Bloomington: Indiana University Press.

Meyer, Birgit. 2009. "Introduction: From Imagined Communities to Aesthetic Formations; Religious Mediations, Sensational Forms, and Styles of Binding." In *Aesthetic Formations: Media, Religion, and the Senses*, edited by Birgit Meyer, 1–28. Houndmills: Palgrave.

Meyer, Birgit, and Annelies Moors, eds. 2006. *Religion, Media, and the Public Sphere*. Bloomington: Indiana University Press.

Meyer, Birgit, et al. 2010. "The Origin and Mission of Material Religion." *Religion* 40 (3): 207–11.

Montgomery, David W. 2007. "The Diversity of Everyday Religious." In *Everyday Life in Central Asia: Past and Present*, edited by Jeff Sahadeo and Russell Zanca, 355–70. Bloomington: Indiana University Press.

Montgomery, David W. 2014. "Towards a Theory of the Rough Ground: Merging the Policy and Ethnographic Fames of Religion in the Kyrgyz Republic." *Religion, State and Society* 42 (1): 23–45.

Moors, Annelies. 1998. "Wearing Gold." In *Border Fetishisms: Material Objects in Unstable Spaces*, edited by Patricia Speyer, 208–23. London: Routledge.

Moors, Annelies. 2000. "Embodying the Nation: Maha Saca's Post-Intifada Postcards." *Ethnic and Racial Studies* 23 (5): 871–87.

Moors, Annelies. 2007. "'Burka' in Parliament and on the Catwalk." *ISIM Review* 19 (5).

Moors, Annelies. 2009. "'Islamic Fashion' in Europe: Religious Conviction, Aesthetic Style, and Creative Consumption." *Encounters* 1:176–99.

Moors, Annelies, and Emma Tarlo. 2007. "Introduction." *Fashion Theory: The Journal of Dress, Body & Culture* 11 (2–3): 133–42.

Morgan, David. 2008. "The Materiality of Cultural Construction." *Material Religion* 4 (2): 228–29.

Mostowlansky, Till. 2017. *Azan on the Moon: Entangling Modernity along Tajikistan's Pamir Highway.* Pittsburgh: University of Pittsburgh Press.

Myer, Will. 2002. *Islam and Colonialism: Western Perspectives on Soviet Asia.* London: RoutledgeCurzon.

Naumescu, Vlad. 2007. *Modes of Religiosity in Eastern Christianity: Religious Processes and Social Change in Ukraine.* Münster: LIT Verlag.

Naumkin, Vitalii Viacheslavovich. 2005. *Radical Islam in Central Asia: Between Pen and Rifle.* Oxford: Rowman and Littlefield.

Navaro-Yashin, Yael. 2002. *Faces of the State: Secularism and Public Life in Turkey.* Princeton: Princeton University Press.

Nazpary, Joma. 2002. *Post-Soviet Chaos: Violence and Dispossession in Kazakhstan.* London: Pluto Press.

Northrop, Douglas. 2004. *Veiled Empire: Gender and Power in Stalinist Central Asia.* Ithaca: Cornell University Press.

Olcott, Martha Brill. 2007. *Roots of Radical Islam in Central Asia.* Washington, DC: Carnegie Endowment for International Peace.

Özyürek, Esra. 2006. *Nostalgia for the Modern: State Secularism and Everyday Politics in Turkey.* Durham: Duke University Press.

Pedersen, Morten Axel. 2011. *Not Quite Shamans: Spirit Worlds and Political Lives in Northern Mongolia.* Ithaca: Cornell University Press.

Peel, John. 2009. "Postsocialism, Postcolonialism, Pentecostalism." In *Conversion after Socialism: Disruptions, Modernisms and Technologies of Faith in the Former Soviet Union,* edited by Mathijs Pelkmans, 183–200. New York: Berghahn Books.

Peletz, Michael. 2002. *Islamic Modern: Religious Courts and Cultural Politics in Malaysia.* Princeton: Princeton University Press.

Peletz, Michael. 2005. "Islam and the Cultural Politics of Legitimacy: Malaysia in the Aftermath of September 11th." In *Remaking Muslim Politics: Pluralism, Contestation, Democratization,* edited by Robert Hefner, 240–72. Princeton: Princeton University Press.

Pelkmans, Mathijs. 2002. "Religion, Nation and State in Georgia: Christian Expansion in Muslim Ajaria." *Journal of Muslim Minority Affairs* 22 (2): 249–70.

Pelkmans, Mathijs. 2005. "On Transition and Revolution in Kyrgyzstan." *Focaal: European Journal of Anthropology* 46:147–57.

Pelkmans, Mathijs. 2006. *Defending the Border: Identity, Religion, and Modernity in the Republic of Georgia.* Ithaca: Cornell University Press.

Pelkmans, Mathijs. 2007. "'Culture' as a Tool and an Obstacle: Missionary Encounters in Post-Soviet Kyrgyzstan." *Journal of the Royal Anthropological Institute,* n.s., 13:881–99.

Peshkova, Svetlana. 2014. "Teaching Islam at a Home School: Muslim Women and Critical Thinking in Uzbekistan." *Central Asian Survey* 33 (1): 80–94.

Pine, Francis. 1996. "Redefining Women's Work in Rural Poland." In *After Socialism: Land Reform and Social Change in Eastern Europe*, edited by Ray Abrahams, 133–56. Providence: Berghahn Books.

Pine, Francis, and Sue Bridger. 1998. Introduction to *Surviving Post-Socialism: Local Strategies and Regional Responses in Eastern Europe and the Former Soviet Union*, edited by Francis Pine and Sue Bridger, 1–15. London: Routledge.

Poljakov, Sergei P. 1992. *Everyday Islam: Religion and Tradition in Rural Central Asia.* New York: Sharpe.

Privratsky, Bruce. 2001. *Muslim Turkistan: Kazak Religion and Collective Memory.* Richmond: Curzon.

Rasanayagam, Johan. 2006a. "Introduction." *Central Asian Survey* 25 (3): 219–34.

Rasanayagam, Johan. 2006b. "Healing with Spirits and the Formation of Muslim Selfhood in Post-Soviet Uzbekistan." *Journal of the Royal Anthropological Institute*, n.s., 12:377–93.

Rasanayagam, Johan. 2006c. "'I'm Not a Wahhabi': State Power and Muslim Orthodoxy in Uzbekistan." In *The Postsocialist Religious Question: Faith and Power in Central Asia and East-Central Europe*, edited by by Chris Hann et al., 99–124. Münster: LIT Verlag.

Rasanayagam, Johan. 2011. *Islam in Post-Soviet Uzbekistan: The Morality of Experience.* Cambridge: Cambridge University Press.

Rasanayagam, Johan. 2014. "The Politics of Culture and the Space for Islam: Soviet and Post-Soviet Imaginaries in Uzbekistan." *Central Asian Survey* 33 (1): 1–14.

Rashid, Ahmed. 1994. *The Resurgence of Central Asia: Islam or Nationalism?* London: Zed Press.

Rashid, Ahmed. 2002. *Jihad: The Rise of Militant Islam in Central Asia.* New Haven: Yale University Press.

Redfield, Robert. 1960. *The Little Community and Peasant Society and Culture.* Chicago: University of Chicago Press.

Reeves, Madeleine. 2010a. "A Weekend in Osh." *London Review of Books*, 8 July.

Reeves, Madeleine. 2010b. "The Ethnicisation of Violence in Southern Kyrgyzstan." *Open Democracy*, 21 June. https://www.opendemocracy.net/od-russia/madeleine-reeves/eth nicisation-of-violence-in-southern-kyrgyzstan-0.

Reeves, Madeleine. 2012. "Black Work, Green Money: Remittances, Ritual, and Domestic Economies in Southern Kyrgyzstan." *Slavic Review* 71 (1): 108–34.

Rinaldo, Rachel. 2008. "Envisioning the Nation: Women Activists, Religion and the Public Sphere in Indonesia." *Social Forces* 86 (4): 1781–804.

Roche, Sophie, and Sophie Hohmann. 2011. "Wedding Rituals and the Struggle over National Identities." *Central Asian Survey* 30 (1): 113–28.

Rofel, Lisa. 1994. "*Yearnings*: Televisual Love and Melodramatic Politics in Contemporary China." *American Ethnologist* 21 (4): 700–722.

Rofel, Lisa. 1999. *Other Modernities: Gendered Yearnings in China after Socialism.* Berkeley: University of California Press.

Rogers, Douglas. 2009. *The Old Faith and the Russian Land: A Historical Ethnography of Ethics in the Urals.* Ithaca: Cornell University Press.

Ro'i, Yaacov. 1984. "The Task of Creating the New Soviet Man: 'Atheistic Propaganda' in the Soviet Muslim Areas." *Europe-Asia Studies* 36 (1): 26–44.

Ro'i, Yaacov. 2000. *Islam in the Soviet Union: From the Second World War to Gorbachev.* New York: Columbia University Press.

Rubinov, Igor. 2014. "Migrant Assemblages: Building Postsocialist Households with Kyrgyz Remittances." *Anthropological Quarterly* 87 (1): 183–215.

Rumer, Boris Z. 1989. *Soviet Central Asia: "A Tragic Experiment."* Boston: Allen & Unwin.

Sahadeo, Jeff. 2007. *Russian Colonial Society in Tashkent, 1865–1923.* Bloomington: Indiana University Press.

Saktanber, Ayse. 2002. *Living Islam: Women, Religion and the Politicization of Culture in Turkey.* London: I. B. Tauris.

Salvatore, Armando. 1997. *Islam and the Political Discourse of Modernity.* Reading: Ithaca Press.

Salvatore, Armando. 2006. "Power and Authority within European Secularity: From Enlightenment Critique of Religion to the Contemporary Presence of Islam." *Muslim World* 96:543–61.

Salvatore, Armando. 2007. "Authority in Question: Secularity, Republicanism, and 'Communitarianism' in the Emerging Euro-Islamic Public Sphere." *Theory, Culture & Society* 24 (2): 135–60.

Saroyan, Mark. 1993. "Rethinking Islam in the Soviet Union." In *Beyond Sovietology: Essays in Politics and History,* edited by S. Gross Solomon. Armonk: M. E. Sharpe.

Saroyan, Mark. 1997. *Minorities, Mullahs, and Modernity: Reshaping Community in the Late Soviet Union.* Berkeley: University of California Press.

Sartori, Paolo. 2010. "Towards a History of the Muslims of the Soviet Union." *Die Welt des Islams* 50:315–34.

Schielke, Joska Samuli, and Liza Debevec. 2012. *Ordinary Lives and Grand Schemes: An Anthropology of Everyday Religion.* New York: Berghahn Books.

Schoeberlein-Engel, John. 1994. "Identity in Central Asia: Construction and Contention in the Concepts of 'Özbek,' 'Tâjik,' 'Muslim,' 'Samargandi' and Other Groups." PhD diss., Harvard University.

Schulz, Dorothea E. 2006. "Promises of (Im)mediate Salvation: Islam, Broadcast Media, and the Remaking of Religious Experience in Mali." *American Ethnologist* 33 (2): 210–29.

Schwab, Wendell. 2011. "Establishing an Islamic Niche in Kazakhstan: Musylman Publishing House and Its Publications." *Central Asian Survey* 30 (2): 227–42.

Schwab, Wendell. 2012. "Traditions and Texts: How Two Young Women Learned to Interpret the Qur'an and Hadiths in Kazakhstan." *Contemporary Islam* 6 (2): 173–97.

Schwab, Wendell. 2014. "How to Pray in Kazakhstan: The Fortress of the Muslim and Its Readers." *Anthropology of East Europe Review* 32 (1): 22–42.

Sershen, Daniel. 2007. "Kyrgyzstan: Revolution Anniversary Prompts Hopes, Doubts about Democratization." *Eurasianet*, 22 March. http://www.eurasianet.org/departments/insight/articles/eav032207.shtml.

Sezneva, Olga. 2013. "On Moral Substance and Visual Obscurity in Policies and Practice of State Expansion." *Environment and Planning D: Society and Space* 31:611–27.

Shahrani, Nazif M. 1984. "From Tribe to Umma: Comments on the Dynamics of Identity in Muslim Soviet Central Asia." *Central Asian Survey* 3 (3): 27–38.

Shahrani, Nazif. 1995. "Islam and the Political Culture of 'Scientific Atheism' in Post-Soviet Central Asia: Future Predicaments." In *The Politics of Religion in Russia and the New States of Eurasia*, edited by M. Bourdeaux, 273–92. Armonk: M. E. Sharpe.

Shahrani, Nazif M. 2005. "Reclaiming Islam in Uzbekistan." Paper presented at the conference "Post-Soviet Islam," Max Planck Institute for Social Anthropology, Halle, Germany.

Slezkine, Yuri. 1997. "Naturalists versus Nations: Eighteenth-Century Russian Scholars Confront Ethnic Diversity." In *Russia's Orient: Imperial Borderlands and Peoples, 1700–1917*, edited by Daniel R. Brower and Edward J. Lazzerini, 27–57. Bloomington: Indiana University Press.

Slezkine, Yuri. 2000. "The USSR as a Communal Apartment, or How a Socialist State Promoted Ethnic Particularism." In *Stalinism: New Directions*, edited by Sheila Fitzpatrick, 313–47. London: Routledge.

Smith-Hefner, Nancy J. "Javanese Women and the Veil in Post-Soeharto Indonesia." *Journal of Asian Studies* 66 (2): 389–420.

Smolkin-Rothrock, Victoria. 2010. "'A Sacred Space Is Never Empty': Soviet Atheism, 1954–1971." PhD diss., University of California at Berkeley.

Smolkin-Rothrock, Victoria. 2014. "The Ticket to the Soviet Soul: Science, Religion, and the Spiritual Crisis of Late Soviet Atheism." *Russian Review* 73:171–97.

Soares, Benjamin F. 2005. *Islam and the Prayer Economy: History and Authority in a Malian Town*. Ann Arbor: University of Michigan Press.

Starrett, Gregory. 1995. "The Political Economy of Religious Commodities in Cairo." *American Anthropologist* 97 (1): 51–68.

Starrett, Gregory. 2010. "Islam and the Politics of Enchantment." In *Islam, Politics, Anthropology*, edited by Filippo Osella and Benjamin Soares, 213–30. Oxford: Wiley Blackwell.

Stephan, Manja. 2006. "'You Come to Us Like a Black Cloud': Universal versus Local Islam in Tajikistan." In *The Postsocialist Religious Question: Faith and Power in Central*

Asia and East-Central Europe, edited by Chris Hann et al., 147–68. Münster: LIT Verlag.

Stephan, Manja. 2010. "Education, Youth and Islam: The Growing Popularity of Private Religious Lessons in Dushanbe, Tajikistan." *Central Asian Survey* 29 (4): 469–83.

Tapper, Nancy. 1985. "Changing Wedding Rituals in a Turkish Town." *International Journal of Turkish Studies* 9:305–13.

Tapper, Nancy. 1991. "'Traditional' and 'Modern' Wedding Rituals in a Turkish Town." *International Journal of Turkish Studies* 15:137–54.

Tarlo, Emma. 2005. "Reconsidering Stereotypes: Anthropological Reflections on the Jilbab Controversy." *Anthropology Today* 21 (6): 13–17.

Tasar, Eren. 2010. "Soviet and Muslim: The Institutionalization of Islam in Central Asia, 1943–1991." PhD diss., Harvard University.

Tazmini, Ghoncheh. 2001. "The Islamic Revival in Central Asia: A Potent Force or a Misconception?" *Central Asian Survey* 20 (1): 63–83.

Tishkov, Valery. 1995. "'Don't Kill Me, I'm a Kyrgyz!' An Anthropological Analysis of Violence in the Osh Ethnic Conflict." *Journal of Peace Research* 32 (2): 133–49.

van de Port, Mattijs. 2006. "Visualizing the Sacred: Video Technology, 'Televisual' Style, and the Religious Imagination in Bahian Candomblé." *American Ethnologist* 33 (3): 444–61.

van der Veer, Peter. 1994. *Religious Nationalism: Hindus and Muslims in India*. Berkeley: University of California Press.

van der Veer, Peter, and Hartmut Lehmann. 1999. *Nation and Religion: Perspectives on Europe and Asia*. Princeton: Princeton University Press.

Verdery, Katherine. 2006. "After Socialism." In *A Companion to the Anthropology of Politics*, edited by David Nugent and Joan Vincent, 21–36. Oxford: Blackwell.

Verkaaik, Oskar. 2012. "Designing the 'Anti-Mosque': Identity, Religion, and Affect in Contemporary European Mosque Design." *Social Anthropology* 20 (2): 161–76.

Verkaaik, Oskar. 2013. Introduction to *Religious Architecture: Anthropological Perspectives*, edited by Oskar Verkaaik, 7–24. Amsterdam: Amsterdam University Press.

Verkaaik, Oskar, and Rachel Spronk. 2011. "Sexular Practice: Notes on an Ethnography of Secularism." *Focaal* 59:83–88.

Waite, Edmund. 2006. "The Impact of the State on Islam amongst the Uyghurs: Religious Knowledge and Authority in the Kashgar Oasis." *Central Asian Survey* 25 (3): 251–65.

Wanner, Catherine. 2007. *Communities of the Converted: Ukrainians and Global Evangelism*. Ithaca: Cornell University Press.

Wanner, Catherine, ed. 2012. *State Secularism and Lived Religion in Soviet Russia and Ukraine*. Washington, DC: Woodrow Wilson Press; Oxford: Oxford University Press.

Warner, Michael, Jonathan VanAntwerpen, and Craig Calhoun, eds. 2010. *Varieties of Secularism in a Secular Age*. Cambridge: Harvard University Press.

Werbner, Pnina. 2007. "Veiled Interventions in Pure Space: Honour, Shame and Embodied Struggles among Muslims in Britain and France." *Theory, Culture & Society* 24 (2): 161–86.

Werner, Cynthia. 2004. "Women, Marriage, and the Nation-State: The Rise of Nonconsensual Bride Kidnapping in Post-Soviet Kazakhstan." In *The Transformation of Central Asia*, edited by Pauline Jones Luong, 59–89. Ithaca: Cornell University Press.

White, Jenny. 1999. "Islamic Chic." In *Istanbul: Between the Global and the Local*, edited by Çağlar Keyder, 77–91. Oxford: Rowman and Littlefield.

White, Jenny. 2002. *Islamist Mobilization in Turkey: A Study in Vernacular Politics*. Seattle: University of Washington Press.

Yalçin-Heckmann, Lale. 2001. *The Political Economy of an Azeri Wedding*. Halle: Max Planck Institute for Social Anthropology.

Yaroshevski, Dov. 1997. "Empire and Citizenship." In *Russia's Orient: Imperial Borderlands and Peoples, 1700–1917*, edited by Daniel R. Brower and Edward J. Lazzerini, 58–79. Bloomington: Indiana University Press.

Yurchak, Alexi. 2006. *Everything Was Forever, Until It Was No More: The Last Soviet Generation*. Princeton: Princeton University Press.

Zanca, Russell. 2005. "Believing in God at Your Own Risk: Religion and Terrorisms in Uzbekistan." *Religion, State and Society* 33 (1): 71–82.

Zigon, Jarrett. 2009. "Hope Dies Last: Two Aspects of Hope in Contemporary Moscow." *Anthropological Theory* 9 (3): 253–71.

INDEX

Note: Page numbers in *italics* refer to figures.

Bolsheviks, 19, 20, 56
Borbieva, Noor, 100
Bukhara, 87, 103, 104, 194n21
Burbank, Jane, 17
byt, 20, 21, 23

capitalism, 3, 121, 134, 155, 189n4; actu-
    ally existing, 124; adoption of, 113,
    152; democracy and, 5, 6, 31, 35, 36;
    mosques and, 34
Casanova, José, 10, 11, 58, 190n7
Catherine the Great (Catherine II), 18,
    191n13
Catholicism, 12, 14
changes, post-Soviet, 112–13, 115, 117–18
Christianity, 12, 14, 15, 26, 45, 190n11
citizenship, 19, 40; ideas of, 27, 192n21
civil registry office, 64, *65*
civilizing mission, 18, 29, 190n11
Clone (soap opera), 179; characters in,
    156, 159, 160–61; DVD of, *167;* gen-
    der issues and, 152; imagery of, 156–
    57, 159–60, 170; influence of, 161,
    163, 164; Islam and, 156, 164–65;
    materiality of, 166–70; Muslimness
    and, 163, 166, 168; objectification
    and, 152; production of, 156, 169,
    170; screen shot from, *157, 158, 161,
    162;* subjectivities and, 153; watching,
    151, 160–64, 165, 166, 172, 175
"close to Islam" (*dinge jakyn*) or "come
    close to Islam" (*dinge jakyn kelde*), 36,
    46, 49, 50, 51, 85, 103, 117, 123, 125,
    128, 148, 164, 165, 185, 199n7. *See
    also* "turned and gone to Islam"
Cold War, Muslim unity and, 56
collective action, 27, 29, 143
collective farms, 35, 38, 40
collective life, 18, 58, 143
Collier, Stephen, 110

community, 164; cohesion, 147; fissures
    on, 102–7; Islamic, 84, 89, 150; mor-
    al, 25; religious, 32, 91, 113
Connolly, William, 190n7
conscience, freedom of, 5, 36, 112
Creed, Gerald, 77
Crews, Robert D., 17
culture, 28, 92, 123, 175; Arab-Muslim,
    152; depoliticization of, 77; ethnona-
    tional, 77; incumbent, 130; local, 20;
    Moroccan, 160; national, 23, 25, 26,
    32; politicization of, 196n15; religion
    and, 24, 76, 77
culture houses, *135,* 141, 200n5

damla, 81, 98, 100
davat, 46, 57, 82, 96, 97, 99, 101, 102,
    107, 118, 194n16; opening of, 100
Davie, Grace, 10, 11, 14, 15
da'wa, 96, 97, 99
democracy, 189n4; capitalism and, 5, 6,
    31, 35, 36; mosques and, 34; transi-
    tion to, 189n4
demographics, 50, 51, 52, 54, 136, 140,
    186, 187
Deobandi, reformist groups in, 198n23
Dewey, John, 57
Djamoldin, Imam, 87
dress: codes, 76, 164; public, 108–9,
    115, 117; Uzbek, 123; women's, 119,
    120–21, *122,* 126, 127
drug trafficking, 51, 194n18
Dudoignon, Stephané, 89, 93
DUMK. *See* Spiritual Board of Muslims
    in Kyrgyzstan
Durkheim, Émile, 191n13
Dushanbe, 87, 100, 196n14

economic environment, 19, 28, 80, 145,
    149